THE AGE OF
INVINCIBLE

THE AGE OF
INVINCIBLE

THE SHIP THAT DEFINED THE
MODERN ROYAL NAVY

NICK CHILDS

Pen & Sword
MARITIME

First published in Great Britain in 2009 by
Pen & Sword Maritime
An imprint of
Pen & Sword Books Ltd
47 Church Street
Barnsley
South Yorkshire
S70 2AS

ISBN 978 1 84415 857 7

A CIP catalogue record for this book is available from the British Library.

Typeset in 11.5pt Bembo by Mac Style, Beverley, East Yorkshire
Printed and bound in the UK by the MPG Books Group

Pen & Sword Books Ltd incorporates the imprints of Pen & Sword Aviation,
Pen & Sword Maritime, Pen & Sword Military, Wharncliffe Local History,
Pen & Sword Select, Pen & Sword Military Classics, Leo Cooper,
Remember When, Seaforth Publishing and Frontline Publishing

For a complete list of Pen & Sword titles please contact
PEN & SWORD BOOKS LIMITED
47 Church Street, Barnsley, South Yorkshire, S70 2AS, England
E-mail: enquiries@pen-and-sword.co.uk
Website: www.pen-and-sword.co.uk

Contents

List of Plates

Acknowledgements

As a teenager in the 1970s, with an already well-developed interest in the Royal Navy, I grew up with artists' impressions depicting HMS *Invincible* as the shape of things to come. Now she is in the twilight of retirement. I must start by thanking the Royal Navy for its help in compiling this story of her career and times, in particular Captain Mike Davis-Marks and Lieutenant Commander Harvey Burwin of Defence Public Relations (Navy). Through their good offices, it was a great privilege for me to be able to speak to the Navy's most senior serving officers, the First Sea Lord, Admiral Sir Jonathon Band, the then Commander-in-Chief Fleet (and former *Invincible* commanding officer) Admiral Sir James Burnell-Nugent, and his successor, Admiral Sir Mark Stanhope, as well as the then Assistant Chief of the Naval Staff, Rear Admiral Alan Massey. Thanks are also due to the officers and crew of HMS *Illustrious*, who welcomed me aboard to demonstrate how the Navy's carriers have evolved. In an even greater dazzle of gold braid, I was also most grateful and privileged that some of the most distinguished former First Sea Lords of the modern era agreed to talk to me: Admiral of the Fleet Sir Henry Leach, Admiral of the Fleet Sir Julian Oswald, and Admiral Sir Jock Slater. I was also fortunate that *Invincible* is blessed with a very strong First Commission Wardroom Association, many of whose members also responded enthusiastically to my project. The other former *Invincible* commanding officers who kindly gave up their time and memories were Admiral Sir Jeremy Black, Vice Admiral Sir Fabian Malbon, Rear Admiral Roy Clare, and Admiral Sir Ian Forbes. Other eminent former naval persons whose experience and knowledge I happily plundered included Admiral Sir Raymond Lygo, Admiral Sir James Eberle, Vice Admiral Sir Jeremy Blackham, and Rear Admiral Richard Hill. From the world of naval architecture, Professor David Andrews of University College, London, Professor Louis Rydill, and Arthur Honnor all gave their perspectives on the events recorded here. From the world of politics, Lord Owen and Sir John Nott kindly offered their reflections, as did some of the country's most distinguished civil servants in the defence field, Sir Patrick Nairne, Sir Michael Quinlan, Alistair Jaffray, and Sir David Omand. Professors Eric Grove and Gwyn Prins gave much focus to my thoughts. My researches were also greatly aided by Captain Christopher Page, Dr Malcolm Llewellyn-Jones, and the staff of the Naval Historical Branch, Graham Mottram and the staff of the Fleet Air Arm Museum, and Edward Hampshire at the National Archives, Kew. Thanks, in different ways, are due to the naval commentators and analysts Dr Norman Friedman, Richard Scott, Michael Codner, Jason Alderwick, and – posthumously – Antony Preston, who was a friend for many years with an infectious interest in all matters naval. Of course, I would not have had the excuse to inflict myself on this great armada of naval expertise without Pen & Sword, and especially my editor, Philip Sidnell, who gave me the chance to write this tale of an emblematic ship. Thanks also to David Stanford for scrutinizing the manuscript. And, finally, to my wife, Jill, for her loyal support, encouragement, and advice.

Foreword

I was fortunate enough to command HMS *Illustrious* in the mid-nineties which saw a period of continual change and concluded with the Ocean Wave Global Carrier deployment in 1997. The Invincible class was a product of the 1966 Wilson Government's cancellation of the CVA-01 aircraft carrier programme. The CVA-01 decision was precipitated by a change in foreign policy that dictated a withdrawal of national interest East of Suez which was the main argument for sea- based air power at the time. The result was the loss of independent power projection by the UK and a refocusing of defence priorities on the heartland of NATO's central front shaped by Cold War threats. The RAF were to provide air defence to the Fleet in conjunction with surface-to-air missile systems in new destroyers.

Within this smaller role for the Royal Navy, CVS was originally designed to accommodate twelve anti-submarine helicopters as defence against a large Soviet submarine force assessed as the main threat to the NATO alliance at sea. The offensive capability of the navy was to rest in its nuclear submarine fleet and amphibious capability deployed to protect NATO's northern flank.

The Soviets invested heavily in long range patrol aircraft such as the Tu-95 'Bear'. RAF interceptors could not meet response times which put surface units at risk from long range anti-ship missiles, most notably amphibious shipping. To counter this threat the Sea Harrier was born, increasing the CVS aircraft complement to seventeen.

The 1981 Nott Defence White Paper directed a swathe of cuts in the naval order of battle including amphibious shipping and the sale of *Invincible* to Australia. 1982 highlighted the white paper's erroneous assumption as *Invincible* and our amphibious forces became the bedrock for success in the Falklands. Another lesson re-learnt was the lack of organic airborne early warning (AEW) resulting in the loss of six ships. Post conflict, 849 Squadron re-commissioned with AEW Sea Kings and *Invincible*'s air group swelled to 21.

By 1991 the Soviet Union and Warsaw Pact had collapsed – 'Options for Change' heralded the promise of a 'defence dividend'. 1991 also saw the first Gulf War and the beginning of an unpredictable world after the Cold War's relative 'stability'. The Balkans conflict, increased tensions in Iraq and the

Kosovo War followed in quick succession with an Invincible-class ship always present.

The RAF's Harrier force had lost its *raison d'etre* with the fall of the Berlin Wall and became vulnerable to defence restructuring that followed. New Labour's Strategic Defence Review resulted in the formation of Joint Force Harrier (JFH); this drew together the strengths of land-based and maritime-based aircrew expertise. Concluding that an expeditionary force structure required assured combat air power, the UK once again committed to carrier air power thirty-two years after the cancellation of CVA-01. Sierra Leone in 2000 witnessed an amphibious operation, supported by JFH embarked in *Illustrious*. The next year *Illustrious* was conducting Exercise Saif Sareea off Oman when New York's Twin Towers were struck. The US response was swift with a surprise attack from the sea and *Illustrious* was re-configured with CH-47 Chinooks to deploy Special Forces into the mountains of Afghanistan.

As Nick Childs amply demonstrates in this excellent and very readable account of the life of one of the Royal Navy's most significant modern warships and the worlds from which she sprung and into which she emerged, the 'Age of *Invincible*' can be summarised as one of continual change. Designed for one role, developed for another within a Cold War strategic context, *Invincible* was pivotal for air power provision during the Falklands War and grew to accommodate a variety of global tensions spawned from the collapse of the Soviet era and ensuing unforeseen conflict areas. An agile ship in every respect, she has demonstrated the range of effects that aircraft carriers provide. Her gift was to extol the virtues of carrier air power and give the compelling operational evidence for CVF. Now and in future years UK forces on can be assured of air power provision at a time and place of military and political choice. CVF will be a Joint Defence asset, fit for the twenty-first century and at the heart of expeditionary operations – this will require an education process. Wielding significant influence amongst our US and European allies she will offer military planners a wider range of options and effects against potential threats to UK interests.

Admiral Sir Jonathon Band GCB ADC
First Sea Lord and Chief of Naval Staff

Introduction

The grey, overcast skies that day were hardly auspicious. But this really was the dawn of a new era for the Royal Navy. On 19 March 1980, HMS *Invincible*, the sixth ship in history to bear that name, slid gingerly into Portsmouth harbour for the first time and tied up at the South Railway Jetty.

There was certainly a sense of anticipation among the officers on *Invincible's* bridge. Most of those gazing out from the bridge windows had entered Portsmouth many times before in other ships. But they were more used to the compact dimensions of destroyers or frigates. The fact that *Invincible's* bridge towered a full nine decks above the waterline gave a hint that this was no ordinary arrival. Few of those staring out from that lofty perch had seen a view like this across the ancient naval base.

And, despite the discouraging weather, there were more than the usual knots of onlookers and well-wishers who have, through the ages, from the Round Tower and the other vantage points at the entrance to the historic Portsmouth dockyard, witnessed the comings and goings of Royal Navy vessels. For the inaugural appearance of a major new warship in what is to become her home port always stirs a special interest. And HMS *Invincible* was the biggest warship to have been designed and built in Britain since the Second World War.

Her commanding officer, Captain Michael Livesay, RN, surveyed this scene. He was certainly conscious of the moment, and of the excitement running through the ship's company. Tall, trim, with sharp good looks, he was one of the Navy's brightest and best, marked out since his earliest days of training at Dartmouth. He was keeping a very close eye on the navigator and pilot as they brought this valuable ship in to her berth. Strictly speaking, she was still in the hands of the shipyard that had built her. But he wanted to make sure nothing went wrong on what was *Invincible's* debut before the rest of the Fleet.

Above the mechanical hum, the clicks, whirs, and crackle of instruments, gauges, and intercoms that are the ever-present accompaniment in the enclosed, almost clinical surroundings of a modern warship's bridge, there was a special edge in people's voices as orders were issued and acknowledged. And a special intensity as the bridge team scanned the banks of new consoles and radar screens. But Mike Livesay had enough time for a joke or two with those around him, despite the responsibility which he knew was on his shoulders. It was typical of his air of unflappability.

Among those with him on the bridge that day was his second-in-command, Dermot Rhodes, who had been a year behind his captain at Dartmouth. Both men knew that, in a few hours, the ship would be theirs. Both also knew that, already, as well as the casual spectators gathered in clusters at the harbour's entrance, there would be countless pairs of professional eyes scanning every detail of the gleaming flanks and tall, modern, uncluttered upperworks of this new pride of the Navy to make sure that nothing was amiss. And, soon, it would be Dermot Rhodes' responsibility to make sure that nothing was, and that all the right protocols and rituals that the Navy holds so dear would be observed every time from now on whenever *Invincible* left or entered port. But, for Commander Rhodes too, it was a moment of great honour and satisfaction.

Because *Invincible* was not just another big, brand-new ship. She was also a new concept in warship design. And, perhaps more than any British warship for generations, she was a symbol of the fortunes of the Navy itself, and maybe even of where the country saw its place in the world. And those fortunes had certainly taken a dramatic turn in recent years.

There had been many other ships before which had left their mark on the naval and international scenes. Among them, at the beginning of the twentieth century, there was HMS *Dreadnought*, another new concept of warship produced to confront the growing German naval challenge. She created a revolution and defined an era.

There was the mighty battle-cruiser *Hood*. She was not a novel design herself. But, between the two world wars, she seemed to represent the very essence of British imperial might, at least as Britons themselves perceived it. A beautiful ship, her huge but flowing lines spoke of grace and strength, but not menace.

However, she also mirrored the growing gap between the image and reality of empire. HMS *Hood* became a legend. But, like the country's imperial pretensions, she failed to keep pace with the pressures of the changing world around her. And she was found devastatingly wanting when she was exposed to the harsh realities of modern conflict against the new German battleship *Bismarck* on a bleak May morning in the icy north Atlantic waters off Greenland in 1941. Whether it was a lucky shot or not, she was literally blown to pieces, with just three survivors from her crew of more than 1,400.

It was part of the essence of *Invincible*'s symbolism, and a sign of the times, that she was born with an identity crisis. She was an aircraft carrier, albeit not like any that had gone before. But that fact had only recently been officially acknowledged. Indeed, a great many people seemed to have gone to great lengths to conceal it, because to have done otherwise would have been to court disaster, at least as far as the Navy was concerned, and threatened the survival of the ship and what she represented.

And she was conceived out of what had been, for the Navy, a calamity. After the Second World War, aircraft carriers had become its heart. Their squadrons of aircraft had taken over from the battleships' guns as the foundations of the Navy's striking power and its ability to range the oceans, and were the *raison d'être* for much of the rest of the Fleet.

The Navy had been devoting huge resources, and heroic efforts, to staying at the cutting edge of the business of flying fixed-wing aircraft from ships at sea. As the aircraft had got bigger and more powerful, so the challenges too had grown. And the necessary accompanying paraphernalia of steam catapults, arrester gear, landing aids, radar direction, and support facilities had got ever more complex.

In the early 1960s, the Navy had seemed to invest all its hopes in a new generation of big and expensive aircraft carriers, the first of which was to have been the now almost mythical – at least in naval circles – CVA-01. Those hopes were shattered when the plans were abruptly cancelled in early 1966, and it was announced that what had seemed an essential prop to modern naval power was to be taken away.

It looked as if fixed-wing flying at sea would be coming to an early end for the Royal Navy. It was a skill which the Navy had helped pioneer, and of which it was still a leading exponent. And with its passing, it seemed, would also pass the Navy's ability to sail the oceans independently.

It was, of course, a huge shock for the Navy. For many outside naval circles, though, and even some within, it was more akin to a self-inflicted wound. Was not the real story that, not for the first time, Their Lordships of the Admiralty had failed – or refused – to acknowledge the changing times and adjust their ambitions accordingly?

After all, the decades after the Second World War had appeared to be the era of trying to manage, and in the eyes of many actually mismanaging, Britain's relative and absolute global decline. How much could, and should, Britain afford to do in the world? And by what means? What was genuinely in the country's best interests, and what was simply trying to cling on to an illusion of national grandeur?

Perhaps inevitably, the Navy, and in particular its quest for carriers, found themselves at the eye of this particular political storm. In very different circumstances, they still are. Of all conventional weaponry in the modern age, aircraft carriers are perhaps the most telling signal of how a country views its place in the world. Indeed, the giant carriers of today's US Navy have been – apart from nuclear weapons – probably the most influential instruments of war of this age, and possibly any. Such associations have become both a strength and a weakness, especially when their fate has come to be debated in Britain.

It is something of an irony that the Navy's past glories and supremacy have almost become a handicap to its recent fortunes and potential future. The story of the last few decades has been one of painful adjustment for all the services, and for the country. For the Navy, though, it has often seemed a particularly anguished experience. Its past achievements and reputation meant that, like Nelson's Column, the pedestal on which it stood seemed tallest, so its fall has appeared the furthest and hardest. And every time that it has tried to defend its position or revive its fortunes, its leaders have been accused of dwelling on the past. Had not the Navy's main function and purpose been to help build and defend an empire? Now that the empire was going, perhaps the country's maritime pretensions should logically subside with it. This natural impulse in the minds of many has been the hardest hurdle that the Navy has had to overcome.

Already, by the beginning of the twentieth century, when HMS *Dreadnought* took to the water, the Navy was having to reconcile itself to a dwindling supremacy. Maintaining its ascendancy in all the oceans was not possible – it was increasingly a matter of calculation, risk, priorities, and alliances. Industrialization – once the rest of the world had caught up with Britain's initial lead – inevitably shifted a balance of power which had favoured the maritime nations more towards the continental ones. The advent of air power also brought a new vulnerability to the British Isles. So, in two world wars, sea power remained indispensable to the nation's survival, but no longer a sufficient guarantor. It could not, in isolation, in a world of total war, keep the country safe.

Following the end of the Second World War, the Royal Navy was as large and powerful as it had ever been. But both it and the country were having to adjust to subordinate roles, completely eclipsed by the power of the United States. What should be the Royal Navy's role, when Britannia quite clearly no longer ruled the waves, when the legacy of empire now appeared to be more of a burden than a benefit, when Britain's most likely adversary was overwhelmingly a continental power, and when the advent of nuclear weapons seemed to be calling into question the very functions of naval forces and the slow-acting levers of maritime power, since full-scale war could be over almost literally in a flash?

Outward appearances were actually reassuring. The post-war contractions were obvious. But throughout most of this period Britain still had comfortably the most significant Western navy after the United States. The Fleet consisted of many fine, imposing ships, with a full range of capabilities.

And yet, for many, there was an underlying sense that it was beleaguered, struggling to find a coherent and consistent rationale for itself, even that it was living on borrowed time. And the admirals were often frustrated in their many attempts to make the maritime case.

Perhaps they did not always make that case as effectively as they could have done. And maybe, on too many occasions, the critics were right and the admirals were clinging to old thinking, and holding on to the Navy's traditions like a crutch.

Many of those admirals probably were too steeped in the past. As late as the 1980s, some of those in charge had joined the Navy when it was still the most powerful in the world, and they had done their initial seagoing training in battleships that had fought at the Battle of Jutland in 1916.

Of course, the world has changed, and so has the country. The Navy's place and role in both are also clearly different. People's perceptions of it – in as much as they think of it at all in this day and age – are not what they were, and that has become a major part of the challenge. But the Navy, beneath its veneer of traditions, has also become something different.

Most of those responsible for running it in the past few decades have been driven by a conviction that the Navy still can and should play a special role as an instrument of British policy and arm of the country's defence. That was true in the Cold War. It was true even more after the Cold War ended. And it is true in what might now be called the post-post-Cold-War era after the attacks of 11 September 2001 on the United States, as policymakers try to get a clearer perspective of what the new strategic and security landscape actually looks like now, what the real and enduring threats are, and how they can be kept at bay.

The basis of the Navy's case remains that, for a country like Britain, with its traditions and its modern circumstances, a relatively small but very wealthy nation reliant on globalisation and global trade, naval forces – perhaps more than any others – provide the greatest range of possibilities, options, and flexibility in deciding whether, when, and how to exercise influence and, if necessary, to project real power. And the evidence for that is there, the Navy contends with increasing exasperation, if only people will look and think hard enough. The questions are whether they really want to or can be persuaded to, and whether the country really wants to be that kind of international actor.

When HMS *Invincible* emerged in the last quarter of the twentieth century, it had been after an almighty struggle in the corridors of Whitehall. It was a story of inter-service and even intra-service rivalry, of infighting and intrigue, of personalities pitted against each other, of hopes dashed and at least partially revived.

The fact that the story of fixed-wing flying at sea in the Royal Navy did not quite come to an end in the 1970s was due to the appearance of HMS *Invincible* and her sisters. And many different individuals, from different backgrounds, with different outlooks and often sharply opposing views, had a variety of parts to play in the unfolding drama.

So *Invincible* was at the heart of the revised vision of what the Navy should be and what it should do in the late 1970s and beyond, after the upheavals that had gone before, with both the nation's and the Fleet's seemingly reduced horizons. At the time, the Cold War appeared to be stretching endlessly into the future. *Invincible* also arrived on the scene at perhaps the nadir of Britain's post-war economic fortunes.

For some in the Navy, and especially those who had served in and flown from the decks of the old carriers, *Invincible* and her sisters yet to come were pale shadows of the ships that they were succeeding. In place of their thundering squadrons of fighters and heavy strike aircraft, the new ships would carry to sea just a handful of small jets and some helicopters.

For most of those officers and sailors gathered aboard *Invincible* as she edged in the gloom towards her berth for the first time on that March morning in 1980, *Invincible* very much represented the promise of new hope; a link to the past for sure, but more importantly a lifeline to a new, cohesive, and effective future for the Fleet more in keeping with the nation's real security priorities. Yes, the aircraft that she would carry would be smaller, slower, and more limited than those that had gone before. It was only the fact that they would be 'jump jets', relying on vertical/short take-off and landing (V/STOL) to operate, that made them viable aboard a ship like *Invincible* at all. But the package would maintain at least some of the crucial skills and capabilities for operating aircraft at sea, and with it the Navy's ability to act independently and flexibly around the world. Many of those aboard knew that they were lucky to have her.

And yet, to other sceptics, *Invincible* still looked like an extravagance in a period of chronic national financial strain, the incarnation of the continuing dreams of 'big ship' admirals to hold on to at least a semblance of the past. She was expensive, vulnerable, and of dubious value.

But none of the people involved, on whichever side of the debate they stood, and certainly none of the people who lined her decks or waved her in as she arrived in Portsmouth, can have foreseen how tumultuous her early career would be. Barely a year after she was commissioned, another series of political decisions looked set to bring her Royal Navy service to a premature end. Within months of those developments, much larger crowds than had greeted her on that gloomy morning in March 1980 would be waving her and her crew off to war.

She and her sisters would be modernized and adapted as the world moved on from the Cold War. In an ironic twist, they would become the bridge to a longed-for new generation of big carriers. These would become the focus of a debate with so many echoes of the CVA-01 rows that it must have made those who were involved in the arguments of the 1960s almost wince with painful memories. Where, in the end, it will all leave the Royal Navy remains very much open to question.

But, on *Invincible*'s first day with the Fleet, all that lay in the future. Even the ceremonial commissioning of the ship by Her Majesty the Queen was still to come. Once *Invincible* was firmly tied up at her berth in Portsmouth, with very little delay and the minimum of fuss, Captain Livesay signed for the ship in a low-key ceremony in the hangar. The Red Ensign, which signified that, up to that moment, she was still the property and responsibility of her builders, was lowered, the White Ensign was raised, and she officially entered Royal Navy service.

CHAPTER ONE

Reviewing the Fleet

It is a tradition that dates back at least to the fifteenth century: the royal review of the Fleet. In 1415, Henry V inspected his ships before sailing for France for the campaign that culminated in the Battle of Agincourt.

Now it was Monday, 10 June 1953, at Spithead, between Portsmouth and the Isle of Wight. The Royal Navy mustered nearly 200 warships for the Coronation Review. The year before, Queen Elizabeth II had ascended to the throne. Indeed, there was talk of a new Elizabethan age. Given that the reign of the previous Elizabeth conjured up images of Drake and Raleigh, of defeating the Spanish Armada, and of the country establishing itself as a power on the high seas, it seemed to bode well for the Navy. Also, the Labour government that had taken office at the end of the Second World War had been replaced by a Conservative administration under Winston Churchill which would surely not turn its back on the Navy or a world role for Britain.

Riding at anchor were plenty of fine-looking cruisers and destroyers, but now just one battleship, HMS *Vanguard*. The long line of aircraft carriers was confirmation that they were now seen as the Fleet's capital ship, even though some of these were just training ships with no aircraft of their own.

Aboard one of those carriers, HMS *Implacable*, just a few weeks after entering Dartmouth Naval College, was a young Dermot Rhodes. For him, it was a dramatic and inspiring introduction to the Navy.

He came from Sheffield and went to Rotherham grammar school. But he did not relish the prospect of an office job in South Yorkshire. When he announced that he wanted to join the Navy, his father arranged through a friend for him to spend two weeks at sea on a Hull fishing trawler headed for the Arctic. Fortunately for him, the weather was kind, and he enjoyed it. On his return, he applied to the Navy and was accepted.

After two years at Dartmouth, and initial sea training, Rhodes would be sent as a midshipman to the still-considerable Mediterranean Fleet. He would be based mainly in Malta, still a substantial headquarters and very much a major naval base. There would be anti-arms-smuggling patrols off Cyprus, with shore leave in Beirut and a memorable taxi ride to Damascus – these were more innocent days in many ways. Then, after more courses at home in England, it would be back to the Mediterranean and Malta aboard HMS *Girdle Ness*, the trials ship for the new medium-range surface-to-air weapon, Sea Slug, the Navy's first real home-grown introduction to the missile age, and a great hope for the Fleet's future effectiveness. So, it was a not-untypical progress for a young naval officer through Britain's imperial and colonial twilight of the 1950s. But, beneath the surface, these had been troubling times for the Admiralty.

For Britain, the legacy of the Second World War was a swirl of contradictions. There was the mantle and euphoria of victory. The country still saw itself as a great power, with trappings of empire and obligations to discharge. But it also stood increasingly in the shadow of the United States and the growing power of the Soviet Union. And it was exhausted. The atmosphere for a long time in the period after 1945 was grim and austere, and years of persistent and chronic economic underperformance lay ahead.

Many in the Admiralty believed that there would be a return to something close to the pre-war state of affairs. The Navy would resume its role of protecting the sea routes and the country's world-wide possessions and interests. Many of the great ships did quickly disappear to the scrap yard, as the Navy suffered the same massive post-war contractions that the other services had to face. The huge building programmes under way at the end of the war were massively curtailed.

In 1948, Julian Oswald was a 15-year-old about to embark on a Navy career that would take him to the very top – although he obviously did not know that then, and had applied to join Dartmouth as a way of escaping Latin at school. So he was rather alarmed to pick up a newspaper and see a front-page picture of a cruiser and four destroyers and, under it, a caption stating that this was the entire operational strength of the Home Fleet.

Of course, the Navy had other fleets. Serving out in the Far East at the time, aboard the destroyer HMS *Cossack*, was a young James Eberle. This was the real Royal Navy, he felt, rather than the Home Fleet. Out here, the conflict had not really ended, and there was a proper job to do, far from home, continuing to defend the empire. This was the period of the Yangtze Incident, with the frigate HMS *Amethyst* trapped by communist Chinese forces, and then managing a daring escape. There were patrols to be carried out in the Malacca Straits. The Korean War was not very far into the future. As for the Mediterranean Fleet, that was all about nice foreign postings with the family, and polo in Malta.

The state of the Home Fleet may have been an extreme, but the realisation did begin to dawn in the Admiralty that its plans for the future were too ambitious, that it would have far less money and far fewer ships than it had expected. While much of the Navy may never emerge again from the half-life of post-war reserve, there were still plenty of ships with reassuringly familiar names and outlines; cruisers that had done great service in the war, and even some of the most modern battleships survived for a few years, albeit in the reduced circumstances of training roles. This would continue to be a time of painful adjustment. This was a navy in which sailors still slept in hammocks. In the ranks of officers, there were many whose attitude and outlook would not have been out of place in Victorian times. But it had turned out to be another world compared to what had gone before, and it would keep on changing.

There was the afterglow of military victory, a respect still for the military and affection for the Navy, and an expectation that the country would resume a role if not as a superpower, then at least as one of the world's leading powers. Its industrial base was dilapidated, but still in better shape than most of its leading rivals, and it was producing world-beating designs. The fact that they were the products of what would soon come to look like cottage industries in world comparisons had not yet dawned on most people in Britain.

The creation of the North Atlantic Treaty Organization – NATO – was prompted and encouraged from London. Since a defining element of it was keeping the transatlantic link between North America and Europe, the Navy could hardly complain – it seemed as if it was, fundamentally, a maritime alliance. But, as time passed and the shape of the East–West strategic balance shifted, the dominating factor in Britain's membership – and the dominating perspective along the corridors of Whitehall – would come to be the continuing commitment of substantial British land and air forces on the continental mainland.

Throughout this period, the Royal Navy remained an indisputably large and powerful fleet – albeit with many material and manning shortfalls – set apart from every other western navy bar that of the United States. But the drag of a stumbling economy was taking its toll. The Naval Staff saw most of its ambitious post-war plans for new classes of aircraft carriers and powerful new cruisers repeatedly deferred or shelved. For the most part, it had to be content with modifying what major ships it had as best it could, and busying itself with the bread-and-butter business of modernizing its smaller escorts for whatever role would be required of them.

The most troubling problem from the early post-war years and into the 1950s was the developing debate, which simmered and occasionally raged, over what precisely the role of traditional naval forces would be in the context of all-out nuclear war and its aftermath. Indeed, did they actually have a major role in the age of the thermonuclear weapon? Or should the Navy's focus be on more limited conflicts? After all, these were contingencies that seemed more likely actually to occur, given the instabilities in the Middle East and Far East, and the contraction pains of British imperial decline.

The siege mentality in the Admiralty by the mid-1950s was unmistakeable. The Army, somehow, had a more defined role. And the image of the RAF seemed far more in tune with the mood of the times, of galloping and exciting technological change in areas like radar, rockets, and jet aircraft. As it took delivery of its amazing new V-bombers, and took custodianship of the British nuclear deterrent, it seemed to be the dominant service, a bitter pill for those in what was supposedly the Senior Service. In contrast, the Navy, with perhaps still too many big old ships and an unclear strategic outlook, appeared in some ways like an anachronism.

What is more, there was, in 1956, the trauma of the Suez Crisis. That unhappy confrontation seemed to deal a devastating blow to the country's self-image as a great power, and brought home many of the realities of its actual position in the global pecking order.

But, a year earlier, in 1955, Admiral the Earl Mountbatten of Burma had taken over as perhaps the most remarkable First Sea Lord of modern times. It was, perhaps, something of a reflection of what kind of country Britain still was then that the uncle by marriage of The Queen should be taking up the position of professional head of one of the fighting services. But Mountbatten's outlook was very much more modern than that of many of his naval peers.

As he was preparing to take up his assignment, he was warned in a letter by the man whom he would succeed, Admiral Sir Rhoderick McGrigor, that 'we are having a continual battle for the very existence of the Navy'.[1] Treasury demands for savings following the massive Korean War rearmament programme, increasing questions about the Navy's role in the age of thermonuclear weapons, and the first serious skirmishes over its carriers, had all been sounding alarms. Another of Mountbatten's senior colleagues complained to him that the Navy was now regarded as the 'Cinderella' of the fighting services, and that it had not been putting its case sufficiently firmly. That was something of which Mountbatten would never have been accused.

But the aftermath of Suez would inevitably mean more uncomfortable upheaval for everybody. The Prime Minister, Anthony Eden, resigned and was replaced by Harold MacMillan. He in turn appointed Duncan Sandys as a forthright, combative Minister of Defence. Sandys had a mission to shake up the services. As well as the unsatisfactory outcome of Suez, there was a crippling hangover still from the Korean rearmament programme. Sandys also had a track-record of antipathy towards aircraft carriers.

In just three months, the new minister would push through a radical defence review. The aim was smaller, cheaper forces. The thrust was a greater reliance on nuclear weapons and missiles, because that would supposedly be cheaper, and an end to compulsory National Service.

For the Navy, officially, the carrier was without question its modern capital ship, what made it a first-rank fleet in terms of prestige and capability, if not in terms of size, and what made the difference as far as being able to take on an independent world role was concerned. And yet, among many of the traditional seamen and gunnery officers in the Fleet, and the submariners, the attitude seemed still to be grudging and equivocal.

That is certainly how many of the naval aviators in the Fleet Air Arm (FAA) felt their art was regarded. And, to some extent, they were looked upon in turn as a rather renegade band, in the Navy but not quite of it, a breed apart even from other aviators, and perhaps dangerously over-committed to their cherished carriers and aircraft. But the naval aviators had had to struggle through much of their history with inferior aircraft compared to their land-based counterparts, and that was true through much of the 1950s with the transition to the jet age.

Mountbatten was himself an enthusiastic advocate. Like many of his contemporaries, he had bitter first-hand experience of the price the Navy paid in the Second World War for inadequate air cover.

Sandys, however, was seen not only as anti-carrier, but also as sceptical that the Royal Navy had any important role at all to play in an all-out, East–West conflict. Again, Admiral McGrigor warned Mountbatten that the Sandys view was that 'the Navy is no longer needed and it is a luxury the country cannot afford'.[2]

Sure enough, Sandys' 1957 Defence White Paper memorably described the role of naval forces in the context of total war as 'somewhat uncertain'. However, events had provided Mountbatten and the Navy with some ammunition. The First Sea Lord privately opposed the Suez invasion. But, for all the grim political fallout of the crisis, and complaints that the armed forces were initially unprepared, the actual operation in military terms – like the Korean War just a few years earlier – was a text-book demonstration of the usefulness of the Navy and its carriers in limited conflict. It was also the proving ground for a new type of ship that would become of key importance to the Navy: the converted aircraft carrier, equipped with helicopters, which could put ashore a battalion of Royal Marines and their equipment. The Commando carrier was born.

Mountbatten was able to win backing for the Navy's role as a flexible and mobile force for limited conflict and international policing, utilising task forces of carriers, amphibious ships, and the Royal Marines. And the White Paper conceded the value of carrier-centred naval forces in the context of limited conflict. Mountbatten also steered through big cuts in the reserve fleet which were long overdue. In the end, it was the RAF that was to feel the impact of the Sandys axe most sharply, while the Army was most deeply affected by the decision to phase out National Service in favour of an all-volunteer force.

But the Navy had no reason to be complacent. Under Mountbatten, it had apparently won a respite, but also created a hostage to fortune, as the rationale for its major units and forces was now firmly attached to an 'East of Suez' role, protecting Britain's position in the Far East.

In other ways, too, Mountbatten's tenure as First Sea Lord was to store up trouble for the future, at least as far as the Navy's case for new carriers would be concerned. First, he antagonised the RAF over his lobbying for the new naval strike aircraft, the NA.39 or Buccaneer as it was to be called, against their own cherished TSR.2. He was also a great enthusiast for the nuclear-powered submarine. And, by personally charming the US Navy's mercurial nuclear guru, Rear Admiral Hyman Rickover, he helped unlock the door to US co-operation, and accelerated the Navy's own nuclear-powered submarine programme. He thus promoted a rival to the carriers not only as capital ships of the future fleet but also as another conspicuous consumer of scarce resources.

The other ticking bomb for the Navy was Mountbatten's leading role in and enthusiasm for moves to centralize the organization of defence. The logic may have been difficult to fault, as the different elements of war-fighting – land, sea, and air – seemed ever more to overlap. And the problems of furnishing the services' ever more challenging needs on limited resources seemed increasingly to overwhelm their individual ministries and require the rationalization of a central authority.

The trend somehow seemed to hit the Navy hardest. It would steadily undercut and ultimately supersede the Admiralty, which had been such an influential and historic power-base on which so much had rested. It had been a great office, and great decisions had been taken in the ornate Admiralty Boardroom by men who were truly national figures, around the great polished table with a semi-circle carved out of one end to accommodate the proportions of an exceptionally hefty member of the Board. There was the great long-needled gauge on the wall depicting the Channel, attached to a weather vane on the roof, so that in the days of sail when the wind was from the west, the admirals and ministers could sit easily sipping their port and say, 'the "Frogs" can't get us now'. The sense of history was enormous, perhaps too great.

The venue would remain, at least for a few years, but not the power. The Admiralty, the War Office, and the Air Ministry would all disappear in April 1964. The Ministry of Defence, from its modest beginnings as a co-ordinating organization, would become the single, overarching body. It was a double blow for the Navy, since its officers, who had always looked down on the idea of staff work, were ill-equipped to fight in the corridors of power on equal terms with their Army and RAF counterparts. Julian Oswald, as a young officer, would cheerfully tell a friend that he had been sent on a staff course, only for the friend to shake his head gloomily and respond: 'Oh dear, you've been "parked", have you?'

The 1960s dawned with the Navy finally beginning to bear the fruits of much painful effort in the decade before. On 10 June 1960, the Navy's very first guided-missile destroyer, HMS *Devonshire*, was launched at the Cammell Laird shipyard in Birkenhead. Four months later, on Trafalgar Day, 21 October, the first British nuclear-powered submarine, a new HMS *Dreadnought*, went down the ways at the Vickers Armstrong yard at Barrow-In-Furness. In between those two events, in August, the Royal Navy's only remaining battleship, HMS *Vanguard*, began her last, sad voyage from Portsmouth to the breaker's yard.

There was also much to and fro within the Navy's carrier force. The eve of the new decade, November 1959, had finally seen the commissioning of the aircraft carrier HMS *Hermes*. She had been an astonishing fifteen years in the building, the delays the result of financial stringencies and constantly changing requirements as technology had evolved. She was really too small to be fully effective now. The Navy's most powerful carriers, the modern ships of the line almost, were 'fleet carriers', as opposed to the hum–drum 'escort' carriers, mainly merchant ship conversions, that had become so vital in the Battle of the Atlantic and beyond in the Second World War. *Hermes* was a 'light fleet carrier'. And her existence would become an Achilles heel in the Navy's fight for new carriers in the coming years. But at least she emerged with all the latest carrier developments, like steam catapults and an angled flight deck. And she would ultimately prove her worth.

Precisely as HMS *Hermes* emerged, one of the Navy's two biggest fleet carriers, HMS *Eagle*, disappeared into Devonport dockyard for a major modernization. But the beginning of 1958 had also seen the return to the Fleet after an amazing seven–and–a–half years in dockyard hands at Portsmouth of the only Second World War British carrier to have been fully modernized, HMS *Victorious*. She, like *Hermes*, could now – just – operate the latest naval aircraft.

Also like *Hermes*, and later *Eagle* on her reappearance after refit, *Victorious* carried prominently on her new, modern island superstructure the extraordinary long–range 3-D radar, the Type 984, with its unique antenna like a giant rotating dustbin. This huge radar, like the cumbersome new Sea Slug missile system that was HMS *Devonshire*'s main armament, was a testament to British technical ingenuity in the face of chronically limited resources. So, too, were the new generations of aircraft that would be the carriers' 'big guns' – the Scimitar, Sea Vixen, and Buccaneer. These three carriers – *Hermes*, *Victorious*, and *Eagle* – with their unique radar, new profiles, and new aircraft would be the symbols of how the Admiralty saw the Navy in the 1960s. They would all take turns at being a prominent, potent, and confidence-inspiring presence on the Navy's main foreign stations at this time. But the Naval Staff was also looking once more at the longer term.

If the carrier force was to continue, the Navy really did need some new ones. After the abortive studies in the early 1950s, the Admiralty had begun to consider the matter afresh. Briefly, some of the carrier enthusiasts even entertained the hope they might be driven by nuclear power.

On the same day that HMS *Devonshire* took to the water, 10 June 1960, a large group gathered at the Admiralty in London to discuss the characteristics of the planned new aircraft carrier, CVA-01 as it was called, on which the Navy had set its heart. The 'A' stood for attack. This would be a carrier capable of launching the most potent, up-to-date strike aircraft. This would be a strike carrier.

In the chair for the meeting was a thoughtful 39-year-old captain, Terence Lewin, who would go on to rise to the top of Britain's military chain of command as a particularly influential Chief of the Defence Staff at a critical time. He opened proceedings with the thought that, 'we are now starting on a long road which might perhaps end in 1971 with the first of these new carriers entering service'.[3] The road, as it turned out, was much longer and more twisting than anyone at that meeting, including Lewin, could have imagined at the time.

But the Navy knew, after the anguish that it had experienced already in the Whitehall maelstrom, that it would have a fight on its hands. Various design studies were now being considered, ranging from 42,000 tons to a monster of 68,000 tons and 1,000 feet in length – essentially an equivalent of the American Forrestal-class of super-carriers, which had recently appeared on the scene and was clearly having an important influence on thinking in the Royal Navy. It was perhaps a reflection of the ambitions still held in some quarters in the Naval Staff that the biggest design seemed to come closest to meeting their operational requirements, and even then it did not quite measure up. But it was quickly realized that such a ship would never be authorised.

The controversial Duncan Sandys was replaced as Minister of Defence by the more low-key Harold Watkinson. In May 1961, in front of him and a large audience from all the services and beyond, the Admiralty presented its views of what forces it would need in the next two decades. It had been given three potential scenarios to consider: first, with commitments as they existed then; secondly, with no East of Suez commitments, and forces confined almost entirely to NATO; and thirdly, an East of Suez role, but no bases except in Australia. The three scenarios were a reflection of how everyone, at the start of what was to prove to be a tumultuous decade in so many ways, was groping to understand what the future might hold, when everything seemed so uncertain.

At that point, the Navy had an unsatisfactory mixed bag of seven small, medium, and large carriers, modernized and un-modernized, operational and in reserve. For the first scenario, the Navy reckoned that it would still need five carriers. For the second, strikingly, it said it could not see a case for replacing its existing carriers under the current NATO strategy, even for anti-submarine warfare (ASW) against the growing Soviet submarine threat. It would make do instead with an emerging new design idea, the escort cruiser, with ASW helicopters. This was the real first forefather of HMS *Invincible*.

But if that gesture gained the Navy credit for being willing to entertain the prospect of painful change, it was probably immediately undone in the RAF's eyes by the fact that the Admiralty suggested that the carriers' nuclear strike capability could be replaced by American-built Polaris submarine-launched ballistic missiles. Polaris was the spectre that threatened the RAF's most prized possession – guardianship of the country's nuclear deterrent.

And there was more. In front of the assembled gathering, the Navy unveiled its third option – Fleet C – for a world in which Britain wanted to retain its military capability East of Suez, but would be able to rely on bases only in Australia. That, it argued, would need six carriers. Even so, it admitted, on its own it could still only provide one or two Royal Marine Commandos – in effect, two battalions of troops – if some sort of land intervention was required. Anything more, it acknowledged, would require a joint effort.

This was the crucial moment, not least because this was the scenario that seemed to be the most plausible rendition, from the vantage point of 1961, of Britain's likely predicament by the end of the 1970s – of a country straining to maintain its position in the Far East with fewer and fewer footholds. So the Navy made its sales pitch, for the other services to club together with it in a 'joint service seaborne force'.

At this point, the First Sea Lord got up before the assembled gathering. By now, that was Admiral Sir Caspar John, the first naval aviator to hold the office, and a strong and effective leader and advocate. He did not want to make extravagant claims for the Navy, he said, but if the country failed to retain its foreign bases and had increased problems with staging posts and over-flight rights, the sea would surely become all the more important.

The Admiralty felt that 'a world-wide maritime strategy deserved examination', he said. Admiral John clearly meant it to be inclusive. For many in the audience, though, it must have sounded like a challenge. As for the Navy's carriers, he went on, 'I should like for a moment to take them out of the purely naval context. I should like to present them as national assets; as mobile self-contained airfields'.[4]

The First Sea Lord was clearly doing his best to sound statesman-like. In no sense did he see naval and land-based air power as in competition. They were entirely complementary. It is sensible for the Navy to own and operate the carriers, he argued, 'but we should welcome as much flexibility between seaborne and land-based aircraft squadrons as the Admiralty and the Air Ministry could devise'. In other words, the RAF could fly from carriers, and the Fleet Air Arm from the shore, if the situation required.

These ideas were not entirely new. They had been brewing in the Admiralty for some time – especially the concept of wrapping the new carriers that it wanted so badly not in the White Ensign but the Union Flag. The political mood, too, was for a greater coming together of the services as a way of reducing duplication and cost in these straitened and straining times.

The gesture may have seemed like a grand one, the idea that RAF squadrons should inhabit the places until now reserved for the Fleet Air Arm. Many of those in the light blue uniforms of the RAF, though, clearly viewed this as the Navy's Trojan horse. And the very words 'a world-wide maritime strategy' must have set off alarms in the other service ministries and the fledgling Ministry of Defence. This really must have appeared to some as a grandiose scheme by the admirals to wrest back the position of strategic pre-eminence, at least in the context of national if not NATO interests. But maybe, in terms of the political battleground of Whitehall, the Navy went too far, too soon. Whatever the motives, the results of its initiative were in the end to fan the flames of what would be a terrible inter-service rivalry in the years ahead.

There were discordant notes behind the scenes at the Admiralty as well. The Admiralty Board meeting on 26 June 1961 – less than six weeks after it had laid out its maritime vision – was one of many dominated by the carrier issue. And the Vice Chief of the Naval Staff, Vice Admiral Varyl Begg, was uncomfortable.

Carriers, he argued, already consumed huge resources, including in terms of how much of the rest of the Fleet was needed to protect them. Perhaps they could not be dispensed with in the short term, especially if the Navy's world-wide tasks remained unchanged. But surely it was possible that, in the long term, many of their tasks could be performed more cheaply, perhaps by submarines armed with long-range missiles. And he doubted that the Navy could afford everything that it needed or wanted – new carriers, new guided missiles, and nuclear-powered submarines. For now, he suggested, the Navy's position should be that it accepted the need for them reluctantly, not that it was pressing for them.

But Begg was overruled. The Navy pushed ahead with its plans. Not only that, it decided that it wanted a ship of 53,000 tons – bigger, although not by much, than even the biggest of its existing ships.

However, the arguments within the Navy were as nothing compared with the brewing inter-service acrimony between it and the RAF. At this time the civilian head of the Navy, the First Lord of the Admiralty, was Lord Carrington. His ministerial counterpart as Secretary of State for Air, Hugh Fraser, was to confess to him that 'he so loathed the bitterness and unseemliness of the quarrel', and that the whole business made him ill.[5] But that did not stop either from weighing in strongly for their respective services.

The rivalry between the Navy and the RAF was also being stoked at this time by an even more explosive issue – the future make-up of the British nuclear deterrent force. The RAF's stewardship now rested on a new air-launched missile, the Skybolt, being developed in the United States. In British service, it would be carried by the V-bombers, and would give them a new lease of life.

But Skybolt was in trouble. And, as the problems mounted, the Navy started lobbying and preparing more and more for a switch to the Polaris missile system. Barely had the world caught its breath after the Cuban Missile Crisis in October 1962 than the United States cancelled Skybolt the following month. A month after that, the Prime Minister, Harold MacMillan, flew to Nassau in the Bahamas to meet President John F. Kennedy, one of the most critical encounters in post-war Anglo-US relations, and perhaps in the history of Britain's post-war position in the world. One option might have been that Britain helped fund the completion of Skybolt's development. Instead, MacMillan came away with Kennedy's firm commitment to supply Britain with Polaris. The Navy would take custody of the ultimate nuclear role from the RAF.

The RAF had by now clearly set its sights on the Navy's carriers. But the nuclear decision only increased the antagonisms. The RAF had lost the deterrent. It was not about to concede to a partnership in the provision of long-range air power around the world, now its flagship capability.

The Chief of the Air Staff, Air Chief Marshal Sir Thomas Pike, countered the Navy's carrier case with a proposal of his own for a smaller ship that would not encroach too much on what he saw as the RAF's territory as the provider of offensive air power for the nation, anywhere in the world. Specifically, it would not be a platform for long-range strike aircraft. He called it the 'dual-purpose carrier' – it could act as a Commando ship, or as a mobile platform for land-based V/STOL fighters and light attack planes. It became known popularly as 'the Pike ship'.

Maybe it was a genuine compromise. Carrington was attracted by the idea, and believed that Caspar John was as well.[6] But the Naval Staff as whole was not interested. It would still be up to 40,000 tons. That was too big and expensive to be a commando carrier. But the design was less versatile than a full strike carrier like CVA-01. The Air Ministry complained that the Admiralty was misrepresenting its ideas. But, as the arguments and the studies mounted up, Lord Mountbatten, now as Chief of the Defence Staff, took a crucial hand. He managed to sway the chiefs of staff to accept that carriers would be needed as the number of shore bases went down, and also that a new carrier of 50,000 tons would be better able to accommodate new types of aircraft.

But the guerrilla warfare in Whitehall between the Navy and the RAF was growing in intensity, with broadsides, blasts, and counter-blasts from both sides. The level of resistance and unease in Whitehall meant that the Admiralty Board did whittle down its hoped-for new carrier force from five ships to four. Even so, on the Admiralty Board, there was continuing disquiet. At a meeting in late June 1962, another of the Navy's civilian ministers, the Civil Lord, Ian Orr-Ewing, was obviously worried about the proposed new design. The carrier programme was, he said, 'at risk of pricing itself out of the market'.[7] Maybe, he suggested, there should be serious consideration given to a smaller carrier of 40,000 tons.

The Navy was just about to make a new presentation to Harold Watkinson on the proposed design for its new carrier. But he was swept away in Harold MacMillan's swathe of Cabinet sackings, 'the Night of the Long Knives'. In came Peter Thorneycroft, another man with decidedly ambivalent views towards aircraft carriers. He would come up with his own suggestion for a cheap aircraft-carrying ship. It would be referred to officially as the 'offshore support ship'. Inevitably, at least in naval circles, like the Pike ship, it earned a nickname, 'the Thorney craft'.

But the Navy did not take to it any more enthusiastically. It would have been very basic, about 20,000 tons, and designed to support the Army ashore with a few V/STOL aircraft. The Admiralty saw it as limited and vulnerable. It did not even see it as an alternative to a fully-fledged aircraft carrier. It was another idea that was going nowhere because of Navy opposition.

On the other hand, in the autumn of 1962, Peter Thorneycroft started to hear increasing references to yet another idea that seemed to emanate from the Air Staff. In October, he decided that he needed to know more, and asked for details. This was 'the island strategy', or some preferred 'the island stance'. It was the RAF's real counter-attack to the Admiralty's world-wide maritime strategy.

The RAF was now mounting a two-pronged assault. It had been building its case against carriers. Air Chief Marshal Pike declared that the proposed new ships fell into the category of forces that the country should forego because 'they add much to our costs and little to our capability'.[8]

If the Chief of the Air Staff was leading the charge, he was also ably and enthusiastically supported. A recent arrival as his private secretary was a fiercely intelligent, energetic, and determined civil servant, Michael Quinlan, who would be behind many of the most telling papers emerging from the Air Ministry. The Navy was making the case that the usefulness of carriers had been underlined in recent crises, like the threat to the newly-independent Kuwait from Iraq in June 1961, when HMS *Victorious* and then HMS *Centaur* had been rushed to the Gulf, and their deterrent value had helped, the Navy said, to defuse the tensions. Quinlan was helpfully circulating papers suggesting that the carriers arrived too late to make a difference, and would have struggled in the conditions to have made a military difference if hostilities had broken out.

The second prong was the Air Staff's alternative vision to keep Britain in the military game in the Far East and beyond. The country's traditional bases in the region may soon be dwindling. But the reach of modern military aircraft was getting longer. And, with a chain of new island bases stretched out into the Indian Ocean, it could provide the air power – whether transport planes, fighters, or strike aircraft – for most of the military situations that the country would need to confront, and squeeze the Navy's carriers out in the process.

Indeed, the Air Staff argued that the two competing visions were not really alternatives at all, since no conceivable world-wide strategy could do without staging posts of some description. The question was whether the country needed and could afford the Navy's carriers as well. The Navy plan would cost 800 million pounds, it stated, whereas its island bases would be no more than fifty million.

From an early stage, the Navy conceded the need for a network of staging posts for support aircraft. And it did not dispute that its carrier plan would be more expensive than the Air Staff's proposal. But it bitterly disagreed that the RAF could turn its staging posts into fully-fledged air bases, or provide the necessary numbers of aircraft, quite as cheaply as it suggested. It also disputed that the RAF could maintain the level of cover that it claimed, especially to protect naval forces at sea. And it pressed the argument that the island stance would become an increasing hostage to political fortunes, and would greatly reduce the country's room for manoeuvre.

This was a curious time, when Britain as a nation did not seem to know if it was coming or going. And the RAF's island-hopping vision seemed to be a curious mixture. It was founded, on the one hand, on the promise of technological advance, and the greater performance of exciting new aircraft designs then on the drawing boards. But the response to the prospect of British imperial retrenchment, of attempting to set up new world-wide footholds, seemed at odds with political reality and the mood of the age. It would surely attract a flurry of diplomatic fall-out and charges of neo-colonialism – something the Admiralty was quick to highlight.

The Minister of Defence, Peter Thorneycroft, seemed to be one of the sceptics, doubting the feasibility of the island strategy on political grounds. But, on both sides, these arguments would be rehearsed, repeated, and refined for another three years.

While the First Lord of the Admiralty, Lord Carrington, was privately sympathetic at this time to the idea of cheaper ships for the Navy, he agreed, in the face of the Naval Staff's continued attachment to the 53,000-ton CVA-01, to support the big carrier. He wrote to Thorneycroft that carriers of that size were the ones to go for. The Navy had studied a smaller design, of 10,000 tons less, but the larger vessel 'really does win hands down', he said.[9] And he played a trump card. His own view was that both carriers and island bases remained essential as complements to maintain a world-wide strategy. But he argued that, if the rationalization of British air power was a priority, as it was, the bigger carrier would be a better platform for the future joint Navy/RAF aircraft that Thorneycroft seemed to have set his heart on.

In the end, Thorneycroft also agreed to support the carriers. As he prepared for a crucial set of Cabinet meetings in July 1963, he wrote to his ministerial colleagues that 'when the last word has been said upon the matter, the carrier remains, for us as for the United States, the most flexible weapon for any type of conventional war'.[10]

But it was not going to be an easy fight. The Chancellor of the Exchequer, Reginald Maudling, offered an almost weary observation that could probably have been made by any number of his predecessors or successors. 'Every time we look at defence in the round' he said, 'we decide our commitments in total are too great. Every time we look at one or other commitment in isolation, we decide that it is inescapable. The result is that we go on planning to do more than we can or should afford in the field of defence'.[10]

Thorneycroft had concluded by now that a commitment to one new carrier was the most that could be agreed, in order to sustain a total force of three into the 1970s. But he persisted, 'so long as we sought to discharge a world-wide role, the Navy could not survive as a fighting force without carriers'. In the end, reluctantly, the Cabinet agreed to maintain a three-carrier force.

Thus, on 30 July 1963, the Minister of Defence stood up in the House of Commons to make an announcement. After full consideration, Thorneycroft said, the government had decided it was likely to need a force of three aircraft carriers for the 1970s. Two existing ships, *Eagle* and *Hermes*, could be extended until 1980. *Victorious* and *Ark Royal*, however, would come to the end of their useful lives in the early 1970s, so it had been decided to order one new carrier of about 50,000 tons. He also announced that the Navy and RAF had agreed to develop a common new aircraft.

It seemed that, after years of tortuous Whitehall battles, the Navy had won a victory. It was, in reality, nothing of the sort. And the RAF certainly had not given up.

CHAPTER TWO

1966 and All That

The Prime Minister's room in the House of Commons was not the usual venue for a gathering of the Cabinet. It was an unusual time as well. It was already dark outside, at six o'clock in the evening on that Monday, 14 February 1966.

The assembled ministers had already met once in the morning, in the normal surroundings of the Cabinet Room in 10 Downing Street. It was a big day, and it would end up being a long one. The Prime Minister, Harold Wilson, was in the chair. But at the centre of the day's deliberations was the burly figure of the Defence Secretary, Denis Healey. The topic of discussion was the government's critical defence review. It had been set in motion almost as soon as the new Labour Government had taken office sixteen months earlier, ending thirteen years of Conservative administration. Since then there had been seemingly endless meetings, studies, and papers, and increasingly anguished debate. Now it was time for the Defence Secretary to lay his proposals before his colleagues. It was time for decision.

It was also two-and-a-half years since Healey's Conservative predecessor had apparently given the green light to CVA-01. But the problems, and the questions, had persisted.

Even as Peter Thorneycroft had been making his earlier announcement in the House of Commons, his proposal for a joint Navy/RAF aircraft, the P.1154, was unravelling. Among themselves, senior naval officers were wondering if it was politically feasible to come out in opposition to the project. The two services really had two very different requirements – the Navy for an all-weather interceptor, the RAF for a ground-attack aircraft. And the Navy was increasingly unhappy that it was being asked to accept more and more limits on its version's performance. As a joint programme, the P.1154 would soon founder. By early 1964, Thorneycroft was writing to the US Defence Secretary, Robert McNamara, to enquire politely about the possible purchase of US-built Phantom aircraft.

The Treasury had also continued to place obstacles in the path of the carrier. And Carrington was soon complaining that he was 'very disagreeably surprised' at the lack of progress. Indeed, because of a Treasury embargo on further research and development, and the purchase of long-lead items, the programme had been 'positively set back'.[1]

Strikingly too, even within the Navy, controversy still simmered about whether the course that had been set was the right one. Just a month after the Thorneycroft announcement, the then new First Sea Lord, Admiral Sir David Luce, had felt the need to send an extraordinary signal to senior commanders around the world to explain the thinking behind the Admiralty Board's decision to go for this new carrier. 'I realize,' he said, 'that there are officers in the Fleet who genuinely do not understand why the Board have been so convinced that carriers – and a viable Fleet Air Arm – must continue to be an integral part of the Fleet in the military atmosphere of the 1970s. It is of the greatest importance that such officers should be fully apprised of the background'.[2]

When the Labour Party took office in October 1964, there was a widespread acceptance – even among the chiefs of staff – that the defence programme that it was inheriting was unsustainable. It was in that atmosphere that Denis Healey took up the reins at the Ministry of Defence. Already a strong and impressive political figure, he would certainly leave his mark, although possibly not in quite the way that he had originally intended.

Initially, neither Wilson nor Healey was in the business of cutting and running from Britain's world role. Labour's policy at the outset was to maintain it as far as possible. Healey observed that, when Labour came to office, Britain still had more troops East of Suez than in Germany. And, in his view, given the instability and upheavals in the Middle East and Far East, they were probably of more immediate use in maintaining international peace and security than the British contribution to NATO. There was the very real and ongoing Indonesia confrontation, with Britain's forces apparently providing an effective deterrent to escalation, a firm lid on that particular pressure cooker.

There was no escaping a sense that this was all finite. Britain's possessions overseas would inevitably dwindle. But, for the time being, there were treaty commitments and obligations to allies – key Commonwealth partners, and especially the Americans, who were making it clear that they would take a dim view of a British pull-out. So it was decided that the government's plan should be to achieve the least possible reduction in Britain's status as a world-wide power, against the background of acute economic pressure. The trouble was, that pressure was even more acute than most of Labour's incoming ministers realized.

There was an almost immediate sterling crisis. Cuts had to be made in public spending. At a crunch meeting at the Prime Minister's country residence, Chequers, in November 1964, senior ministers settled on a target – to reduce the strain of defence on the economy by cutting its share of the national cake from seven per cent to six per cent. That equated to a cap of two billion pounds on the defence budget at current prices by the end of the decade – 400 million pounds below the previous government's plan. And the

Treasury clearly had its own specific targets as well – the RAF and Navy 'sacred cows', TSR.2 and CVA-01.

In fact, the first to feel real pain was the RAF. In the early months of 1965 the programme for the P.1154, which the RAF had continued alone after the Navy pull-out, was finally cancelled, and so too an advanced transport aircraft, the HS.681.

Most wounding, though, was the cancellation of the TSR.2, in April 1965. It was an astonishing looking aircraft, and no doubt a technical tour de force that would have been ahead of its time and a world-beater in many ways. It is still referred to in hushed tones and with the same reverence in most British aviation circles as CVA-01 is in naval ones. But it was hugely complex, had become massively expensive, and was set to become even more so.

Indeed, it may not have been, by then, quite the talisman for the most senior members of the Air Staff that CVA-01 was for the Navy. Michael Quinlan knew that his boss, the Chief of the Air Staff, now Air Chief Marshal Sir Charles Elworthy, was one of the doubters. And there was at least a consolation prize for the RAF – instead of the original hope of 150 TSR.2s, there would be an order for 50 of its supposedly cheaper and more cost-effective American rival, the swing-wing F-111, an aircraft to which Denis Healey seemed to have become especially attracted.

These reductions helped carry the government more than half-way to its savings goal. But more cuts were needed. The spotlight was soon focusing once more on the Navy and the carriers.

While the political manoeuvres continued to play out in Whitehall, two hours to the West by train from Paddington Station, a small but dedicated design team of naval constructors in Bath was struggling with another set of problems, of how to reconcile the various conflicting pressures to produce a workable design for CVA-01. It was proving to be a monumental task all by itself.

CVA-01's original chief constructor, the head of its design team, was a somewhat dour but wise Scot, James Lawrence. Under him, much of the key outline design work, and the basic appearance of the new ship, had been agreed. The artists' impressions of the time must certainly have excited high expectations, at least for Fleet Air Arm pilots. The design seemed so much in advance of the ships from which they currently flew, like a scaled-down version of the new American carriers, but with a huge domed structure above the bridge that would house a new Anglo-Dutch radar of great sophistication. For the Navy as a whole, though, such images may have done as much harm as good.

In 1963, there was a change in the design team. Lawrence was replaced as chief constructor by Louis Rydill. For Rydill, the next three years would be a demanding, frustrating, and unhappy time.

A short but determined man of strong views, Rydill was actually born in New York in 1922, after his parents emigrated to the United States. But, with the Depression and unemployment, they returned, disembarking after their transatlantic voyage in Plymouth, where the family settled. Rydill went to work as an apprentice in Devonport dockyard in 1938. The pressures of the Second World War intervened and gave him the chance – unusually for his background – to become a naval architect. But, before taking over the CVA-01 project, he had actually spent most of his professional time working on submarine designs, including for that first nuclear-powered vessel, *Dreadnought*.

Carriers are, of course, a massively complex design proposition. CVA-01 would end up with some 1,200 compartments. And, despite the various studies that were carried out over the years, there had not been a fully-fledged British carrier design since the Second World War. Moreover, the demands had changed so dramatically with the advent of bigger, heavier, and faster aircraft, imposing massively greater shocks and stresses on ship structures, requiring much more complicated support facilities, and setting much more complex operational problems. Rydill certainly had no carrier design experience. He argued strongly that he needed a bigger team. But he was told that the nuclear-powered submarine projects had priority. Yet again, Britain was trying to stay in the game with meagre resources. And, while Louis Rydill and his team had no direct contact with the political arguments and frictions on display in Whitehall, they certainly felt their effect.

In London, all the agitation was over whether CVA-01 was too big, too ambitious, and too extravagant – a potential monument in steel to a persistence of national self-delusion and naval over-ambition. The Navy had carefully marshalled its argument that a ship like CVA-01 was more cost-effective than the smaller options which were being promoted in different quarters.

But Rydill's team of designers were constantly exasperated by the requirement, as they saw it, to squeeze an effective strike carrier with the capabilities that the Navy wanted into a vessel of only 53,000 tons, much smaller than the Americans' equivalent vessels. Rydill himself was frustrated that the Admiralty Board had settled on what seemed like an arbitrary figure. Somehow 53,000 tons was deemed politically acceptable for the size of the ship, but 55,000 tons was not. He could certainly have done with that extra tonnage and more as the designers made their calculations.

Bit by bit, items disappeared from the Navy's shopping list of equipment for the new ship. One of the air defence missile launchers was sacrificed. The Ikara anti-submarine missile system was another casualty. As another saving, the new carrier would do without what had been one of the cherished traditional comforts and conveniences for senior officers on the Navy's big ships – separate sea and harbour accommodation.

Efforts at innovation were made everywhere to try to make the most of the design, and they often provoked heated argument. By the time Rydill took over the design, it had been decided to move the island superstructure inboard from its traditional position on the starboard edge of the flight deck to create an 'Alaskan highway' – a passage outboard of the island just wide enough to manoeuvre aircraft from the aft lift to the forward catapult. Extensive studies had apparently suggested that this would minimize the disruption to operations on the rest of the flight deck. But, when Rydill came in, another set of experts looked at the Alaskan highway and pronounced it a dreadful disaster – just one aircraft breaking down as it was being manoeuvred could completely wreck launch operations at a critical moment. Everyone, it seemed, had an opinion, and every section of the Navy wanted to get involved.

Rydill had made friends with a US naval architect and carrier expert who had been seconded to Bath as a technical liaison officer. His friend had looked at the design and immediately pronounced it too small, with insufficient margins for future growth. At the time, the Naval Staff was arguing in London that the Americans had been nodding approvingly at the British design. Whatever the truth, the US Navy has managed to utilise the same, much bigger basic design for its carriers, with the odd refinement here and there, for half a century.

Back in Whitehall, the various protagonists prepared once again to join battle over the carriers. And, in one subtle but perhaps crucial way, the balance of power in the corridors of the Ministry of Defence had already shifted. In terms of its top leaders, the RAF now seemed to have a decisive edge. There was the new Chief of the Air Staff, Charles Elworthy, a charming, sensible, and persuasive New Zealander, and a lawyer by training. His right-hand-man in many respects was another outstanding officer, the Assistant Chief of the Air Staff (Policy), Air Vice Marshal Peter Fletcher – seen in naval circles very much as the 'hatchet' man when it came to the carriers. And there was Michael Quinlan. In comparison, the then First Sea Lord, Admiral Luce, was serious, honourable, but rather diffident. Neither he nor those others on the Naval Staff who joined the new round in the battle for the carriers really seemed to measure up to the RAF team as 'Whitehall warriors'.

Whether or not Healey had preconceived notions, he gave the Navy plenty of opportunities to argue for the carriers. But August 1965 was a critical month, as the service chiefs submitted their cases. Charles Elworthy's was typically crisp and to the point, with all the hallmarks of a barrister summing up a prosecution case in court. He pulled no punches. Four hundred million pounds a year needed to be saved. It was now estimated that the carrier force would cost 1,450 million pounds over ten years. At times, this would mean only the small HMS *Hermes*, with as few as five strike aircraft, would be available east of Suez. It was a poor return for the money. Carriers were also slow and potentially vulnerable.

Elworthy went on. There had been no scenarios of a war at sea that needed carriers since 1945, and it was difficult to envisage them. The carrier case was founded on intervention, to support the Army overseas, and it was only indispensable in a few highly unlikely cases. What was 'a very narrow specification', he argued, would get narrower as the range, payload, and performance of land-based aircraft increased. Giving up carriers, he declared, would make only a small difference to the range of political and military options available to the government. In fact, it 'would not cause Her Majesty's Government to withdraw from any commitments or to alter its basic strategy'.[3]

In black and white, it looked like a clinical indictment. Admiral Luce's case seemed hamstrung from the outset. As the First Sea Lord acknowledged, 'it has never been suggested that seaborne air power alone could sustain our national strategy throughout the world in the 1970s'.[4]

But this was still a bitter argument over what capability the RAF could really offer to fill the gap that would be left by sacrificing the carriers, as well as how much firepower the carriers could really bring to bear, and how quickly. There was a chasm of understanding between the two services of how the strategic costs of giving up the carriers were weighed against the financial benefits. And it was – in addition – an ideological fight over the provision of a key element of the nation's air power.

Luce argued that, while carriers had some very particular advantages, the case for them rested on more general considerations as well: their flexibility, their deterrent value, the fact that – unlike island bases – they were politically invulnerable. He pointed to the effective use to which the US Navy was putting its carriers in Vietnam, and argued that this was bound to be having an impression on many nations around the world. 'Our force, though smaller, would be similarly regarded', he said.[5]

As well as the case on supporting the Army in an intervention role, the other issue on which the Navy and the RAF would not agree was the extent to which the latter could provide air cover for the former far out to sea in the absence of carriers, and the extent to which the Navy really needed it. The gap between the two positions on this was literally hundreds of miles wide. The Naval Staff was still inhabited by admirals who had seared on their memories the sinking by Japanese air attack of the battleship *Prince of Wales* and the battle-cruiser *Repulse* in the immediate aftermath of Pearl Harbour in December 1941. It was an event so shocking that, for many back in Britain, including possibly Churchill, it was the moment of greatest doubt about whether Britain would emerge victorious in the war.

But, for all that, the Navy was struggling. For all the services, the coming decade was really about a holding strategy, how Britain could best fulfil its remaining obligations in the Far East, and help maintain regional stability, as it liquidated its residual colonial assets. Yet, even so, the way Luce put it for the Navy, it was hardly a clarion call to spend nearly one and a half billion pounds of the taxpayers' money, or an agenda for the way ahead. 'Just as, in the past', he wrote, 'the Navy was the spearhead of British influence, holding our position until it could be consolidated by land-based forces, so in future it will be the rearguard maintaining our presence in an area where we need to exert our political influence until we can withdraw with dignity and safety'.[6]

The Navy was certainly engaged by now in a rearguard action. Opinion against the carriers was hardening rapidly. A crucial blow came just a few days after these RAF and Navy exchanges, when the Army finally got off the fence. The Chief of the General Staff, General Sir James Cassels, summed up his feelings in a memorandum on 17 August. Urgent economies had to be made, he agreed, and cutting the carrier force would be the least painful way of making the necessary savings. It would not, he argued, cripple Britain's defence capabilities.

In October, as the whole process was building to a climax, Healey went to see Harold Wilson to outline the way that his thoughts were leading. Britain could not afford more than three carriers in the 1970s. For all the objective arguments in favour of carriers, that was just not an effective force. It would mean only one East of Suez, and at times that would be the poor, limited *Hermes*. Giving up carriers would inevitably mean Britain's options would narrow; it would no longer have the ability to land troops against a sophisticated enemy. But it all meant, he argued, a stronger case in favour of F-111s.

Maybe it suited Healey to set the services against each other. Maybe he had no choice, since the Navy and the RAF were completely at loggerheads, and it was best for them to fight it out, with the Army as the swing voter. Healey's intellectual sympathy for the analytical approach, and for things American at the time, may have swayed him anyway towards the RAF camp and into believing only the best of the F-111. He relied a lot on scientific advice, but even that was divided. The influential Chief Scientific Adviser, Sir Solly Zuckerman, had tended to favour the carrier case in the various studies that he had been asked to undertake. He continued to argue that the island strategy was untried and – in effect – unworkable. It was, he said, 'a vast system of interacting human and technical components more complex than any we have ever achieved'.[7] Carriers may be expensive, but at least they are proven, was his message.

But Zuckerman had been close to Mountbatten, and was not really trusted by Healey. And one of Zuckerman's deputies, Sir William Cook, had also written to Healey. He said that he believed carriers were unnecessary; their offensive role was better carried out by the RAF, and the defensive role could also adequately be provided by land-based aircraft. He acknowledged that, without carriers, the Navy would no longer be an independent fighting service, but that was only a stronger argument for a root-and-branch review of its mission, size, and shape. As Healey sat and digested these words, he scribbled in the margins the words 'very useful'.[8]

Of course, it was part of the Navy's case as well that abandoning the carriers would have a fundamental impact on the Navy's capabilities. In that sense, it was throwing down a political gauntlet. The abandonment of carriers inevitably meant a step down in prestige and power, since there was no way to replace their capabilities completely in the foreseeable future.

Still the agony continued. Robert McNamara at the Pentagon, answering an enquiry from London, sent Healey an offer of one of the smaller and older American carriers. A Royal Navy team rushed to Washington for talks. The Americans offered to transfer one carrier in 1970. A second might be possible between 1970 and 1974, for a total cost of 150 million US dollars. The best of the ships that might be on offer was the USS *Shangri-La*, although she had been completed in 1944.

The Naval Staff was open to the idea, but hardly enthusiastic, to the exasperation of some Fleet Air Arm pilots who would by now accept any offer to keep fixed-wing flying in the Navy. Other options to whittle away at the costs were put on the table: cutting the number of new aircraft to be bought; abandoning the plan to fit the Phantoms that were being bought with British rather than American engines; or soldiering on with just *Ark Royal*, *Eagle*, and *Hermes*, and no new carriers at all. But it was all too little, too late.

And yet, the Naval Staff seemed to carry on with its hopes for CVA-01 as well. As late as December, 1965, the design was finalized. The size had, in the end, crept up after all, to 54,500 tons. Overall length would have been 963 feet. And for an overall cost of seventy million pounds, the ship would have been able to carry a mix of thirty-six Phantoms and Buccaneers, four airborne early warning (AEW) aircraft, five anti-submarine helicopters, and two search-and-rescue helicopters. It would certainly be a more potent package than even the biggest of the Navy's existing fleet carriers. The Naval Staff was even preparing to send out the formal invitations to the shipyards to bid for the contract.

The New Year dawned. 1966. One of the men who had been intimately involved in all the debates was Patrick Nairne, a highly-respected, serious, deliberate and dedicated civil servant. He had served in the Army during the Second World War. But when, after the war, he joined the civil service, he was assigned to the Admiralty in 1947. He remained there for nearly twenty years. He served as Carrington's private secretary when he was First Lord. But, when Healey arrived at the Ministry of Defence, he called on Nairne to do the same for him.

Patrick Nairne had spent much of his professional life helping to draft the case for carriers in the Admiralty. Now he had to leave all that behind, and any residual loyalties to the Navy. He quickly developed a respect for and rapport with Healey. They were very different characters, but had interests that overlapped. Nairne was an amateur painter. Healey's artistic flair found its outlet in photography.

Even at the Admiralty, Nairne had been uneasy with the development of the Navy's ambitions. He had become increasingly involved in the discussions about the nuclear-powered submarine programme, its potential but also its prospective growing cost. But, at the same time, there was CVA-01, which seemed to him like an elephant lumbering unstoppably forward.

And now, he thought, it was in its almost inevitable death throes. On 10 January, Nairne wrote a long and considered note to Healey in the beautiful, meticulous, almost copper-plate handwriting that was characteristic of many of his submissions. 'The Admiralty is mentally mixed up', he wrote.[9] Perhaps harking back to that Admiralty presentation five years earlier, he argued that maybe a full maritime strategy in the Far East would be the best solution, but the Navy could not construct, man, or afford to run it. The First Sea Lord, he suggested, realized this, but could not face the consequences of it.

Just a few days before, the Navy Minister, Christopher Mayhew, had launched his own final pitch to the keep the carriers. Mayhew and Healey did not get on. The junior minister had been largely sidelined by Healey in many of the discussions. He had become increasingly frustrated. And he had already complained that the government was failing to face up to the political realities: if cuts had to be made in already overstretched forces, then logically there had to be decisive cuts in commitments, he argued. There was at the centre of this defence review 'a political vacuum', he declared.[10]

His latest language was colourful indeed. Abandoning the carriers, he said, would mean 'a Navy that cannot sail the high seas, cannot protect our shipping, and cannot fight'. And, by his estimate, the savings would be just thirty million pounds a year. 'I can think of no more abject conclusion to this Defence Review than that we should risk so much for so little'.[11]

Just under three weeks later, on 27 January 1966, the Admiralty Board approved the final design for CVA-01. It must have been a poignant meeting, since the axe was clearly poised.

At the beginning of February, Admiral Luce made his final plea to Healey for the carriers. There was an impression, he said, that 'we stubborn sailors are completely sold on carriers and have wilfully refused to look beyond'. That was not so, he insisted, but there would be a 'horrifying' loss of capability without them. 'The country will need an effective Navy as far ahead as we are committed to being a "World Power" and the only way of ensuring this is to build CVA-01'.[12]

It was no use. Denis Healey joined the Admiralty Board on 7 February with his mind made up. It was a gloomy affair. Admiral Luce again set out what the Navy saw as the risks of the Defence Secretary's plan. If it was simply a question of cost, maybe there was still a way of bridging the gap at least to keep carriers throughout the 1970s. Denis Healey acknowledged that there would be some risks, and that there was always the possibility of the unforeseen. But, in all recent scenarios, he said, carriers had been useful rather than essential. And he returned to what was now the main theme of his argument, that a force of three carriers – the most that could be afforded – just was not viable.

Alistair Jaffray, who had taken over from Patrick Nairne in the Navy department, had for some time felt that CVA-01 was a lost cause purely on cost grounds. At the same time, he believed that the RAF's island strategy was unworkable, a 'cloud cuckoo land' concept that would also prove expensive if pursued.

There were also clearly doubts elsewhere at the centre of government. The influential Cabinet Secretary, Sir Burke Trend, took issue with the RAF case as well as he briefed the Prime Minister ahead of the crucial Cabinet meetings. Trend also observed that it was doubtful that the Americans or anyone else 'would take us seriously in the Far East if we were seen to be contracting out of the carrier role'.[13]

And yet, on that dark February evening in the House of Commons, the Defence Secretary sat with his colleagues in the Prime Minister's room. He placed his proposal before them. Aircraft carriers could not be regarded as cost-effective. They were relevant only for the Far East, were too vulnerable in the Atlantic, and in the Mediterranean and Middle East air cover could be provided by land bases.

The Navy, he said, could not man more than four carriers, and the country could not afford more than three. One of them would be *Hermes*, with just twelve fighters and seven strike aircraft. It was not to be a good return on 1,400 million pounds. The only operation for which carriers were essential was landing and withdrawing troops against sophisticated opposition beyond the range of land bases. And his proposal did not envisage needing that capability during the 1970s.

There was some concern around the table, and an acknowledgement of the mobility and flexibility of carriers. But then the Prime Minister weighed in. Yes, carriers were a valuable bonus to capabilities. But the Cabinet had to face the fact that they could only be afforded if the government breached its target ceiling of 2,000 million pounds for the defence budget. Indeed, even phasing out the carriers would leave the government a little above its self-imposed ceiling, it seemed. No-one was prepared to go any further.

And that, essentially, was that. The decision was taken. CVA-01 would not be built. The carrier force would be maintained only as a stop-gap until 1975 if that were possible. A week later, it was all confirmed in a statement in the House of Commons, and in an accompanying Defence White Paper.

It was a body blow to the Royal Navy. The First Sea Lord resigned. So too did the Navy Minister. But there was no great public groundswell of disapproval. In the run-up to the First World War, in the 1909 'naval scare', from an age when there were such things, the Admiralty was at loggerheads with the Treasury over the number of dreadnoughts to be built. A public cry had gone up, 'we want eight, and we won't wait'. The Admiralty got their ships. Indeed, Winston Churchill rather ruefully observed that the Navy ended up with more than it originally asked for. 'The Admiralty had demanded six ships. The economists offered four; and we finally compromised on eight.'

But that was when there was real fear of looming conflict, the Navy was still seen as the nation's indispensable shield, and the measure of national security was almost solely the preponderance of British battleships over all likely comers. There was nothing like that this time. There were other preoccupations now. The rest of the country – and the world – seemed to sail on. Within weeks of the carrier decision, Harold Wilson called a general election. Labour was returned with an increased parliamentary majority. And, pretty soon, the country was in the grip of a very different kind of public agitation, in the form of mounting expectation and eventual euphoria over the World Cup.

Louis Rydill declared that the day CVA-01 was cancelled was the happiest of his life. In his view, the design was a disaster. Neither of these sentiments was prompted because he was anti-carrier, but both were the result of his years of frustration over the project. If it had gone ahead, Rydill believed, the design would have been improved as the shipyards got hold of the plans and prepared actually to build the ship. It would not have been ideal, but then no ship ever is. But it would also have ended up being closer to 60,000 tons or more, and a lot more expensive.

In one sense, the explanation for the cancellation of the new carriers was simple. It was the most conspicuously expensive defence programme still in the offing at a time when cuts were still on the table. And yet it still seemed curious. Even those close to the whole argument were uncertain whether Denis Healey was really persuaded that the island strategy would deliver all that it claimed.

Much of the Navy persuaded itself that it was cheated by RAF dirty tricks. The story grew of dodgy RAF maps that were fixed to make the island strategy fit together. But the Navy in its turn was accused of some underhand leaking to the press. That was the spirit of the time. The Naval Staff was subsequently blamed by its own side for displaying arrogance and inflexibility in not being ready to consider something less ambitious than CVA-01 until it was too late. And why was the potential role of carriers in NATO, in the context of anti-submarine warfare, so readily dismissed?

But was CVA-01 really so exorbitant an ambition? It was a bit bigger, and a bit better, than the Navy's biggest and best up till then, *Ark Royal* and *Eagle*. But it was nothing like on the scale of what the Americans were turning out.

In view of what was to follow in just the next two years, what was at stake was not the avoidance of pain, but merely the sequence of it. Even if CVA-01 had not been axed in early 1966, it would probably not have lasted much longer. The plans of everyone at the Ministry of Defence – Denis Healey, the Navy, and the RAF – were all founded on economic quicksand, and they would all in the end be consumed by it.

Ironically, had the Labour government decided at its outset in 1964 that the east of Suez commitment would be wound up as quickly as possible, that might have changed the equation for CVA-01. Without the need to sustain a commitment in the Far East, a more modest Navy proposition at that time of just a twin-carrier force in a NATO role might have looked both viable and affordable. But, by the time that idea was actually mooted, the die had already been cast.

As it was, the RAF would struggle to provide the air cover for the Fleet that it promised. And its ability to provide the support for land operations at the distances suggested by the island stance would continue to look suspect. Indeed, only more than 30 years and at least two generations of weapons later, did it begin to look truly feasible.

CHAPTER THREE

The 'Cruiser'

'This is not the end of the world, or … the end of the Navy'. So wrote the editor of *The Naval Review*, the journal of Royal Navy officers, two months after the fateful announcement. The reaction of this august naval mouthpiece was clearly one more of sadness than anger. But there was real anger on display as well. One retired admiral fumed to another defence journal that Denis Healey had been 'the victim of one of the biggest confidence tricks of modern times'.[1] It was a widespread suspicion in the Navy, and would remain so, that RAF sharp-practice had scuppered the carriers. Officers like Dermot Rhodes felt that they had been brought up to rely on carrier air cover to go about their business; as far as they were concerned, they knew that the RAF could not provide what they needed.

The Navy was aggrieved, but perhaps it felt a little guilty too. Perhaps CVA-01 was a step too far. At the higher levels in the Navy, it was accepted that the job now was to get to grips with a future without carriers. Or was it?

On the day of the announcement, Julian Oswald was in the middle of a training course at Whale Island in Portsmouth. He was called in by the commanding officer, Arthur Power, and told to go away and produce a paper within a week on the possibilities of operating V/STOL aircraft at sea, what ships in the Fleet might take them, and what could be achieved. The answers that Oswald came back with seemed only to underline the Navy's predicament now: such planes could use any ship with a reasonable size of flight deck, but to have any reasonable capability a ship would still need to have a long, flat deck.

On 3 March 1966, the Admiralty Board welcomed Admiral Sir Varyl Begg as the new First Sea Lord, following the resignation of David Luce. A big and imposing man, it was Admiral Begg who had raised questions about the Navy's carrier plans five years before. Whether he had been prompted by great foresight, or because he was a traditional gunnery officer who had never been a real convert to carriers, he now had an unenviable task, to try to refashion the Navy's structure and rebuild its morale.

To consider the way forward, Begg set up the Future Fleet Working Party (FFWP), with the task of rethinking the shape of the Fleet in six months. It was a good idea, but the problems started almost immediately. The FFWP – or at least a large part of it – quickly set off in the direction of finding some way to keep a measure of air power within the Fleet, essentially to find a way around the wording of the Defence White Paper and what had seemed a pretty clear statement of the government's policy.

There was nothing on the scale of CVA-01. But the Working Party – rather like Julian Oswald's commanding officer at Whale Island – finally grasped at the idea of V/STOL aircraft at sea. They may not be any good as fighters for air defence, but they might have a limited reconnaissance and strike role.

The Working Party produced a blizzard of papers and design studies on fleet structures and different types of warships, as it desperately looked for something that appeared both new and workable. It soon developed some fourteen fleet concepts, including an all-small-ship navy, and even an all-submersible one, although that was quickly dismissed as 'illusory'. There were multiple sketches of different types of new destroyers and frigates, big and small.

But the main controversy surrounded various proposals for what were essentially mini-carriers, dubbed 'cruiser/carriers' or 'commando cruisers', to underline their relative modesty and to differentiate them from 'the real thing'. Of 17,000 -18,500 tons, it was proposed that they could carry combinations of helicopters and, eventually, V/STOL aircraft, as well as a sizeable force of Royal Marines.

The fleet concept that many in the Working Party clearly favoured was centred on six of these ships. Allowing for refits, that meant a pair could be kept operational East of Suez, another pair West of Suez. In each pair, one would be configured for anti-submarine warfare, airborne early warning, and what were cautiously dubbed 'probing' missions – in others words, very limited reconnaissance and strike. The other would operate as a Commando carrier. They were, in fact, rather like the offshore support ships that had been rejected just three years before. It was accepted that, initially, they would operate only helicopters. But the advocates of these ships clearly had in mind that they would eventually embark V/STOL aircraft. Their complement might then be, say, fourteen such planes and four AEW helicopters, or eight aircraft, four AEW helicopters, and six ASW machines. In the Commando role, they would carry eighteen assault helicopters.

The lingering indignation of some of those on the Working Party came through in some of the submissions. Without some form of ship-borne air support, one stated, the use of the Navy as an instrument of national policy would be severely limited. 'Until this issue could be examined with full objectivity,' it suggested, 'it does not seem capable of resolution'.[2] On paper, the quasi-carrier design looked flexible and adaptable. These new ships would also be less than half the size of CVA-01 and – at an estimated cost of just over thirty million pounds – less than half the price.

But they were too much for Admiral Begg. He was not happy, and personally intervened to insist on design studies that could not be mistaken for a carrier. His instruction produced annoyance and frustration within the FFWP which he himself had set up, and led also to some bizarre and ungainly designs as the Working Party did what it could to disguise aircraft-carrying design proposals as anything but that.

The tensions were understandable. The FFWP was going about its work against the background of the carriers going, but the East of Suez presence remaining. But that backdrop was beginning to shift again. And then there was the prevailing political reality. Begg was criticised for blocking talk of anything that might be construed as a carrier. But he had a difficult balancing act to perform. He had to judge what would be politically acceptable in the immediate aftermath of the carrier decision, against the urgency of clarifying the future for the sake of the Navy's morale.

Varyl Begg's appearance and manner were those of a very traditional naval officer. But his supporters believed that at least he had a clear vision of the future. Alistair Jaffray felt that he was a true strategic thinker, and the best First Sea Lord of his time. It seems that he did cherish the idea that missiles in their different forms would be able to fill the roles vacated by the carriers. It was a mixture of old and new, and perhaps a typical gunnery officer's solution – the answer was a fleet of vessels that were a bit like traditional cruisers, but armed with missiles instead of guns. But, if carriers had outlasted their natural lifespan in the eyes of some, the vision that the new generations of missiles under development would be good enough to plug the gap completely was and would remain hopelessly optimistic, and that was part of the problem.

Rumours of splits on the Admiralty Board were filtering into the press. One newspaper report in December 1966 carried the headline 'Admirals in dispute with First Sea Lord'.[3] There were certainly strong arguments and dissenting voices. But Begg was a very determined and dominant character and, for the time being, he got his way. The Admiralty Board was to reject key elements of the FFWP's recommendations. The submission on the future shape of the Fleet made to Denis Healey by the Board centred on a new cruiser that would not exceed 10,000 tons. The current generation of V/STOL aircraft was spoken of as not cost-effective, and the Board declared that future ships should be kept as small as possible. It all seemed to go a long way to suggesting that the Navy was genuinely embarked on a new course.

Indeed, it seemed a radical departure for a service that only recently had been contemplating the acquisition of a new 50,000-ton flagship, and while the other major fleets seemed to be planning bigger and bigger warships. It helped change the perception of the Admiralty Board in government. In that sense, Varyl Begg did the Navy a considerable service.

The term 'cruiser' has long been an evocative one in the Royal Navy. Not as imposing as the great battleships, they were nevertheless strong, powerful, and often very handsome ships, capable of independent operation. And, between the world wars especially, they became the real symbols of the Navy's world-wide presence, the colonial policemen of the seas.

Partly for that reason, in the aftermath of the Second World War, the concept of the traditional cruiser began to appear rather outmoded, and its proponents backward-looking. With the battleships too expensive to keep going, a few of the existing cruisers with their gleaming light grey outlines would remain an important part of the Fleet, regularly serving as flagships – ships like HMS *Belfast*, and HMS *Sheffield*, the 'Shiny Sheff'.

But only three more such ships would ever be completed. The rather extravagant studies for new cruisers, even armed with guided missiles, which emerged in the late 1940s and early 1950s, came to nothing. Mountbatten helped push the Navy in the direction of a more modest design for its first guided-missile ship, the County class, which could at least be plausibly termed a destroyer and thus not excite the same suspicions from the Treasury. Even so, the ships were – with a full load displacement of 6,200 tons – in reality closer to the size of Second World War light cruisers than the dashing destroyers of the past.

They were very much transitional ships. They were impressive, fine-looking, and comfortable vessels in a traditional sense. They were at home operating in any of the world's oceans. They had large crews of nearly 500. And, with two twin gun turrets, they were the last ships designed and built for the Royal Navy that could fire a traditional broadside.

But their raison d'etre was their main missile system, Sea Slug. They carried a large anti-submarine warfare (ASW) helicopter as well – another nod to the future. And they were powered partly by the then quite new-fangled gas turbines as well as the traditional steam.

Their technology, however, was quickly overtaken. This fact, and the continuing pressure for cuts, meant that the Royal Navy careers of all eight ships of the class – one of the last designs built with a truly world-wide perspective in mind – were relatively short.

So, large destroyers, plus the new generation of general-purpose frigates that were coming into the Fleet, seemed to be fulfilling most of the traditional cruiser roles at a more modest price. But the Navy's attachment to the cruiser in some shape or other still would not die.

At the beginning of the 1960s, it was resurrected in modified form. The Navy was still keen on a ship with the ability to operate independently, but was also starting to look at a new type of vessel to carry a detachment of large anti-submarine helicopters, to complement the hoped-for new carriers. Part of the idea was that, by relieving the carriers of the need to embark their own helicopters, those ships could pack in more fighters and strike aircraft, and thus become more effective in their primary role.

The outline of the new ship quickly grew from a destroyer-like design of just over 5,000 tons to a 13,000-tonner able to carry nine helicopters. They were originally dubbed just 'helicopter ships'. It was at the suggestion of the then First Lord of the Admiralty, Lord Carrington, that they were re-designated 'escort cruisers' in July 1960.

But the proposition always looked a dubious one in the climate of the day. There were obvious advantages. At a time when the increase in the number of Soviet submarines was beginning to become a real concern, they would be a way of getting more ASW helicopters into the Fleet. They could operate with the carriers, and allow them to pack an extra punch in planes. Or they could operate on their own in a limited war or peacekeeping context. The disadvantage was that this increased flexibility was being bought at the expense of introducing a whole new class of costly warship into the Fleet, and thus raising the price of the overall package. There were also doubts about whether the Navy could afford to man these new ships. Most crucially, some on the Naval Staff feared that the increased cost overall of adding these ships to the Fleet would put the carriers themselves under increased threat.

But, with the axe having fallen on the carriers anyway in 1966, the perspective after that looked rather different. Suddenly, the idea of a new cruiser for the Royal Navy took on a whole new connotation, especially if it was going to be limited to around 10,000 tons. It was also predicted to cost no more than thirty million pounds – less than half the cost of CVA-01. It offered the Navy the prospect of a reasonably significant ship around which to build its more modest task forces of the future. And yet, whatever it was, it was not an aircraft carrier, as far as the suspicious onlookers of the RAF and the Treasury were concerned.

After some persuading, Denis Healey seemed both convinced and mollified. So, in June 1967, he wrote to the Chancellor of the Exchequer, James Callaghan, to plead the case for the new cruiser. The Navy, he pointed out, had been uncertain about its future for three years. Its programme was actually quite modest. He also offered a further sacrifice on the Treasury's altar. Still in the Navy's plans was a new class of large and expensive guided-missile destroyer, the Type 82, which had been envisaged as escorts for CVA-01. The Navy had hoped at one point for eight. It was still thinking that four might be possible. On one hand, the Type 82's role had disappeared with the cancellation of the new carrier. On the other hand, with the impending demise of the existing carriers as well, the Navy was desperate to get the new Sea Dart medium-range anti-aircraft missile system which was the Type 82's main armament into the Fleet as quickly as possible. Healey said that, to help ease the financial strain, he would limit the class to just one ship, HMS *Bristol*, the construction of which was about to begin. It was a significant gesture by Healey. It was also a striking reversal of Churchill's 1909 'we want eight' compromise, and yet another sign of the times.

By now, even the Treasury was acknowledging that the Navy had made considerable economies, at the cost of great pain and anguish. It would still be on its guard about this cruiser proposal, seeing it already as potentially a very expensive new programme. But ministers now endorsed the broad outlines of the new shape of the Fleet that the Navy had set out. It would include three classes of ships: the cruiser, a medium-sized guided-missile destroyer of about

3,500 tons, and a new general-purpose frigate. This all promised a very different look for the Royal Navy by the end of the 1970s.

And yet, in the next two-and-a-half years, the Navy would effect a remarkable coup, shifting the goalposts of assumptions drastically back in its favour almost under the noses of the Air Department and the Treasury. The turnaround would be startling not just in the light of the anguished years that had gone before, and the Naval Staff's failure to press the carrier case to a successful conclusion, but also because it would take place when the political and economic goalposts were also continuing to shift in a contrary and adverse direction.

Pretty soon, the foundations of the 1966 Defence Review were being shaken and put in renewed doubt by the continuing economic pressures on the country. These were also producing convulsions within the government. The East of Suez commitment was coming under intense scrutiny. There were new tensions in the Cabinet, and increased pressure from members of the Labour Party who had always been dubious about the continuing East of Suez presence. All this meant that the proposals that Denis Healey had set out in early 1966 were very far from the last word on what was now turning into a rolling reappraisal of the country's defences.

Further emergency defence cuts of 100 million pounds were required within five months. But the economic gloom was unrelenting. By mid-1967, just as Healey was finalizing the case to Callaghan over the cruiser project, the balance of argument in the Cabinet on how long the country could afford to stay East of Suez was shifting, and the timetable for withdrawal was accelerated to the mid 1970s.

Still, the pressures persisted, not helped by the political and economic fallout from the 1967 Arab-Israeli War. That short, sharp confrontation threw into further doubt the military value of the British forces in the Middle East and Far East, and the Arab oil embargo added to the country's economic woes. By November, the government was forced to accept what it had been trying to avoid ever since it came to office, and the currency was devalued. James Callaghan resigned as Chancellor. There was a further immediate rash of piecemeal defence cuts, including the decision to scrap the old carrier HMS *Victorious* straightaway. Then, on what became known as 'Black Tuesday', 16 January 1968, the Prime Minister, Harold Wilson, made public the decision to pull out from East of Suez by the end of 1971, with an accompanying whirlwind of further defence cuts.

Specifically for the Navy, this meant that the phasing out of all the carriers would also be much accelerated. They would go by the end of 1972. The RAF also suffered a body blow. It would not get its F-111s after all, or its island bases. Its apparent triumph over the Navy, after all the years of wrangling, had lasted precisely twenty-three months.

But the repercussions of the Wilson announcement were more fundamental than that. From now on, the main rationale for British force levels in the future was to be unequivocally within a NATO context.

There was one happy coincidence, and one trend, which looked as if they might work to the Navy's advantage. First, just a month before the Wilson announcement, NATO had made a significant shift in its doctrine from a strategy of immediate and massive nuclear retaliation to any Soviet aggression to a posture of 'flexible response'. It was an acknowledgement that the Soviet Union had caught up sufficiently in the strategic nuclear stakes to make the previous strategy untenable. It put an added emphasis on conventional – including naval – forces as part of an escalating ladder of capabilities that it was hoped would increase deterrence, stability, and the chances of maintaining some degree of rational control in a crisis. But it was not going to be a pretext for any massive conventional rearmament.

Secondly, there was the looming presence of an ever more powerful Soviet fleet, which had, throughout the 1960s, been forcing itself increasingly on the West's attentions. Unfortunately for the Royal Navy, it was now looming so large that it seemed unlikely that anything Britain could do in its straitened circumstances would make a decisive difference in the balance of maritime power, even in the context of NATO and in just one part of one ocean, the eastern Atlantic. The country's traditions, expertise, and geographical location might argue in favour of a significant maritime contribution to the Alliance. But just what shape and size that contribution might be still seemed rather inexact and difficult to calculate, while the established and rather more formalized land and air commitments that the country had made to the Central Front in Europe were entrenched and still going to pull in another direction.

Just four weeks after Harold Wilson's statement in the House of Commons, which had so drastically shifted the country's security perspective, Terence Lewin, now a Rear Admiral, stood up to address an audience at the Royal United Services Institute for Defence Studies, just a short walk up Whitehall from the House of Commons, and in the shadow of the Ministry of Defence. He was now back working in that building as Assistant Chief of the Naval Staff responsible for policy, after a spell in command of the aircraft carrier, HMS *Hermes*, where he had experienced first-hand the challenges of maintaining the morale of the Navy, and especially the Fleet Air Arm, in the wake of the CVA-01 cancellation. It was over seven-and-a-half years since he had chaired that key early meeting setting out the characteristics of what the Navy hoped CVA-01 would become.

The title of his talk now was 'The Royal Navy In The Next Decade',[4] and he tried to paint a seascape of how the Navy saw itself from now on. He had not had much time to collect his thoughts. Quite apart from the fact that the East of Suez announcement was still fresh in people's minds, Lewin had been in his job only a few days when it had been made. Of course, much work had already been done to reshape the Navy. The question was, though, were the decisions still valid?

It was, he acknowledged at the outset, 'a fluid situation and new policies are in the making'. And yet he argued that the more NATO-focused strategy of the future would require a broad concept of operations similar to that which the Navy had employed before, but with more emphasis on the specific Soviet threat. There would have to be general naval forces to maintain a presence, backed up by higher-quality forces with better defensive and offensive capabilities, to match each level of potential escalation in a confrontation with the Soviet Union. This was the justification for the task force concept based on the new cruisers that would be at the heart of the new Navy. Perhaps revealing his personal view of the CVA-01 decision, he pointedly argued that the aircraft carrier combined the virtues of defence and offence, and 'that was why we liked it so much'. Now, though, those capabilities would be split, with the defensive abilities of the planned new cruisers and their ASW helicopters, and the offensive power of the Navy's growing force of nuclear-powered submarines. And, crucially, the Navy's amphibious forces would have a role in protecting NATO's flanks.

So, that was the broad outline of the Navy's vision of its own future. Behind many of Lewin's words on that day, though, was also a thought that has become the wistful refrain of many advocates of a maritime strategy in the modern age. He lamented that precisely those things for which a navy and maritime power had been and remained most valuable, are also those which are so difficult to quantify in analysis and theoretical scenarios: the value of deterrence, of conflicts prevented, and of flexibility to be ready for the unexpected. And, as he concluded, 'it is nearly always the unexpected that happens'.

But the Navy would still have to return many times to the question of why it remained so wedded to its idea of complex task forces centred on ships like the new cruisers. To the sceptics, it seemed as if senior naval officers would often just resort to some variation of the argument that the exercise of sea power was some mystical art with deep, eternal truths that others simply did not understand. Sea power allowed you to sweep your enemy from the oceans, and pursue your own strategic goals wherever you chose by sea or land.

But was it not different now? Fleets surely did not fight fleets any more. What was the justification for formations of large, expensive, and vulnerable ships lumbering along on the surface, when their prospective airborne and submarine opponents in the modern age seemed to have most of the advantages and none of the disadvantages of the maritime environment? And with the focus more squarely on NATO now, were the admirals not really preparing to fight some new version of the Battle of the Atlantic which could not possibly be valid and have time to have a real effect even in the new era of flexible response and some unknown – but short – period of tension or conventional fighting on the way to a nuclear showdown?

Alistair Jaffray, as he helped fight the case for the new shape of the Navy in Ministry of Defence committees and before the Treasury, felt the admirals' exasperation in return. Why was it always the Navy that had to justify its existence?

But that was the political reality, not least because the focus was now so much more on NATO. While a key foundation of the Alliance might have been its maritime element, the prism through which everything was viewed was the Central Front. The role of maritime forces was relevant to the extent that they did or did not give credibility to NATO's Central Front strategy of forward defence, a political imperative for the West Germans.

It may have been acknowledged that a lightning Soviet thrust into West Germany was the least likely scenario actually ever to materialize, but the political appetite to think through the implications of that was limited. Meanwhile, NATO's navies were still puzzling about what the Soviet naval build-up was really meant to achieve. In such circumstances, the best approach seemed to be to focus on the technical issues of how to deal with what remained the biggest threat to the Alliance at sea, the Soviet submarine.

While everyone was still taking stock of the fluid situation that Lewin had referred to in the wake of the East of Suez decision, a remarkable transformation was under way behind the scenes as the Admiralty got to grips with how it really saw its new cruiser developing. Throughout this period it was known as 'the command cruiser', to emphasize that its key function was the control of maritime forces, including the land-based aircraft that were now meant to become the Fleet's main airborne support.

The cruiser's other major functions were to carry the new medium-range surface-to-air missile, Sea Dart, again vital for air defence with the planned withdrawal of the carriers, and to be the platform for a concentration of large helicopters, that were rapidly coming to be seen as the most potent weapon against the Soviet Navy's burgeoning submarine force.

That was all very well, and the Naval Staff had won broad support for the concept. But it was on the basis that, as well as not exceeding 10,000 tons, the planned ship would cost no more than thirty million pounds.

As the Navy got down to its deliberations, the three design options that emerged at the beginning of 1968 all exceeded the original target. One was for a ship of 12,750 tons, to carry six helicopters. Then there were two more proposals, each to carry nine helicopters, of 17,500 and 18,750 tons respectively. Crucially, the first design looked more like a conventional cruiser, with a hangar for the helicopters in the superstructure and a flight deck confined to the aft end of the ship. The other two, though, had what was now being called a 'through' flight deck running the full length of the ship, with a hangar below, and a superstructure sited off to the starboard side – rather like an aircraft carrier.

By then, Varyl Begg had been reluctantly persuaded that a carrier-like design might be acceptable. But, crucially at this stage, there were two important changes of personnel and personality.

The first arrival was a new Navy Minister. At just 30 years old, David Owen became the political head of the Royal Navy. Having been born and bred in Plymouth, and with the parliamentary constituency of Plymouth (Devonport), he had a special attachment to the Navy. He was intellectually confident and ambitious. Even so, the thought of becoming the political master of a man like Varyl Begg, with all his salt-encrusted experience, was a daunting one. The First Sea Lord seemed to Owen to be from another age.

But Begg was in his last weeks in office himself. In August 1968, Admiral Sir Michael Le Fanu succeeded him as First Sea Lord. He was a very different character, more to Owen's liking. He was a charismatic and, by all accounts, exceptional leader. He certainly arrived with a flourish. Immediately on becoming First Sea Lord, he mounted a public relations master stroke. Four Buccaneers took off from Lossiemouth Naval Air Station in Scotland and, with in-flight refuelling and stops on the way, flew 8,000 miles in eighteen hours to land on HMS *Hermes* sailing off the west coast of Malaysia. In the observer's seat of one of the planes was Michael Le Fanu. On his arrival aboard *Hermes*, a signal was sent out: 'Distinguished Chinese Buccaneer observer recovered on deck'. It was a play that the new First Sea Lord often liked to make on his own name, 'Lee Fan Yu'.

Owen saw that the gesture immediately had the Navy, and especially the Fleet Air Arm, eating out of Le Fanu's hand. It may have put others in Whitehall on their guard. But Le Fanu, who had previously been Commander-In-Chief in the Middle East, and had just overseen the difficult withdrawal from Aden, was known well by Denis Healey, who greatly respected him. And he would co-opt Owen into a pact to push for the most carrier-like cruiser that they could manage, that would at least have the ability to take V/STOL aircraft to sea. David Owen agreed, so long as there was no direct confrontation with the RAF. Le Fanu told his minister that he would embrace the idea that the RAF should provide the aircraft, believing that once the principle had been accepted, the Air Force would soon lose interest.

Le Fanu would also be supported by a particularly strong team on the Naval Staff. There was the reform-minded Admiral Sir Frank Twiss as Second Sea Lord. Edward Ashmore, another steely character, was about to become Vice Chief of the Naval Staff. There was Lewin, soft-spoken but highly intelligent, and a reassuring presence. And in the influential post of Director of Naval Plans, there was a strong and straightforward figure in the shape of a Captain Henry Leach. In terms of personality, the balance of power in Whitehall had certainly swung back towards the Navy at this time.

The early months of 1969 were crucial in the development of the ship that would become *Invincible*, as the Navy debated its case extensively, and how to present it in a way that would convince the other services, the Defence

Secretary, and the Treasury. The proposed ship was now 18,750 tons, with an internal hangar and a through deck. Indeed, she was now being referred to as a 'through-deck cruiser'. The complement of helicopters had grown to twelve and the Navy was now firmly attached to the idea that the ship should have the option of operating fixed-wing V/STOL aircraft. But the cost for all of that was an estimated thirty-eight million pounds. It was a long way from 'about 10,000 tons' and 'about thirty million pounds' of just two years previously.

The Naval Staff looked hard for savings where it could. Maybe the cost of the V/STOL provision, two million pounds, should be entered separately, as essentially an optional extra. Again, as with CVA-01, some cherished traditions would be sacrificed. The special facilities for accommodating a Royal Marines band could be cut. That would at least save 100,000 pounds. Perhaps the ship should have cheaper diesel engines, for a monetary saving but also the operational cost of a reduced top speed.

On the morning of 27 March 1969, a group of senior officers gathered in David Owen's room in the Ministry of Defence to present their proposal. Everyone there was clearly conscious of the growth in the cost and particularly in the size of the proposed ship. The key justification was the need for more helicopters – now a total of twelve. The new Sea King was now seen as the Navy's principle weapon for taking on Soviet submarines, and it was deemed to have great potential, but American experience had shown that more needed to be carried in each cruiser to be fully effective. Owen agreed that the ship proposed should make sense to the Navy, but cautioned that the rest of the Ministry of Defence would have to be convinced, and that further cost savings would certainly help. There was an acknowledgement that the Air Staff would have to be sounded out now if the Navy was going to press the V/STOL option.

The Vice Chief of the Naval Staff, Admiral Ashmore, was deputed for the task. Given the recent history of animosity between the two services, he must have left that meeting with a sense of trepidation. Broaching with the RAF the idea of putting fixed-wing aircraft on a new design of ship was a task which would have to be approached with great caution and diplomacy.

Ashmore's letter to his RAF opposite number went through several drafts. It was eventually sent on 8 April.[5] With every line, it tiptoed very delicately towards its point. The new ships, it said, were planned to replace the current Tiger-class cruisers (and not, by implication, the aircraft carriers). But the RAF might be interested to know that there might be potential for the ships to carry V/STOL aircraft. However, Ashmore made it clear that the Navy was thinking only in terms of these being RAF planes. Of course, the matter would need joint study, he went on, but the Navy's preliminary thoughts were that there was a capability gap that would need to be filled between what shore-based aircraft and ship-borne missiles could provide. And, yes, David Owen had authorised trials of the V/STOL Harrier on the existing cruiser HMS *Blake*, which had been rebuilt with a hangar and flight deck to carry helicopters. But these were also played down. They were really to help potential foreign sales of the Harrier.

This delicate memo also pointed out that, in the Navy's view, the most cost-effective design for the new ships would be a through deck with a hangar below. An early draft carried the observation that 'it cannot be denied that, in many ways, the ship looks suspiciously like a mini-aircraft carrier!' That was omitted when the letter was finally sent.

This approach was, it seems, not quite the bombshell that the Navy had feared. As the Vice Chief of the Air Staff pointed out in his reply, since CVA-01 had been sunk, the RAF had suffered its own losses, with the cancellation of the F-111 and a reduction in bases. There was shared grief here, clearly, and possibly the makings of a truce, especially as the Navy was talking about RAF planes aboard its ships. Indeed, in a response typical of the Whitehall mind-set, the RAF even saw this as a possible pretext to propose buying some extra aircraft for itself to do the job.

In fact, the first joint Navy-RAF meeting on the subject took place on 18 April 1969, in Room 4336 of the Ministry of Defence. Formally, it was the Cruiser Sub-Committee of the Sea Air Warfare Committee. It was a Friday afternoon, and the thoughts of the attendees were probably already wandering towards the weekend. But it was a significant moment in the Navy's resuscitation. By the end of the month, the Naval Staff had revised its requirement for the cruiser to include potential combinations of large ASW helicopters and V/STOL aircraft.

The Navy still had to argue its case vigorously. As with the old carriers, questions were asked about the vulnerability of the new ships. As before, the Navy argued that they came as part of a package, with ships like the new Type 42 destroyers to protect them.

Owen himself still had doubts, and was clearly to be no pushover. He continued to query the cost with Le Fanu. He had also become a great advocate of the potential of nuclear-powered submarines. He asked whether the money that would be spent on the cruisers could be better spent on submarines. The Navy's response was that its surface and submarine forces were each complementary parts of the overall naval package, and that the cruisers were vital to the effectiveness of the rest of the surface fleet.

Alistair Jaffray could see that the main appeal for the Treasury would be one of cost-effectiveness. The Navy kept pressing the case that the cruisers were the cheapest way of getting more large anti-submarine helicopters to sea.

And things were starting to move quite quickly now. The RAF had finally decided that it would be unwise to oppose the cruiser; the Navy had set out a good case. And it was clear how much it meant to the admirals, after the loss of CVA-01. The cruiser had, the Air Force Department observed, 'attained a symbolic significance in the future fleet out of all proportion to its military value'.[6]

At the same time, it was clear that the RAF was not fooled by the Navy's tactics. Naval Staff Requirement 7097, as the detailed specification for the new ship was designated, was not just a replacement for existing cruisers, the Air Force Department noted, it was 'for all practical purposes a kind of mini-carrier'.[7]

Denis Healey was no fool and cannot have been misled either. Indeed, the only people who were probably fooled were the sailors themselves, who continued doggedly to call their new prize a through-deck cruiser. By that stage, nobody was taken in by the term 'cruiser'. Reports appeared in the press referring to the Navy's hopes for new mini-carriers. Treasury officials said they were 'difficult to distinguish' from aircraft carriers.

In December, the Navy made its pitch to Healey. By then, the atmosphere in the corridors of the Ministry of Defence was very different from the days of the carrier controversy four years earlier. For one thing, the Defence Secretary had now seen most of his own early plans frustrated. He was also conscious of how much the Navy had been forced to give up.

Indeed, David Owen noted that relations generally seemed much improved between the Navy and its ministerial bosses. He put it in large part down to another move afoot that seemed to underline that things were really changing in the Navy itself, that it was ready to embrace reform and able to adopt a genuinely modern perspective on the world.

There was still one naval 'hangover' from the past, in more senses than one, that was used as ammunition by all those who saw the Navy as a service trapped by its own traditions. The tot was the daily rum ration for all ratings above the age of 20 serving aboard ships. It was usually issued before the main meal in the middle of the day. A fixture since the middle of the eighteenth century, it was now recognized as an anachronism – and potentially damaging to the efficiency of the Fleet in an age of complicated electronics and missiles. A helmsman at the wheel of his ship would have comfortably failed the new breathalyser test which was just being introduced.

The main motive force behind the move to abolish the tot was the Second Sea Lord, Frank Twiss. The Admiralty Board grappled with the issue for some time. It was recognized that the move would be sensitive, especially on the lower deck, and not least given all the other upheavals in the Navy in recent times. There was brief mention of the possibility of mutiny. It was agreed that timing and presentation would be critical. And Le Fanu accepted that the admirals, rather than ministers, should take responsibility for the change, which it was decided should come into effect in the middle of 1970. That was why Owen, and probably Healey too, saw the move as another sign of a rather different relationship now between the admirals and the politicians.

After he heard the Navy's case on the cruiser, Healey had a meeting with Owen and Le Fanu. He said that he accepted the concept, but cautioned that it would still be difficult to convince his cabinet colleagues, especially as the ship had grown so much in the previous two years. He was also clearly dubious about the idea of a V/STOL option, and sceptical that it would cost as little extra as the Navy suggested. But he was willing to go into battle for it.

The Treasury, meanwhile, was clearly caught somewhat off-guard by the speed with which the cruiser proposal was leaping over the Ministry of Defence's various bureaucratic hurdles. But Treasury officials were certainly suspicious about the way the Navy seemed to be trying to nudge open the door once again to some form of renewed ship-borne air power. Why pay for designing a V/STOL option into the new ship, one official complained, when it was very doubtful that the aircraft themselves could ever be afforded?

But the Treasury's mandarins also had to face some new political realities. One was that the Ministry of Defence had by now borne a succession of quite devastating Treasury-inspired cuts over three years. The view of the Chancellor, Roy Jenkins, who had succeeded Callaghan, and who had fought Healey hard already over the cancellation of the F-111 and the withdrawal from East of Suez, seemed to be that, if the defence ministers and their advisers felt that they could afford these new ships within their existing spending, and the Navy insisted it needed them, then that would have to do this time.

Jenkins wrote to Healey in January 1970 in cautionary but conciliatory tones: 'I know you recognize how many eggs you would be putting into one basket in committing to ships of this size and cost. But I know with what careful thought you have reached the conclusion that three cruisers are preferred to the twelve or so frigates you could buy. I would not wish to challenge the conclusion you've reached'.[9]

That was a huge boost. There would be no big cabinet fight, or even the need for cabinet-level approval. The cruiser could go ahead. But Jenkins echoed his civil servants in expressing concern over the V/STOL option. Making provision for it as part of the design of the ship was one thing, but there should be no commitment to exercising the option without much more thought, and it should not in any way call into question the decision to phase out fixed-wing flying in the Fleet Air Arm.

One battle had been won, it seemed. Clearly, another was still in the balance.

There was also a further delicate juggling act that had to be performed. A fleet built around the new cruisers, with other new generations of quite modest but modern destroyers and frigates, all orientated towards NATO, promised to give the Navy a new and sustainable coherence. But proper fulfilment of this vision would still be the best part of a decade away.

And the Navy still had its existing if ageing carriers. Keeping them going effectively for an undetermined but limited time to bridge the gap and cover the withdrawal from East of Suez was still a requirement, but would also be a major challenge. At the same time, there were also a few in the Navy, especially the Fleet Air Arm, who clearly felt that, as long as the carriers were around, there was also still a chance of prolonging life.

Despite, or rather because of the cancellation of CVA-01, the Navy argued that it was vital to go ahead with a major refit for HMS *Ark Royal*, so that she at least could operate the new Phantom aircraft from 1970 onwards. The current Sea Vixen was becoming increasingly obsolete. If the government's position really was that the carriers were still needed for an interim period to cover the withdrawal from East of Suez, an up-to-date fighter was necessary to counter the increasingly sophisticated Soviet-designed aircraft that were finding their way now into the arsenals of countries like Egypt and possibly Indonesia.

But the Treasury's opposition to full-size carriers was undimmed. Along its corridors, the attitude had been that the CVA-01 decision was just one step in the right direction. There were still the existing ships. As one Treasury official put it, his department was still 'gunning for the carriers'.[10]

The cost of *Ark Royal's* refit was considerable – an estimated twenty-six million pounds at the outset. Callaghan, still Chancellor at this stage, said he was very uneasy about it. The Navy did everything it could to reduce the bill. Nothing that was not associated with equipping the ship to carry Phantoms, generally refurbishing her for further service, and improving crew conditions, was included. There would be no general improvement in her equipment, as there had been with her sister ship, *Eagle*. No defensive weapons at all. No new operations room. She would have to make do with less advanced radars. Still, the bill soon crept up to thirty million pounds.

But, in this struggle, Healey was on the side of the Navy. And he was supported by the Foreign Secretary, Michael Stewart. Between them they kept the refit alive.

But the policy shift in January 1968 looked set to tilt the balance again. The Treasury went back on the offensive. How was it justified continuing to spend money on the ship, argued the new Chancellor, Roy Jenkins, when she would now serve for only twenty-one months after she emerged from the dockyard?

The Prime Minister, Harold Wilson, was drawn into the argument. He tended to favour the Ministry of Defence case, but decided that the matter had to be settled in committee. Ministers gathered on 28 February 1968. Healey argued that cancelling *Ark Royal's* refit now would save only six million pounds. Jenkins quibbled with the figure. But the decision, in the end, was to go ahead.

Tensions in the Navy Department at the Ministry of Defence had been running very high all through the months of uncertainty over *Ark Royal's* fate. The sense of exultation after the decision to complete the refit was announced was palpable. One civil servant burst into the office of the Director of Plans, Henry Leach, clapped his hands and exclaimed 'we've got it!'.[11]

Leach looked up from his desk with a rather cold stare. 'What a pity,' he replied. He had opposed the refit, believing that it was indeed a waste of scarce resources, and an exercise in nostalgia. It was not an attitude that would endear him to the Fleet Air Arm. He admired the Fleet Air Arm officers as pilots. But he felt some of them were diehards who had to be restrained, or they would place in jeopardy the real chance of reviving naval flying.

For many in the Navy and especially the Fleet Air Arm, the *Ark Royal* decision looked like a lifeline. And pretty soon, Alistair Jaffray at the Ministry of Defence was warning the Prime Minister's office that Lord Mountbatten had already been lobbying both the First Sea Lord and the Chief of the Air Staff to keep the carriers running on longer. Number Ten should be prepared that he might be heading in the Prime Minister's direction as well.

The Treasury's defeat over *Ark Royal* certainly rankled with its top officials. They knew that many in the Navy still clung to the hope of keeping their carriers. And there were worrying signs. 'We have been very lucky', one Treasury official wrote, that the carrier case was based on the East of Suez role, even though the NATO authorities would certainly have welcomed a European case for keeping the carriers.[12] The new worry was a new focus on the Mediterranean. The Ministry of Defence had announced that it would plan to alternate a carrier and either a Commando carrier or an amphibious assault ship into and out of the Mediterranean in view of the new East–West tensions following the Soviet invasion of Czechoslovakia.

It was 10.27 on Monday, 15 December 1969 when *Ark Royal* slipped her last line and proceeded to sea from Devonport Dockyard for the first time in more than three years. A difficult period lay ahead. In command was Captain Raymond Lygo. A pilot himself, he had flown Seafires in the Second World War. A blunt speaker and a forceful character, he was one of the most trenchant and determined defenders of naval aviation, and was therefore looked upon by many others in the Navy as one of the most difficult and dangerous of that generally awkward breed of Fleet Air Arm officers. Serving in the Ministry of Defence at the time of the carrier debate, he in his turn had looked on with mounting exasperation and, in the end, dismay at the way the senior Naval Staff had handled – or, in his view, mishandled – the case.

Lygo did everything he could in the last months of *Ark*'s refit to make sure that she was as fit as possible to carry on in service for as long as possible. But he also took the ship to sea on those first sea trials with only half her engines working, fearing that any delay in order to finish fixing the others would be used as a new pretext to curtail her service even more. For him, the prospect of keeping her going for just one more short commission, with the crews of her Phantoms and Buccaneers continuing to take the risks of flying their jets at night and in all conditions with no future, was a gloomy one. Like Mountbatten, he was pressing to extend not only her service but that of her sister ship, *Eagle*, as well.

And a new turn of events seemed to offer a further glimmer of hope.

CHAPTER FOUR

Invincible and the Sea Harrier

It was still the case that, in the political battles for carriers, cruisers, and fixed-wing flying at sea, there had as yet been few decisive victories or defeats. CVA-01 was dead. But, otherwise, the fight was still on. It was helped by a new political twist. In the middle of 1970, Harold Wilson called, fought, and expected to win a general election. He lost. The Conservative Party under Edward Heath upset the predictions.

The Treasury suddenly saw the opportunity to snatch victory from the jaws of defeat over the cruisers. On 19 June, the day after the election, as Harold Wilson was conceding, a Treasury official suggested that the Ministry of Defence should be asked to put its plans for the new cruisers 'into cold storage' while the new government worked out its position.[1]

That official's motivation was probably in part a suspicion that the Conservatives might want to revisit the whole issue of phasing out the carriers; not reviving CVA-01, of course, which was never going to be on the cards, but at least extending the lives of the current ships, as Raymond Lygo was arguing.

With the change of government, the carrier enthusiasts in the Navy Department certainly looked seriously at the options for keeping a force going throughout the 1970s after all. It would amount to just two ships, *Ark Royal* and *Eagle*. But *Eagle* would need a two-year 'Phantomization' from 1973 to 1975. And there would be serious manpower implications. One assault ship would have to go into reserve, as well as the cruiser *Blake*, plus two County-class destroyers, one of which would be scrapped early.

In the end, in October 1970, while *Ark Royal* was in Malta, the government announced that it had agreed to keep her going until 1978 at the minimum cost possible to plug the gap until the new cruisers arrived. Lygo heard the news in Malta, and his first response, typically, was 'what about *Eagle*?'. But it was too much. There would no reprieve for her. She would go in 1972. With this solution, the government argument went, the Navy would get the maximum value out of the money spent on *Ark Royal*. She would thus be available to cover the withdrawal from East of Suez, and would then 'provide a valuable asset' for NATO in the Atlantic and Mediterranean.

Ark Royal would soldier on. So long as she remained in service as a fully fledged strike carrier, she appeared to confer on the rest of the Royal Navy a certain elite status not enjoyed by anyone else except the Americans – not even the French, whose own two carriers at the time never quite seemed to measure up in comparison. But as a single unit, the Navy would find it increasingly difficult to fashion a worthwhile role for her. She really did seem like a floating monument to the past, increasingly at odds with the concept and the capability of the future Fleet, rather than the shape of things to come. Still, at least she kept certain important skills alive.

But to what end? The Navy still had a fight on its hands with *Invincible* and, even more significantly, with what aircraft she and her prospective sisters would carry.

Detailed design work on the new cruiser was well under way. A key early decision, as the outline studies were turned into a fully-fledged design, was that the new ship would be powered by gas turbines, in keeping with the other new classes that would make up the future Fleet. This would have a very great bearing on the appearance and operation of the new cruiser.

As this process unfolded, there were some subtle and not-so-subtle changes. The ship's estimated displacement crept up again to 19,200 tons. A provision to carry four Exocet surface-to-surface missiles also appeared, with the weapons to be sited alongside the Sea Dart missile launcher.

It was also becoming apparent just how deft the Naval Staff had been this time in winning agreement from the other services, and especially the Treasury, for rather more than they actually realized. The outline requirement was for the design to accommodate twelve helicopters or V/STOL aircraft in its hangar. But, because of the length of time that the ships would be in service, the Navy had successfully argued that provision was also to be made for possible growth in the next generation of aircraft that they might operate – a generous margin of ten per cent in dimensions and twenty per cent in weight for the anticipated follow-on to the current large ASW helicopter, the Sea King.

That meant, studies now showed, that the ships would safely and sensibly be able to operate not twelve but seventeen of the current generation of aircraft, and twenty-one at a pinch for short periods. To some, that looked like an Admiralty sleight-of-hand. Whatever it was, it was going to prove its value.

But, to the frustration of the Naval Staff, getting political agreement to place an actual order for the new ship continued to prove hard work. Two years into the new government, it was still not forthcoming. Time was running out if the first of the class was going to be ready by 1978, when HMS *Ark Royal* was due to retire. And the prospect of further defence cuts was looming.

And, in August 1972, no doubt to the consternation of the Admiralty Board, the Defence Secretary, Lord Carrington, a veteran from the struggles over CVA-01, asked once more for the reasoning – on just one sheet of paper this time – behind why the Navy wanted the new cruisers rather than more frigates and destroyers. The distillation that the Navy sent back was illuminating. It remained government policy, it said, to maintain a fleet capable of a full range of maritime operations. And, for once, the Navy had seemed to grasp the broader political inclinations of the government of the day, and especially the Prime Minister, Edward Heath. The Royal Navy was the only navy in Europe with that broad range of capabilities, it said, and it might one day form the basis of a European navy.

The paper went on to argue that two critical elements in its capabilities were the deployment of one of the most effective anti-submarine weapons, the Sea King helicopter, and the ability to command and control British and NATO maritime forces. The most cost-effective way of carrying out both tasks, it said, was with the proposed cruisers, with the bonus that they might also be able to operate V/STOL aircraft.

Carrington's problem, as he pointed out, was that giving the go-ahead for even just the first ship would imply a commitment to the whole, very expensive programme, which was for three such vessels. But the Navy shot back that, even if it was to be faced with new cuts in its budget, unless there were to be a major change in government policy, it would still want to go ahead with the cruisers, accepting that the later ships might have to be delayed somewhat.

Just then, the Treasury relented just a little, agreeing to allow an invitation to go out to Vickers Shipbuilding to tender for construction of the first new cruiser. It made it clear that this was still no commitment to a first order. But things were inching forward at last.

At about this time, one other decision of great symbolic importance was taken. For a while, the Navy had been mulling over what names to give the new ships. And, perhaps not surprisingly, the favourites were former aircraft carrier names.

But it was recognized how politically sensitive this would be. So, in the end, for the first ship at least, it was decided that discretion was the better part of valour. The Admiralty Board decided that, because of the emphasis on the command and control aspect of the ships' design, the first-of-class should bear the name of a battle-cruiser or heavy cruiser of the past which had seen service as a famous flagship.

In the end, it came down to two names. One was *Invincible*, the flagship of Vice Admiral Sir Frederick Doveton Sturdee at the Battle of the Falkland Islands in 1914. The other was *Lion*, from which the legendary and controversial David Beatty, at the time a vice admiral, had commanded the British Battle-Cruiser Squadron and Battle-Cruiser Fleet, including at the Battle of Jutland in 1916.

The problem was that there was an HMS *Lion* in the Fleet at the time, albeit in reserve, and she might not have been scrapped by the time the first through-deck cruiser arrived. So the Admiralty Board's choice, finally, on 27 February 1973, was *Invincible*, little knowing what a coincidence the Falkland Islands connection would prove to be.

There was another connection as well. The previous *Invincible*, like this one, was a novel design, and one that divided opinion. She had appeared in 1908, two years after the revolutionary battleship HMS *Dreadnought*. She was the first battle-cruiser. The man behind both ships was the mercurial, inspirational, visionary, and galvanizing First Sea Lord of the time, Jackie Fisher. He saw battle-cruisers as great hunters of the sea. They would be a cut above the armoured cruisers of the day. They would have the big guns of battleships, but would sacrifice armour protection for greater speed.

When the fifth *Invincible* appeared, she was a captivating sight: a great three-funnel vessel of 17,000 tons, with characteristic tall tripod masts. But she and her sisters were a flawed and fragile concept, especially after Germany switched to building battle-cruisers as well. As the prototype of the breed, *Invincible* would be quickly overtaken by newer classes in the Anglo-German naval arms race that preceded the First World War. She would perform much as Fisher had envisaged in that first Battle of the Falkland Islands. But her flimsy protection would mean that she would be shattered and literally blown in two – and lose all but six of her crew of over a thousand – in a duel with German battle-cruisers at Jutland a year and a half later.

Two months after the decision on the name, the order for the new *Invincible* was placed with Vickers Shipbuilders at Barrow-In-Furness. As yet, though, the aircraft that the Navy wanted her to carry were still seemingly beyond its grasp.

The Admiralty had not been slow to consider the possibility of using V/STOL aircraft at sea, even back in the 1950s. But, for the most part, it was with a high degree of scepticism. The penalties associated with such planes seemed too high. On one hand, they did not have the performance of the conventional aircraft that the Navy had set its sights on. On the other hand, the V/STOL idea posed a potential threat to them, and more particularly to the big carriers. Similar suspicions would stifle the prospects of V/STOL in the US Navy.

Many in the Royal Navy, like many in the RAF, dismissed the early V/STOL models as toys. The public may have marvelled at the early prototypes of the P.1127, which became first the Kestrel and then the Harrier, as shining examples of British technical ingenuity. Despite its rather hunched-shoulder design, and its peculiar appearance when hovering like some kind of giant insect, the aircraft was a thing of fascination, and well in tune with the spirit of bounding technological change of the 1960s. But it had very limited performance, especially when operating from a ship. It made its first deck landing at sea on *Ark Royal* on 8 February 1963. But, even when the Navy was forced to take a fresh look at it after the CVA-01 cancellation, it was still easy to dismiss it as a very questionable proposition.

In fact, the P.1127 nearly died on the same day as CVA-01. At that same fateful Cabinet meeting, the Chancellor, James Callaghan, raised it as a potential sacrifice. But it survived.

Two things changed the balance of the argument in the late 1960s: the determination of the Naval Staff, particularly under Admiral Le Fanu's leadership; and the development of a more powerful version of the Harrier's Pegasus vectored-thrust engine. So, in a debate on the Navy Estimates in the House of Commons in March 1969, David Owen had declared that, now the engine had been up-rated, 'it makes it worth looking at for flying from ships'.[2] He knew, of course, exactly what the Naval Staff's hopes were by this time. He insisted that there was no question of building ships specifically to carry the Harrier, only that it might operate from ships already planned. And he clearly still held to the position in public that any aircraft that went to sea would be the RAF's. But the rumour, the speculation, and the political mood seemed to be moving the Navy's way.

The Treasury had been reluctant to endorse the provision of a V/STOL capacity in the proposed cruiser, fearing – correctly, of course – that it was opening the door to further expenditure down the line. But it, like other potential adversaries, was probably lulled into a false sense of security by the very limitations of the aircraft under consideration.

The Navy began to press the case as a limited capability, not to provide full air defence for the Fleet, or as a major strike weapon, but to fill a gap between what ship-borne weapons and land-based air cover could provide. The Navy raised the spectre of fast patrol boats armed with anti-ship missiles which might escape detection in time for anything other than an on-the-spot aircraft to take on. But the principal threat that the Navy focused on was the long-range 'shadower' out to sea, the reconnaissance aircraft which could direct weapons from other planes, ships, and submarines against a western task force.

Again, the Navy was haunted by a Second World War spectre – the long-range, four-engined Focke-Wulf Fw-200 Condor, which used to patrol far out into the Atlantic, and circle convoys out of the range of the ships' defences, radioing their positions to the marauding U-Boats. It was the advent in growing numbers of small, cheap 'escort' carriers based on merchant ship hulls that helped put paid to the Condor threat. Now, though, it had a very direct modern equivalent, the Tupolev Tu-95 Bear. For the Navy's task forces, when they were operating far out into the Atlantic, beyond the range at which the RAF could quickly provide air cover, that was a problem. The term 'hack the shad', the Navy's main rationale now for taking the Harrier to sea, would become something of a mantra in the years ahead, indicative of a real need that, at the same time, would supposedly not usurp the main role of the RAF in defending ships at sea.

So, as the Ministry of Defence had considered options for the incoming Conservative Government in 1970, the Navy had managed to slip past the chiefs of staff a statement that it had agreed with the RAF. It acknowledged that 'an embarked force of fixed-wing V/STOL aircraft could provide a valuable quick-reaction capability, dealing with shadowers, for reconnaissance and probing, and for surface strike to supplement shore-based air support'.[3]

But any brief truce that had existed with the RAF on the question of actually equipping the new cruiser with V/STOL aircraft had quickly faded as it became increasingly clear that the Navy wanted to put its own planes on its ships.

The air marshals may have come to regret their moment of weakness in agreeing that statement, basically acknowledging in principle something that they probably did not think would ever come to pass in practice, except on their terms. But it would still take another five years of hard Whitehall infighting, another change of government, and another defence review, before there would be a ministerial green light.

As it started to regroup, the RAF now basically reversed its position, arguing that the Navy's proposition was in fact so limited as not to be worth the money. It also had its eyes fixed on something altogether more ambitious and more to its liking, an 'Advanced Harrier' to be developed in conjunction with the Americans, much more expensive than anything the Navy either felt it wanted or could afford. The RAF argument was for delay, to find out exactly what US plans were and maybe eventually to press for a joint programme with the Americans. The Navy proposal it described as 'pointless'.

So what exactly was the Navy proposing? In early 1972, it produced an outline specification for the new plane that it would like, in Naval Staff Requirement 6451. It was 'to provide the Fleet with an organic capability for air interception, reconnaissance, probe, and limited surface strike based on the Harrier aircraft'. It would be as similar as possible to the Harrier GR3, the RAF's latest version. But it would have a lightweight air intercept radar, which the Harrier lacked. There would also have to be the provision of air-to-air and air-to-surface missiles. The proposal was for just fifteen aircraft in all, with eighteen pilots, to be ready by 1977.

For once, the modesty of the Navy's proposal seemed to be getting it into trouble. On one key central committee, the non-Navy members wondered if the proposed plane would really be up to the job of an interceptor at sea. And the RAF was dismissive of its strike capability. Attacking a large warship would require five to seven Buccaneers; the proposed maritime Harrier force would not come even close to that capability. It must have been a bitter pill for the Navy to have its old Buccaneers – which the RAF had been so reluctant to operate – used against it in Whitehall arguments. But it insisted that its proposal was a 'worthwhile' capability, albeit not everything that it would have liked. The committee remained unconvinced.

The Navy was looking for just 900,000 pounds for a nine-month project definition study. Still, it would be difficult to over-estimate the Treasury's hostility. It expressed grave reservations, and 'the most serious objections' to the cost-effectiveness of a maritime Harrier.[4] There were the costs of development, balanced against the limited numbers envisaged, and the limited performance of the aircraft itself.

The Treasury believed that it had plenty of sympathizers in the Ministry of Defence, not just within the RAF. But it also acknowledged that this was something that the Navy was very keen on. Rather sneeringly, one official described the combination of the through-deck cruiser and the V/STOL as 'the next best thing to the aircraft carriers that some sailors still secretly hanker after'.[5]

He was right, of course. But, this time, the Navy had more political sympathy behind it. Questions were being asked in the House of Commons about what was happening and why a decision was taking so long. Eventually, the Ministry of Defence squeezed reluctant agreement out of the Treasury for the project study to go ahead, but only on the understanding that there would be a public statement that this committed the Government to nothing further.

And then the political pendulum swung again. In February 1974, in the midst of economic turmoil and a confrontation with the coal miners, the Prime Minister, Edward Heath, called a general election, and lost. The Labour Party under Harold Wilson was back and, within days of taking office, the new administration decided that what was needed was … a defence review.

Under this review, the Navy actually fared relatively well. Its most vulnerable capability was its amphibious forces. They were almost as high on the Treasury's target list as the carriers. The review did see the abandonment of a British presence in the Mediterranean, which the Treasury had continued to fret was still a half-open door to wider naval ambitions. But the Navy managed to save the Royal Marines and its amphibious forces when it was deemed in the review that reinforcement of the NATO Northern Flank was vital to the security of the United Kingdom.

The maritime Harrier had by this time had more scrutiny from the chiefs of staff and within the Ministry of Defence than most other projects involving a similar, and by implication relatively limited, sum of money. But still there was no definite approval. Was the investment of an estimated 100 million pounds really worth it, some asked, when the return would be no more than ten operational aircraft at sea at any one time? And would the maritime Harrier be able to cope with the kind of threat that it was likely to have to face in the 1980s? Still, the Navy continued to press hard. And, perhaps reluctantly, the other chiefs of staff agreed at least to keep it alive.

At this time, there was an unlikely potential benefactor who played a part in the debate. It was hoped that the Shah of Iran would buy a through-deck cruiser for the Iranian Navy. And it was thought that his decision could hinge on whether the maritime Harrier went ahead, so that he could equip his ship with them. So, potentially at stake were orders for both a cruiser and perhaps sixteen Harriers worth an estimated 200 million pounds. Some in Whitehall argued that the maritime Harrier should not go ahead until there was an unequivocal commitment from the Shah. Others, briefly, suggested that perhaps Iran could help fund development, although the potential complications that this could pose meant that the idea quickly faded.

The maritime Harrier was kept going – just – during 1974 with a drip-feed of funding. Each month the Ministry of Defence went to the Treasury to ask for a cheque – 38,000 pounds one month, 23,000 another, 21,000 the next. Meanwhile the wrangling went on.

By the beginning of 1975, pressure was mounting again for a decision. Still the doubters persisted. One official questioned how a project that had teetered on the brink of cancellation for the last twelve months of the previous government could now survive a full-scale defence review. And the outward appearance of consensus among the chiefs, it was argued, hid a different reality – a lengthy and at times bitter argument in which the Chief of the Naval Staff was essentially isolated, but attached such importance to the project that he was willing to bear almost any other cut to keep it going. In such circumstances, it was said, the other chiefs would not risk a split by standing against him.

Critically, the new and pugnacious Defence Secretary, Roy Mason, a sceptic at first, seemed to be won over. And, in the final analysis, the Treasury decided that, if the Defence Secretary believed that the project was important enough that he would find the money, the Chancellor of the Exchequer should not stand in the way. In May 1975, finally, the go-ahead was agreed.

The order was for just twenty-four examples of what would become the Sea Harrier. It had the designation FRS.1, for fighter, reconnaissance, and strike. For its interception mission, it would have a radar, called Blue Fox, and a raised cockpit, which helped the pilot with visibility. It would carry two short-range Sidewinder air-to-air missiles. And it would have a new anti-ship missile. But perhaps the most important thing for the Navy was that it would appear in the traditional colours of, and be operated by, the Fleet Air Arm.

It had been such a fight for so long for just a couple of dozen aircraft of rather modest performance. But – like the stay of execution for HMS *Ark Royal*, and the go-ahead for the new cruisers – it kept an idea alive. And those aircraft would pay almost incalculable dividends in a very short space of time.

Did the Navy in this strange period from the mid 1960s to the mid 1970s lose the big battles and win the small ones, or was it the other way around? It lost a new generation of full-size fleet carriers, but the rusty old *Ark Royal* was allowed to soldier on honourably for a few more years. The alternative perspective was that a flawed CVA-01 concept finally fell foul of its own contradictions, and what was salvaged was the continuation of fixed-wing flying at sea in another and potentially more exploitable form.

CHAPTER FIVE

A New Genus

It was 1977, and celebrations up and down the country marked Queen Elizabeth II's Silver Jubilee. Of course, the services paid their own tributes. For the Navy, the climax at the end of June was that time-honoured tradition, a royal review of the Fleet at Spithead.

It was still an impressive assembly of naval power, even if not on the scale of the Coronation Review that Dermot Rhodes had witnessed nearly a quarter of a century earlier. There were some sixty major British warships present, including four nuclear-powered submarines, as well as numerous minor vessels, survey ships, and auxiliaries.

But it was also a twilight parade of the old Navy. The ships which took pride of place had all seen their origins in the Second World War: *Ark Royal*, with just a year still to serve; *Hermes*, now a Commando carrier; the cruisers *Tiger* and *Blake*, both of whose days were numbered. As The Queen, as Lord High Admiral, reviewed the Fleet from the deck of the Royal Yacht, *Britannia*, she saw only rare glimpses of the future. There was a clutch of rakish new Type 21 frigates, bought as a stop-gap measure. But, from the three classes of warship that had been at the heart of the new Fleet agreed ten years previously in the wake of the CVA-01 cancellation, there were but two examples: the brand new Type 42 destroyer, HMS *Birmingham*, following the Royal Yacht and carrying the Admiralty Board, and her older sister ship, HMS *Sheffield*, which had been the first of the Type 42s.

However, just a month earlier, there had been another significant royal event for the Navy. At the Vickers shipyard at Barrow-In-Furness, in front of a home-grown crowd brimming with pride in what they had created, The Queen had named and sent down the slipway HMS *Invincible*, the first of the new through-deck cruisers. Inevitably perhaps for such a red-letter day for the Royal Navy, the date had historical significance. On that very day, 3 May, exactly 230 years earlier in 1747, the ship that was to be the very first HMS *Invincible* had been captured from the French at the first Battle of Cape Finisterre.

Also among the crowd at Vickers was the then Chief of the Defence Staff and former First Sea Lord, Admiral of the Fleet Sir Edward Ashmore. He had been at the heart of much of the manoeuvring over the years that had brought matters to this point. It was, he reflected, the end of a long road, at least as far as he was concerned.

He looked up at the gleaming new hull on the slipway, and then as *Invincible* thundered into the water, riding high as the tugs gathered her up. As a man who had been familiar with the carriers of old through his career, she seemed very small he thought, even compared to HMS *Hermes*. 'But given her presence,' he concluded, 'the surface fleet could consider itself viable in wide areas of the sea that would otherwise be denied to it by the air threat'.[1] And that was the important thing.

In truth, she was not that small compared to most of her predecessors, but only really in comparison to what might have been. She was dwarfed by the American super-carriers, and undoubtedly overshadowed by the biggest of Britain's traditional carriers, *Ark Royal* and *Eagle*. And, of course, CVA-01 would have been significantly larger. Her modern, clean-cut lines and relatively light construction also made her look almost dainty, and even rather un-warship-like, next to the carriers of the previous generation. Indeed, by the most traditional measure of warship size, she was a genuine lightweight. She displaced just under 20,000 tons, compared to 28,000 tons for *Hermes*.

But, despite Admiral Ashmore's impression when he saw her at her launch, she was almost exactly the same size as *Hermes*, at least in terms of the internal volume of her hull and superstructure, and similar to most of the other carriers that had seen service in the Royal Navy. She stood taller than most of her predecessors too. From her bridge, her commanding officer would be able literally to look down on his counterpart in *Hermes*.

And, in terms of scale, nothing like *Invincible* had been designed and actually built for the Royal Navy for a quarter of a century. But she did clearly represent a step down in ambitions, prestige, and capability. And translating the transition and upheaval that she represented into a coherent and workable whole had not been easy for her designers.

From the naval architects' perspective, she sprung from no single tradition of warship design, neither truly the cruiser that she started life as nor a carrier in its purest sense. She was, as two of those involved intimately in her construction were later to explain in a paper before the Royal Institution of Naval Architects, a 'new genus' of aircraft-carrying ship.[2]

The major characteristics of the final design were settled in the early 1970s under the stewardship of Anthony Austin, a clever designer, but with a reputation for being somewhat difficult and dictatorial. However, the design that emerged largely during his time was elegant in many ways. Ship design, so the naval architects contend, is one of the ultimate exercises in the art of compromise. *Invincible*, like her predecessor, would divide opinion. But what she embodied was a remarkable achievement, given the pressures and constraints being applied.

From the outset of *Invincible's* career, when naval aviators looked at her, they would grumble at the odd and inefficient shape of her hangar – maddeningly narrow in the middle like a dumbbell or a dog's bone. It hindered her capacity to carry aircraft. The same was true of the island superstructure, which was far larger than on a traditional aircraft carrier, and encroached on vital flight deck space.

The naval designers had a rather different perspective. First, they had not been asked to design a pure aircraft carrier, far from it. It had been a difficult birth to say the least. Secondly, the shape of the hangar and the size of the superstructure were the results of two other decisions that the Admiralty Board had taken – to move to gas turbine engines instead of steam, and to maintain its ships in future by exchanging major machinery rather than repairing it where it was installed. Gas turbines need vast amounts of air flow, and hence huge amounts of ducting. And exchanging heavy machinery requires large passageways up and down through the ship. These clearly encroached on aircraft operations. But, without these elements of the design, *Invincible* would have had to be bigger and more expensive, and would have required a much larger crew. In fact, *Invincible*'s complement was half that of an aircraft carrier of similar size from an earlier generation.

None of that would have set the pulse of a Fleet Air Arm pilot racing. But, in the hard-fought battles in Whitehall, it might have made the difference between the ship being built at all and her going the same way as CVA-01.

The other point was that, for all that a maritime Harrier had by now been a gleam in the eyes of the Naval Staff for some time, the order for the aircraft did not actually materialize until two years after that for the ship, when construction was well under way. The designers had made what allowances they could, but without more definite decisions, they were hamstrung.

In the spring of 1975, a young naval architect, David Andrews, joined the design team. His responsibility would be integrating the ship's weapons systems and aircraft. As he toured her under construction in Barrow, he came across empty compartments labelled 'Dedicated to V/STOL', which his predecessors had set aside without really knowing what would fill them. That would be his job.

Andrews would soon discover that it was one thing to design what was essentially a helicopter carrier with a vague thought that it might one day carry V/STOL aircraft as well, but it was quite another to make it all work. It was going to be a tight squeeze. The aircraft itself was quite small. But it had to do everything the old aircraft on the previous carriers did – it was meant to be a fighter, reconnaissance aircraft, and strike plane all in one. And each job required different weapons, equipment, and support facilities. He was going to need all those empty compartments, and more.

There was, however, one beneficial side-effect to the fact that the designers' main concerns had been to do with how to operate helicopters rather than Harriers. They had made the hangar particularly tall, so that the helicopters' maintainers could work on the rotors and engines. As David Andrews soon found out, the fact that the Harrier had not been designed originally to go to sea presented some extra difficulties. One was that, to change an engine, the engineers had to remove the entire wing. On land, the RAF used a massive steel rig that would never fit on a ship. But, with the height available in *Invincible's* hangar, David Andrews and his team were able to devise a new system that worked.

As he reflected further, Andrews also marvelled at the cleverness of the design from the naval architect's point of view – the way his predecessors had incorporated all the different demands for the gas turbines, the ducting, the routes to move the machinery between the engineering spaces and the hangar. To him, *Invincible* was a mass of innovation, and it had all been neatly incorporated. The same was true of the way the crew would be accommodated, the spaces in which they would work, and how they would move about the ship. Of course, there were compromises here, too, that would lead to further grumbles. *Invincible* would be a labyrinth of some 800 individual compartments. But serving aboard her would be a totally different experience from that aboard the carriers of old. She would seem more like a giant frigate than the bewildering, often uncomfortable warren of a ship like *Hermes*.

Again, compared to the previous generations of big warships, *Invincible* would not have sturdy belts of armour to help protect her from damage in battle. As with the other new generations of warships that were being built, the Navy would have to think hard about how to use her in ways that did not expose her to unnecessary danger. Her key to survival in battle would chiefly be avoidance through manoeuvrability, good strategy, and destroying or decoying incoming attacks.

In fact, what had been taking shape on the stocks at Barrow-In-Furness was an undoubtedly proud-looking ship, with an exceptionally clean and modern appearance, that was also handsome, and whose coherence – like many of the best engineering designs – made her look smaller and more compact than she actually was. Except for one thing. At the bows of the ship, everything seemed to have gone horribly wrong. The flight deck stopped short of the bows and there was an open, untidy forecastle, which had the appearance more of a cargo ship than a warship, let alone a carrier.

Invincible's construction was well under way, and she was progressing towards launch day, when the mild-mannered Arthur Honnor had joined the team as the new design project manager. As he surveyed the ship on the slipway, he asked the same question that virtually everyone did when they saw her for the first time: 'why doesn't she have a carrier bow?'

It is part of the mythology that has built up around *Invincible* and her sisters that this was an element of the disguise, to fool their opponents that they were not really carriers. Honnor suspected there was an element of that, although there were also good design reasons for doing it too. The specification for the ship required a flight deck of 550 feet, and that was achieved, without the need to extend it any further forward. In this way, it also meant that the big Sea Dart missile system could be mounted forward, with a good arc of fire, almost on the centre-line of the ship, and the standard missile magazine could be fitted without major modification. However, the plan also to fit Exocet anti-ship missiles on the forecastle alongside the Sea Dart was abandoned at the end of May 1973, just over a month after *Invincible* had been ordered.

Arthur Honnor had other things about which he needed to worry. The state of industrial relations and shipbuilding capacity meant *Invincible* was falling behind schedule. Finding enough skilled labour to complete the mass of plumbing for the ship was a major headache. The pressures on the schedule were mounting. And then another complication cropped up.

In November 1976, the Harrier's chief designer, John Fozard, had delivered a lecture to the Royal Aeronautical Society detailing studies that he and his team had been carrying out on launching a Harrier from an upward-curving ramp structure. For many in the audience, it was a revelation. For one man, though, it was a long-overdue vindication.

The ramp was already widely referred to as 'the Ski-jump', and it was the brainchild of a naval officer, Lieutenant Commander Doug Taylor. Taylor had joined the Navy on 1 August 1945, in the dying days of the Second World War. He had a fascination for aeroplanes that anyone who had grown up as a schoolboy in southeast England during the war would have had as they watched RAF and German pilots duelling overhead, and saw the fleets of bombers droning back and forth. But he was even more interested in big guns, so entered the Navy as an ordnance artificer apprentice. He knew little about the Fleet Air Arm, but his career would become inextricably linked with it, and especially with its survival in the business of flying fixed-wing aircraft.

Taylor came to serve in a remarkable array of Navy carriers in the 1940s, 1950s, and 1960s – *Ocean*, *Implacable*, *Glory*, *Eagle*, *Ark Royal*, and *Victorious*. It was while aboard *Victorious* in 1964, when she was the mainstay of the Far East Fleet, that an incident occurred which would be one of the spurs to the creation of the Ski-jump. The ship was returning from Australia to Singapore. It was a period of particular tension in the Indonesian confrontation. As the carrier picked a careful course past Indonesia, the crew was on alert. Taylor was the flight deck engineer. There were two Sea Vixens poised on the ship's two catapults, ready for launch, their crews roasting in the brutal heat.

On the flight deck, too, conditions were grim. And, for Taylor, there was the dawning realisation that there was a serious potential problem. Such little breeze as there was had been coming from right aft, so there would be no wind assistance for any launches. On top of that, the steam heat from the primed catapults, plus the blazing heat from the sun, meant that the steel of the flight deck had expanded, and the catapults would probably have jammed. The ship would have been defenceless. For all the talk of a carrier's main armament being its aircraft squadrons, they were themselves totally reliant on what were, in effect, two steam cannons. And if they went wrong, any carrier would be horribly exposed and vulnerable. It certainly seemed to Taylor a lot on which to hang an entire naval strategy. This incident helped start him thinking about alternative ways to get aircraft airborne from ships at sea.

He had another, related issue on his mind. For all the attachment he had developed to naval aviation, he, like a number of others in the Navy, was increasingly concerned that the Fleet was becoming over-reliant on fewer and fewer bigger and ever more valuable ships. He came to the view that the Navy needed to get aircraft to sea in ships that not only it could afford, but also that it could afford to lose.

It was a while before all these ideas gelled together for Taylor into a coherent whole. It happened at home on Christmas leave in 1969 – the Ski-jump, the use of V/STOL aircraft, the possibility that, with a combination of the two, ships as small as frigates could take fixed-wing aircraft to sea. He put his thoughts down on paper and submitted them to his bosses. But his proposals fell on deaf ears.

One of Taylor's superiors, however, did take note and – not without some difficulty – arranged a sabbatical for him at Southampton University to work up his ideas into something that would carry more academic respectability. His thesis duly appeared in 1973. The Ski-jump was basically the marriage of the unique design qualities of the Harrier, the laws of physics, and a simple idea. By helping to propel the V/STOL aircraft upwards on a short take-off run, the Ski-jump allowed it carry a considerable extra payload of fuel or weapons into the air for a given length of flight deck. While the basic idea was straightforward, there was a lot of complicated mathematics to back it up.

But still there was resistance. Taylor went to see John Fozard, who was polite but non-committal. It was a chance meeting with an acquaintance on Fozard's team that led to the breakthrough. He had access to computer programmes of experimental Harrier launches from ships. Taylor's findings were incorporated. The transformation was dramatic. The Ministry of Defence would finally authorise a set of tests from a prototype ramp built at the Royal Aircraft Establishment, Bedford.

The fact was that trials of the Harrier at sea were producing some troubling results for the Navy. Rolling take-offs from the flat deck of HMS *Hermes*, to simulate the 550-feet run available on the new cruisers, had been showing that, in rough weather, to stay within safety limits, the Harrier would be launching with virtually no endurance or payload.

Far from eliminating the hazards of flying fixed-wing aircraft from ships, V/STOL aviation was substituting one set of problems for another. For conventional aircraft, there were the inherent risks of the shuddering and violent take-offs and landings by catapult and arrestor wire. With the Harrier, the very fact that its departure was quite leisurely in comparison was itself a major issue. From a standing start, the take-off run took ten to twelve seconds. In a rough sea, with a pitching deck, it was difficult to judge the right moment with confidence, to know that the ship and the aircraft would not be dipping dangerously towards the sea and oblivion at the critical moment. The Ski-jump appeared to add that extra margin of safety that made a vital difference.

The designers on the cruiser project were keen, therefore, to incorporate the ramp. There were discussions with the Naval Staff, and with Vickers. Arthur Honnor wrote a paper stating that the ship would not be delayed, and that there would be no increase in the overall cost, if a ramp were fitted. There were some doubts, and worries that there might be hidden costs in having to modify the aircraft. So would it really work? David Andrews was present at Bedford on 5 August 1977 when the first ever Harrier launch from a Ski-jump took place. It did work.

Invincible had already been launched herself by then, and was well on the way to completion. So only a modest seven-degree gradient of ramp could be incorporated at such a late stage in construction. It was literally just welded on to the forward end of the runway. There was, however, one happy bonus from the installation. There had been concerns that the ship would need some ballasting on the port side at around flight deck level to compensate for the weight of the superstructure to starboard. The ramp solved that problem too.

In the decade before *Invincible*'s launch, a profound narrowing of the Navy's horizons appeared to have been taking place. The multiple fleets of the past had dwindled to just one. April 1967 had seen the last Commander-In-Chief South Atlantic depart. Just two months later, the Mediterranean Fleet – which had numbered Nelson himself among its historic commanders – ceased to be. The ships remaining in the Mediterranean were to come under the Commander-In-Chief of the Western Fleet, which superseded the Home Fleet – again, a historic formation which had been the Navy's backbone in two world wars. But the Western Fleet did not last long. At the end of October 1971, the Far East Fleet was disbanded. The inevitable next step, in May 1972, was that responsibility for all of the Navy's seagoing forces was brought under a single command, designated Commander-In-Chief, Fleet.

And yet, the Navy's determination to maintain a presence on the wide oceans did not end there by any means. There were still token forces scattered around, including East of Suez. But, more significantly, in May 1973, a squadron of Royal Navy warships led by the cruiser, HMS *Tiger*, set off on a 'group deployment' to the Far East. Other similar deployments would follow, with the specific intention of maintaining the Navy's expertise to operate in distant waters.

Just over a year later, *Tiger*'s sister ship, HMS *Blake*, set off at the head of another significant squadron, this time under the command of Henry Leach, now a vice admiral. In a sense, these cruisers were in their element, showing the flag in far-flung ports across the Pacific and beyond. *Blake*'s group, in fact, completed a circumnavigation. But *Tiger* and *Blake* were old, and showing it. Leach had to nurse his flagship along. The Navy desperately needed new ships with new capabilities, as technology and the likely threat continued to change.

But these were the years of 1970s 'stagflation', of desperate British economic performance and even more desperate industrial relations. Construction timetables seemed to stretch out. Costs mounted. The new ships and their weapons seemed to be taking an awful long time to materialize.

Of the other two classes of major warship besides the cruisers which had been authorised as part of the future Fleet, the destroyer had turned into the Type 42. It was deliberately a smaller and simpler ship than its predecessors, with a target displacement of some 3,500 tons to their 6,000 or so. Even as the Type 42's final design was approved in November 1968, it was acknowledged that it had been drawn up within some very tight limits, with little margin for future improvements. Still, it was considered by the Admiralty Board to be a good design in the circumstances. The key to the Type 42 was its Sea Dart medium-range air defence missiles. It was critical to get these ships into the Fleet in good numbers as quickly as possible, to help fill the air defence gap that was being left by the departure of the carriers, and with the County-class destroyers and their Sea Slug missiles already looking prematurely obsolete.

The other class was meant to be a general-purpose frigate of 2,000 to 2,500 tons. Its job would be to replace the Leander-class frigates that were by now the backbone of the escort fleet. Virtually everybody who became anybody in the Navy of the 1970s, 1980s, and even 1990s commanded a Leander at some point or other. They were the best British post-war frigate design, and probably the best vessels of their type in the world at the time. They were the signature ships of the Royal Navy then. They were well-balanced and smart, with a handy gun armament, a short-range missile system, a helicopter, and a reliable power-plant. They were the true successors to the colonial cruisers of the inter-war period. Like those ships, some said the Leanders were not as well-armed as certain foreign contemporaries. But they were good enough to be able to operate independently, and cheap enough to be ordered in quantity, and therefore to help the Navy to maintain a widespread presence, again like the inter-war cruisers. Twenty-six in all were built for the Royal Navy over fourteen years.

But the Navy soon got into trouble trying to produce something better to replace them. The size and cost of what was now known as the Type 22 soon began to mushroom. In 1972, the Navy was hoping that, by the beginning of the 1980s, it would have some 20 of these ships either in service of building. That was going to prove a forlorn hope.

It also seemed as though the Naval Staff was displaying an almost exaggerated determination to emphasize the new mid-ocean anti-submarine focus of the new Fleet. So the Type 22 was designed without any main gun armament. This move also seemed to reflect a misplaced faith in some of the missile systems that the Navy was developing at the time, which saw the ships of this period – including *Invincible* herself – emerging with what, to the lay person, looked like very scant weaponry. One Treasury official, no doubt equating missile systems with extra cost compared to guns, bemoaned this aspect of the Type 22's design, and how it would preclude these ships from some of the traditional applications of sea power. The Type 22 was, he argued, 'totally incapable of firing a shot across anyone's bows, as it might have to do in an Argentine/Falklands or Caribbean situation'.[3] That was in 1972.

This trend also led the Naval Staff to do what many regarded as unspeakable things to the Leanders themselves, ripping out their gun armament and replacing them with various types of missiles as well. There were, perhaps, good operational reasons for this – especially the desperate need to get new weapons into the Fleet. Ikara torpedo-carrying missiles were fitted to some of the class, and Exocets to others, to help fill gaps in anti-submarine and strike capabilities. But the costs – both in purely financial terms and with respect to the operational flexibility that the Navy itself argued lay at the heart of sea power – may have been too high.

But the vision remained clear. Artists' impressions in the mid-1970s showed a modern and impressive-looking *Invincible* thrusting through the waves, with Harriers and helicopters on her deck, and Type 42s and Type 22s powering along in company as a model Royal Navy task group of the future. Yes, the strike carriers would be gone, with the capabilities that they embodied. But this was still an attractive image, exactly as the Naval Staff envisaged it, and it seemed to enshrine a real purpose for the Fleet.

Despite the continuing economic crisis, the 1970s were largely a period of gently dwindling force levels rather than stark upheavals, as had occurred in the late 1960s. And there was the promise of considerable modernizaton of the Fleet. Given that the country, by this stage in its post-war history, seemed to be barely holding on to its national self-esteem as those around it forged ahead, the condition of the Navy could have been a lot worse.

To some extent, the pressures on the services for more cuts were relieved by the mounting concern over the advances in Soviet military capabilities. That was certainly the case for the Royal Navy, as the spectacular development of the Soviet fleet showed no signs of abating. Remarkable new warships seemed to keep appearing one after the other, bristling with weaponry and extraordinary arrays of radars. In the mid-1970s, the first grainy, snatched photographs appeared of the Soviets' own version of the aircraft-carrying cruiser. The ship, the *Kiev*, at 40,000 tons and over 900 feet in length, completely dwarfed *Invincible*, and cut a far more imposing dash with her towering superstructure, multiple radars, and bristling array of missiles and guns.

But while the appearance of the *Kiev* on the scene certainly had a huge impact, two other strands of developments were also of great concern: the quickening pace of Soviet submarine building; and the appearance of the supersonic, long-range Backfire bomber, with the ability to penetrate deep into the eastern Atlantic from its northern bases. Both the submarines and the bombers came with deadly anti-ship missiles attached.

The age of the anti-ship missile had arrived quite literally with a bang on an October evening – perhaps poignantly, on Trafalgar Day – in 1967. Cruising in the Mediterranean, a few miles north-east of Port Said, the Israeli destroyer *Eilat* was first crippled and then sunk by four Soviet-made Styx missiles fired from one or more Egyptian patrol boats in harbour. Of course, the fact that such weapons had been developed and were coming into service was well known. But this one event had sent shockwaves around the world.

The particular demon that concerned the Royal Navy was the Soviets' Charlie-class submarine, which carried the supersonic SS-N-7 anti-ship missile. Crucially, the Charlie class could fire its main armament while still submerged. So these submarines could approach western task groups and fire their weapons at short range with little warning time. Studies being carried out seemed to show alarmingly low levels of survivability for surface forces that might be exposed to these threats.

The Royal Navy was just developing a new short-range, quick-reaction missile, Sea Wolf, which might be a partial solution. But it was expensive, and only the Type 22s and a handful of Leanders were scheduled to be fitted with it. The Navy talked about 'defence in depth', or 'layered defence', for its task groups, including air support from the shore, the handful of Sea Harriers that were being bought, and US Navy aircraft carriers, with stiffer defences the closer the attackers got to their target. But, for much of the Fleet, there seemed precious few of those layers, even with NATO allies to help. In one of the presentations on the layered defence concept, one naval officer boasted proudly of it as being as if the attacking Soviet forces would be moving down 'the jaws of a crocodile'.[4] A growing band of sceptics among the Ministry of Defence's analysts were wondering if it was not the Navy that was placing itself – or at least its surface ships – in a Soviet crocodile's mouth.

Arthur Honnor, as head of the design team for *Invincible* and her sisters, was all too aware of the debates going on over new threats. He wondered whether *Invincible* herself was also already being overtaken by developments, at least as far as her weapons and equipment were concerned. Was Sea Dart the best defensive missile for the ship after all, especially given how big an impact it had had on the design? Suddenly, with just one missile launcher, and nothing else but a few decoy rockets, she looked terribly under-armed.

It may have been too late to do anything about *Invincible* for now, given that her construction was well advanced. The same was probably true also for the second ship. She had been ordered in May 1976, and – in a sign of how the political climate had relaxed in one respect at least – she had been allocated the famous carrier name *Illustrious*.

The planned third ship was tentatively to be called *Indomitable*, another name with recent carrier connotations. Maybe it was not too late to modify her so that she would be better equipped to meet the new and more challenging operational environment. In late 1976, the Naval Staff began to consider the question.

But one thing that it did not want to do was to delay her too much longer, or indeed suggest so many changes to the design that it would open the door to renewed arguments in the Ministry of Defence over whether to go ahead with her at all. There were already worries that, such was the bleakness of the economic outlook, she could be delayed by up to ten years anyway.

A working party was set up. It set itself a limit that it would not consider any modifications that would hold completion of the ship up for more than twenty-two months. But, at the same time, it had at its disposal studies that showed the scale of challenge. These suggested that a task force of half-a-dozen ships centred on a cruiser would attract considerable attention from Soviet naval air forces. The estimate was of a co-ordinated attack by Soviet bombers armed with air-to-surface missiles, arriving in three waves, with each wave launching a dozen missiles. It was judged that, with existing defences, a significant number of missiles would get past the ships' own weapons, and then it would be up to decoys and luck.

Naval officers have always maintained that, in scenarios like this, there would be many other factors at work, and that pressing home attacks on ships at sea is never as straightforward as the scientific studies suggest. They are, in that sense, very artificial scenarios. The working party pointed out that the Navy's task forces would be operating as part of a vast network of forces. But these were still sobering statistics. It was these kinds of estimates that were reigniting a significant debate with which the Royal Navy, and indeed all major navies, was having to contend, over the whole issue of the vulnerability of surface ships in the missile age.

The working party considered a number of options for the new ship – an improved version of Sea Dart, substituting the Sea Wolf system, or even fitting both. The problem with all of these proposals was that they would delay construction by two years or more. Removing the Sea Dart, even if Sea Wolf could be fitted instead and it left room to carry an extra aircraft, was considered too high a price to pay anyway. In the end, the group concluded that the best that could be achieved in the time allowed would the fitting of a better radar.

But there were also some more positive technical developments that needed attention. The Navy was finally getting to grips with the potential of its big Sea King helicopters in the fight against submarines. But one thing that had become clear was that, to operate efficiently, they would need much larger numbers of sonobuoys – the small listening devices that they dropped into the sea in patterns to detect hidden submarines. The cruisers could do with more storage space to carry more of these. The working party recommended that as a key modification.

The whole business of anti-submarine warfare was also changing in a significant and elaborate way. The successful development of towed array sonars – long cables trailed behind frigates and fitted with complex hydrophones – promised greatly increased detection ranges. That would extend the cover that ASW task forces could provide. But the increase in the amount of information to be processed, and the greater dispersal of forces that was both possible and necessary, also greatly complicated the task of command and control. Another key improvement, therefore, was to be even better facilities for directing the battle. The Navy's view was clearly that, while the vulnerability of these ships may have increased, so too had their value and that of the task forces that they would lead in the overall East–West maritime struggle. That, however, would not be the view of others.

The Naval Staff was also by now sufficiently enthusiastic about the Ski-jump that it wanted a bigger and better one fitted than those that could be installed in the first two ships. Other minor modifications were considered and discarded – like fitting landing craft to improve the ship's ability to act as a Commando carrier. In March 1979, the modified design was approved. A few of the improvements would be incorporated into *Illustrious* while she was being built. *Invincible* would have to wait until her first major refit.

Things were moving. But still not as quickly as the Naval Staff would have liked. *Invincible*, it seemed, was going to be two years later than originally planned. The Navy was faced with what it came to call 'the flat-top gap'. The old *Ark Royal* was rapidly approaching the end of her planned life. She was scheduled to retire at the end of 1978. But *Invincible* would not be ready by then. There was one alarming report that she might not be fully in service until 1984.

To fill the gap, the Naval Staff looked at extending *Ark Royal*'s life yet again. The admirals knew that any further stretching out of the career of their last traditional aircraft carrier would be politically sensitive, not least with the RAF, which was already waiting to take over her aircraft. There was thought given to her operating in a reduced carrier role, keeping her Phantom fighters, but having Harriers instead of Buccaneers. Or maybe she could carry just Harriers and helicopters, in the same way as the new cruisers.

But then the alarm bells began to ring. *Ark Royal* would need a refit to keep her going. The Treasury suggested that, if that were the case, with the economy in such a bad state, the only way for this option to make sense would be if *Ark Royal* were to be kept going for some time and the third cruiser deferred indefinitely. The Navy did not like that. *Ark Royal* was also very manpower intensive, at a time when the Navy was beginning to suffer even more chronic personnel shortages. The Naval Staff decided against keeping her going. Instead, another old but smaller ship, the Commando carrier HMS *Bulwark*, which had just been put in reserve, would be brought back into operation as an anti-submarine helicopter carrier.

That was not quite the end of the story for *Ark Royal*. In early 1978, in her last year of operational service, NATO's Supreme Allied Commander Atlantic, SACLANT, US Admiral Isaac Kidd Jr, approached the First Sea Lord, who was now Admiral Sir Terence Lewin. He was anxious about what he saw as a shortfall in Western carrier forces in the Atlantic. Was there any chance, he asked, that HMS *Ark Royal* could be kept in service? It was a reflection of the importance the Americans placed on carrier forces in the Atlantic, but also of the value they placed on the British ship.

Once again, Britain's chiefs of staff looked at the question, but decided that it was just not on. *Ark Royal* had never been modernized to the same extent as her sister, *Eagle*, apart from her ability to operate Phantoms. She had an antique operations room. And, with a crew requirement of 2,600, it would probably have required the paying off of two destroyers, the cruiser *Blake*, and two or more frigates to keep her going. Lewin replied to Kidd that, regretfully, after careful consideration, the Ministry of Defence could not agree to the request. 'Frankly,' he said 'as far as organic air is concerned, we are going full ahead for V/STOL, and hope to help you plug the gap with these aircraft before too long'.[5]

Clearly, in the circumstances, it did not make any sense to keep *Ark Royal* plodding on any longer. But the American approach was perhaps a reminder of how things might have been different. A British fleet based on a couple of full-size aircraft carriers might have made a difference in NATO, when the Americans were feeling the pressure of global overstretch themselves. An extra carrier would have been a significant part of the NATO maritime whole.

So it was then that, on 4 December 1978, on a tranquil morning, the last of Britain's conventional aircraft carriers slipped into Plymouth Sound for her final homecoming. She was a tired ship, and she looked her age. But she still had a rugged and imposing presence. And, like many great ships, she seemed to have acquired a real character, and had certainly attracted great affection. Her name, however, would live on. In naval terms, it was a name that was far more ancient than *Invincible*'s, with battle honours that stretched back to The Armada. But, in modern times, it had been more associated than any other with the business of carrying aircraft to sea. It was announced that the third new cruiser, which was to have been named *Indomitable*, would in fact be the fifth *Ark Royal*.

Three-and-a-half months later, on 20 March 1979, far to the north at Barrow-In-Furness, Captain Michael Howard Livesay joined his new ship, *Invincible*. He was thrilled, certainly, at this opportunity, but also fully conscious of the challenges, complexities, and responsibilities that lay ahead.

Michael Livesay had joined Dartmouth Royal Naval College in 1952 at the age of 16. He eventually qualified as a fighter direction and radar specialist. He served in a destroyer and the carrier *Hermes*. His first commands were the mine-hunter *Hubbertson* and the frigate *Plymouth*. Just before being appointed to *Invincible*, he worked on the Naval Staff in the Ministry of Defence, and was heavily involved in a joint project with the US Navy on a new concept of maritime operations to support NATO. He was clearly destined for great things. And yet he told his wife that, while delighted, he was surprised to have been given *Invincible* as a command.

But he had little time to reflect. Less than a week after he arrived, the ship went to sea for the first time to begin her builder's sea trials. She headed to

Greenock. She was in dry dock there over the Easter weekend. On the Saturday, one of the engineering officers, Lieutenant Michael Price, picked up a signal from the Ministry of Defence in London. It announced that the ship's visual recognition sign would be R05 – not the traditional 'C' prefix for a cruiser, but 'R'. Price called the second-in-command, Dermot Rhodes, and asked him to pass the news on to the Captain. *Invincible* was officially an aircraft carrier at last.

CHAPTER SIX

Invincible Emerges

It had been two months short of six years after the first keel plates had been laid that *Invincible* had headed out to sea for the first time. She was still very much in the shipbuilder's hands, flying under the Red Ensign. But, in the previous weeks and months, the nucleus of what would be her crew for her first crucial commission in Royal Navy service had begun gathering in and around Barrow. For many, it was their first visit to this isolated outpost of industrial empire, on the edge of the Lake District and some of the country's most beautiful countryside.

The first senior man to arrive had been the marine engineering officer, Commander Peter Ridley. That was January 1978. His first reaction to the ship was one of awe. That was not just because of her size, but also because she was so new in so many ways. The ship's main engines were not the sort of things that got most people excited, but they were enough to make an engineer's mouth water: four Olympus gas turbine engines, like those in Concorde, except that, instead of powering a 100-ton airliner through the air at twice the speed of sound, they would be pushing a 20,000-ton aircraft carrier through the water at just under 30 knots. Even more importantly, to a marine engineer, four equal engines was a classic layout that meant great flexibility. So long as it all worked.

Commander Lionel 'LG' Scovell would join as the senior officer during this period. He was an air engineer. He had done his early training in the light fleet aircraft carrier HMS *Vengeance*, about the size of *Invincible* but with a much bigger crew. His view of *Invincible* was that she was about as small as the Navy could get away with for what she was meant to do. One of his responsibilities would be to suggest any changes that needed to be made as the construction worked proceeded … so long as they did not increase the cost or delay the completion date of the ship. He would hand over to the ship's executive officer, David Dobson, when he arrived. And precisely because of the amount of sea time and experience that he had already accumulated aboard carriers, the Navy would insist that somebody else would take over his job of air engineer as well before the ship was actually accepted into Royal Navy service. So he would leave *Invincible* before she was commissioned.

Another engineer who joined the ship soon after was a young lieutenant, Richard Pelly. He was renewing a family connection with the name *Invincible*: an ancestor had been a captain of the previous HMS *Invincible*. He would make a name for himself, and help forge the camaraderie of that early, close-knit group of Invincibles by organizing walking expeditions the length and breadth of the Lake District.

And then there was Mike Price, one of those salt-of-the-earth characters, who could be a bit difficult and argumentative at times, but which every ship's company should have. He arrived in November. Mike had joined the Navy in May 1951 as an ordinary sailor. But, in the 1960s, he decided to become an officer. He would be the oldest officer aboard *Invincible*, also working on the engineering staff. Mike had been involved in many of the proving trials ashore for these strange new gas turbines. Now he was going to get to grips with them in an actual ship. For all of them on the engineering team, *Invincible* was a window onto a new world. They had been used to engine rooms where they stood on steel footplates amid boilers and turbines and turned huge brass handles and valves. Now they would be sitting in an air-conditioned control room, at a console with dials and levers. It was another sign of how the Navy was changing.

For Commander Dermot Rhodes, his appointment as executive officer to *Invincible* was a complete surprise, since David Dobson already had that job. But he had just been promoted to captain and given his own command himself. Rhodes was euphoric. He had had two frigate commands already. But he had also always enjoyed his first lieutenant appointments. And this meant being second-in-command of a brand new major warship and brand new concept. For him, there could not have been a better job at the time.

So he headed for Barrow with a certain amount of trepidation but also tremendous pride and excitement. And, in contrast to Admiral Ashmore just a couple of years earlier, when he saw *Invincible* for the first time, he thought she was huge.

Of course, the first person he called on was the commanding officer. Rhodes had known – or rather been aware of – Captain Livesay when they were both at Dartmouth. The Naval College at the time was a place of strict hierarchies. Even those a term ahead of you were considered to be on a pedestal. Livesay was a whole year ahead of Rhodes, but even then stood out as sensible and approachable. For Dermot Rhodes, Michael Livesay would be easily the best commanding officer with whom he ever served, and perhaps the finest naval officer he ever met.

The two men would come to complement each other well. Rhodes would stand out in *Invincible*'s formative years for the great touch that he had with all of those aboard, especially his ability to communicate with the ordinary sailors. To him fell the task of knowing what was really going on in the ship. Every day at sea, he would tour *Invincible* and talk to members of the crew. After the

Captain, Rhodes was the man most instrumental in making sure morale was buoyant.

Another two members of that first wardroom were Lieutenant Commanders Noel Cartwright and Peter Lansdown. They had joined the Navy together in September 1962, had known each other on and off through their careers, and now got lodgings together in Barrow. For them, it was a remarkable experience, witnessing what at first seemed to Noel Cartwright like little more than a rather scruffy heap of metal being transformed into a fine ship in a very short time. He was to be signals communications officer and Lansdown was an advanced warfare officer, responsible for underwater warfare. In other words, two critical roles for what *Invincible* was supposed to become.

Along with the mounting excitement were some frustrations. The Navy was very much a guest of the shipyard at this stage, the crew allowed to observe, but not really to touch. And, as in any relationship between client and builder, there would be some tense moments along the way. Crew members had to be escorted everywhere by Vickers staff, and they were all living ashore. The key moment for Peter Lansdown was when the ship's company finally moved on board, just a week or so before *Invincible* was to leave Barrow. She was exactly the same ship, but, all of a sudden, there was the smell of soap. People were using the bathrooms and the showers. *Invincible* was coming to life.

The central figure, of course, was the captain. He was not charismatic in a showy way. But he had great energy. And the people around him came to want to do well for him. He was approachable and sympathetic, but also firm, and knew what he wanted. Commanding a ship like this was the reason why he had joined the Navy. He came to earn the respect and admiration of his crew because he had mastered all the key aspects of the job – how to handle the ship, how to fight it, and how to fight its corner in the bureaucracy of the Navy and the Ministry of Defence.

One of those who was quickly infected by Mike Livesay's enthusiasm for his new ship was the deputy supply officer, Lieutenant Commander Anthony Hallett. The two men would become firm friends. In Tony Hallett's opinion, Mike Livesay would be instrumental in the future success not only of *Invincible*, but of the whole class. And he felt that everyone around him in those early days in Barrow was starting to get excited by the potential of their new vessel, and were impatient to get their hands on her properly.

But it was not all plain sailing. Creating a ship like *Invincible*, with her hundreds of compartments and a million different components and design features, is a journey in itself for the naval architects and engineers. And then, finally, the theory has to be put to the test. Thus, she had set off on her builder's trials.

First, there were little things which cropped up. After one outing, the project manager, Arthur Honnor, received a report that *Invincible* had dragged her anchor on one occasion while in the Firth of Clyde. He looked again at the design, and realized that she had been given rather small anchors for her size. So he ordered some bigger ones. But it was too late to order thicker and heavier anchor chain as well. Also, the new anchors were too big to fit in the recesses designed to house them in her bows. So those had to be plated over, and the new anchors stood proud on the bows. The new anchors solved one problem. But during her career she would develop a habit of losing anchors in rough weather.

Another issue which appeared early on would saddle *Invincible* with a reputation from which she would never really escape. It quickly became apparent that, at certain speeds, she vibrated. Some called it a 'wobble'. The problem was most apparent at the stern. Everyone had their own theory. It was because she was designed with a short keel. It was the fact that all the power from her engines was channelled through just two propeller shafts. Maybe one of the shafts was bent.

The naval architects believed that the problem was exaggerated. It was not that *Invincible* vibrated any more than previous ships, it was just that it happened at unexpected speeds. Generations of officers who would serve aboard *Invincible*, and whose cabins occupied the aft part of the ship, would take a different view.

In truth, nobody ever really found the definitive answer. The theory that Arthur Honnor preferred had to do with the novel, lightweight design of her aircraft lifts. They were attached to only one bulkhead, instead of on each side like the lifts in the old carriers. That, according to one engineer, created a 'structural hinge'. Honnor had never heard of such a thing before. But it meant – according to the theory – that there was a particular harmonic associated with the lift at the stern, and that resonated throughout the ship.

Later on, there would be a serious problem with *Invincible*'s diesel generators. There were eight in all, and they supplied the ship with her electrical power. But they started breaking down one after the other. The issue started to become critical, and threatened to jeopardise the ship's trials. But, just in time, the problem was traced to faulty bearings.

But these would be the stories of any new ship, let alone one with all the innovations and untried theories of *Invincible*. It was time to see whether she could deliver as a warship. It was time to leave Vickers and Barrow behind.

By now, Commander Brian Goodson, the ship's supply officer, had joined. As he navigated the ship's many passageways and compartments, its many decks, and explored and inspected his storerooms and storage spaces to see how best to make use of them, he noticed something about the emerging character of the ship. He spotted precisely that aspect of *Invincible*'s layout which the designers had hoped would make a difference to the atmosphere aboard. Of course, she was not on the scale of the old *Ark Royal* and *Eagle*. But she was still a big ship. So what else was different? It was a generational difference in design philosophy, the result of more than three decades of the changing demands and the habits of life at sea against the background of social change ashore.

On *Invincible's* main deck below the hangar deck, there was a long, wide passageway that ran like a ring-road right round the ship, up and down each side for a great part of her length. On this deck were the main galley and dining room. It was the ship's 'high street'. Sooner or later on that deck, you met everybody aboard. It took away the remoteness that people sometimes felt on the old aircraft carriers. The ship shrank, and a tight community was created. An inanimate object became a thing with character and personality. Almost from the outset, *Invincible* would gain a reputation as a happy ship.

And so it was, on Saturday, 15 March 1980, the ship which had, over more than six years, grown in the midst of Barrow, set sail to be accepted into Royal Navy service. She had become enough of a landmark that she even featured on the cover of the local telephone directory. Barrow, with evident pride in what it had created, gave her a rousing send-off.

That first evening after *Invincible* had finally left Barrow behind, a group of officers gathered in the wardroom. Between them, they were to parcel out responsibility for the various community and social activities aboard that are part of creating a community at sea and would be another factor which would help to turn *Invincible* into a bonded, breathing whole. Tony Hallett would earn a permanent place in the annals of *Invincible* when he put his latent entrepreneurial skills to work in aid of the ship's social fund. His idea of marketing as gift items ladies' underwear complete with the ship's name – '*Invincible* knickers' – became a roaring success, although they earned the unwelcome attention of the tax inspector when they were featured on the BBC.

Four days after leaving Barrow, on another grey March morning, the Isle of Wight and Portsmouth hove into view for the first time. *Invincible* was about to join the Fleet. But she, and the Royal Navy as a whole, were already sailing in choppy waters, even if that was not immediately apparent.

A couple of years before, in August 1978, while *Invincible* was still clad in scaffolding, draped in awnings, and lying in the shadow of the giant cranes of the Vickers yard, Admiral Sir Terence Lewin, as the First Sea Lord at the time, had written in optimistic terms: 'As the economy emerges from the dark days of the mid-'70s, a certain stability has returned to the naval programme'.[1]

At the beginning of the 1970s, the Fleet was still headed by the two big sister carriers, *Ark Royal* and *Eagle*. There were two Commando carriers and two assault ships, to make up the Navy's amphibious forces. The four Polaris ballistic missile submarines or SSBNs had entered service. But, partly because of that urgent programme, there were still only three of the nuclear-powered but conventionally-armed Fleet submarines, SSNs. They were far outnumbered by the twenty-seven conventionally-powered boats. All eight of the first-generation guided-missile destroyers of the County class had entered service, and there were still a couple of other gun-armed destroyers. The frigate force totalled some sixty-four ships.

As Lewin was writing, a year after the Silver Jubilee Review, the last of the big carriers, *Ark Royal*, was just four months from retirement. The Navy still had carriers of sorts – the Commando carriers were doing service mainly as interim anti-submarine ships until *Invincible* arrived. But that meant that amphibious forces were certainly weaker. There were fewer conventionally-powered submarines, but the flotilla of nuclear-powered Fleet boats had grown substantially, and was still unique in a European navy. The SSNs had, for some time now, been hailed as the real offensive capability of the Navy, the true successors to the battleships of old. It was hardly surprising, therefore, that their names should include *Dreadnought, Warspite,* and *Valiant,* among the most evocative battleship names of the past. More of the modern Type 42 destroyers were joining the Fleet. But frigate numbers were continuing what seemed like an inexorable decline.

With the loss of its big carriers, the Navy was undoubtedly being demoted a league in terms of all-round capability and independence of operation. Some would argue that it was no longer truly a balanced fleet, as it lacked real power to take the offensive: the SSNs and a scattering of Exocet missiles around the Fleet hardly made up for the loss incurred. There was also the moderate indignity that the French Navy would now be the only one in Europe that operated conventional carriers. But the Royal Navy had always rather disparaged their design. And Britain still had more new, high-quality warships overall.

The Naval Staff could certainly reflect with some satisfaction on the fact that all the warship programmes that had been agreed over a decade earlier remained. There had even been the important addition of the Sea Harrier to the scheme of things. By most standards, this was still a major fleet. Clearly it could still, in certain circumstances, operate beyond its strictly NATO commitments and the country's home ocean. But, behind Admiral Lewin's confident front, there had been a growing worry that the Navy was spread too thin, with too many gaps, to be truly effective as the kind of fleet that the admirals would have liked.

The Soviet Navy was still transforming itself into an ever greater, world-wide maritime presence. The debates of the western naval strategists as to the purpose of that fleet were endless. Was it just to deny the West use of the sea, or to help Moscow exercise a growing international influence of its own? The arrival of carriers like the *Kiev*, and more classes of ever-bigger surface ships, seemed to be tipping the balance of the argument in favour of the latter.

The West still had some advantages, of geography and technology. At least the Soviet naval forces had to run some sort of gauntlet to get out of their northern bases – the relatively restricted waters between Greenland, Iceland, and the United Kingdom that was 'the GIUK Gap'. The West could, and did, erect barriers of seabed listening devices, submarines, and long-range maritime patrol aircraft. And then there was the promise of the towed array sonar technology, with its much greater detection ranges – at least until the Soviet Union's submarine technology caught up, and its vessels got quieter.

In 1976, an extensive new study for the Naval Staff on the size of fleet needed to counter the growing challenge at sea had produced some more alarming results – it suggested, ideally, a force much larger than seemed remotely affordable.[2] The 'baseline fleet' included, for example, thirty-four ships equipped with Sea Dart, in addition to the cruisers – that was nearly double the planned number. Overall, for air defence, ASW, and shadowing Soviet forces, the Navy reckoned it needed seventy-four destroyers and frigates, and twenty-four SSNs – again, fifty per cent more than were actually planned.

The Navy was also already looking to the need for an improved V/STOL aircraft, even before the Sea Harrier had arrived, and to equipping each of the new cruisers with extra planes – nine instead of the planned five. It would all add to the bill. Different, cheaper fleets were considered, but flexibility went down accordingly, and vulnerability went up. Such was the scale of the challenge that there were the first serious questions being raised about whether the concept that the Royal Navy had been building towards throughout the 1970s may well be overtaken before it had had a chance to come to fruition – that maybe the Navy, once again, was being too ambitious in what it was setting out to achieve.

The tensions that all this was creating started to spill over into frictions behind the scenes. How could the Navy respond in terms of maintaining its capabilities and the numbers of its ships?

As the ship planners looked at what would happen when the last of the *Invincible* class had been completed, there was thought for a time that there might be room in the plans for a further class of cheaper big ships. It would be a way of getting more of the valuable Sea King helicopters to sea. They would have simpler diesel engines and a lower speed than *Invincible*, and could perhaps be used for convoy escort work. They could perhaps carry up to fifteen helicopters. And they might also be useful in the amphibious role. There was a definite echo here of some of the cheap aviation ships that had been mooted in the 1960s. For that reason, perhaps, the idea seemed to go nowhere.

But the biggest disagreements would be over destroyers and frigates. The official aim at this stage was a fleet of sixty-five ships if possible. The Navy was putting much faith in a bigger and better destroyer to replace the Type 42s. The Type 43 would be part of the answer to the growing air defence problem. But was there a way to cut the costs of frigates from what was increasingly being referred to as the 'gold-plated' standards of ships like the Type 22s, the first of which was finally just coming into service?

A paper for the Naval Staff on escort ship policy called the concept of a cheap escort 'illusory' – it would be inflexible or just a liability.[3] The paper was heavily derided. Certainly, designing a cheap ship of real value was a major challenge. But the head of the ship design department asked contemptuously if the Navy really expected that it would be able to afford sixty-five Type 43 destroyers.

James Eberle had, from his early career in the Far East, now risen to the point where he became Commander-in-Chief, Fleet, in 1979. He was intellectually sharp, politically astute, and something of an iconoclast – which made him a bit suspect as far as some of his more traditional colleagues were concerned. He was one of those who worried that the Navy was again pricing itself out of the market. His views would put him at odds with some of his senior colleagues, including the man he was relieving as Commander-in-Chief, and who himself became the new First Sea Lord, Henry Leach. In a sense, they were both right. Leach had long worried that even some of the Navy's best ships had been under-armed. Admiral Eberle feared the navy was repeating the same mistakes that it had made in the past, and was refusing to face reality.

The naval architects would continue to produce designs for lighter, cheaper frigates. The Navy would reject them. So the designers went back and tried again. The debate would become muddied by an unsatisfactory argument over whether a 'short, fat' hull form would offer intrinsic advantages over traditional 'long, thin' ships. The debate would attract public attention, but shed little real light. Eventually, the budget pressures would force the Naval Staff to accept something of a middle course in the size, shape, and cost of its next frigate. But would that be enough to maintain the vision of the Fleet that *Invincible* represented?

All these years that the Royal Navy had been struggling to make its case in the corridors of Whitehall, the US Navy had been fighting similar battles in Washington.

In terms of scale, of course, it was all very different. And the fact that there was a clear understanding that the United States, as a superpower, needed to maintain a global presence, obviously worked to the advantage of America's admirals. But the senior ranks of the US Navy often seemed to feel as unloved in Washington as their British counterparts did in Whitehall.

With the experience of the Pacific War, those in charge of the US Navy were even more wedded to the carrier concept than the Naval Staff in London. American carriers had seemed to prove their worth in limited wars time and again since 1945 – not least in Korea and Vietnam. But there were always sceptics even within the US Navy's own ranks – not least among the submariners. The question marks over vulnerability kept recurring. It was an uncomfortable fact that the Soviet Navy was being built up as a largely anti-carrier force.

The US Navy's carriers had come under the most intense scrutiny themselves within the Pentagon during the McNamara years in the 1960s – a fact that may have influenced Denis Healey. The US Navy was also handicapped by the same doubts that the Royal Navy had faced over what contribution sea power made to the defence of NATO.

And, by the late 1970s, it also seemed to be facing its own big-carrier showdown. The administration of President Jimmy Carter had come into office with a determination not to order another full-size nuclear-powered carrier. It cancelled the next order planned by the previous Ford administration, and directed the US Navy to consider smaller, conventionally-powered ships.

The US Navy had been looking at a variety of designs, from a 'medium-sized' 50,000-ton carrier down to a 'sea control ship' of about 14,000 tons, to carry V/STOL aircraft and helicopters. This was, in many respects, an 'economy' version of *Invincible*. But American admirals did not like any of them.

In Senate hearings in 1978, the Chief of Naval Operations, Admiral James L Holloway, disagreed publicly with Carter's Defence Secretary, Harold Brown, over carrier policy.[4] The US Congress was on the US Navy's side. It reinstated the nuclear-powered carrier, which went on to become the USS *Theodore Roosevelt*.

Despite, or perhaps because of, their different fortunes in their respective carrier battles, the American and British navies were clearly anxious to try to stick together as closely as they could on maritime strategy. Hence the new staff talks involving Mike Livesay, while he was still on the Naval Staff in the Ministry of Defence and before he was appointed to *Invincible*.

A major US concern was clearly whether the Royal Navy would be able to keep up in the technological race. The United States was making big advances in its communications and the way it was processing information for the modern maritime battle. And one major question was how that would affect the ability of the two navies to operate together. The Americans also did not have the same assessment of the Royal Navy's ability to defend itself against Soviet air attack as the British themselves had.

What was also clear was that the shape of any naval battle would depend on how much warning time there would be in a crisis. With just a short build-up of tension, the better the chances of bottling up the Soviet naval forces behind the barrier defences of the GIUK Gap. The down-side was that there would be a far greater onus on NATO's European navies – with the Royal Navy supposedly in the lead – to operate virtually on their own early on, since it would take the US Navy carrier battle groups seven days to come steaming across the Atlantic to the rescue.

If the warning time was longer – say, up to thirty days – NATO would have more time to assemble its forces. But, equally, Soviet surface and submarine forces could stream out into the Atlantic before any shooting started, to take up positions that would inevitably force NATO onto the defensive. And, in a period of tension but no actual shooting, would NATO have to start escorting convoys across the Atlantic? Would all ships be convoyed, or only some, or none? The Americans and the British would have differing views on these questions.

The Royal Navy may no longer have had carrier battle groups of its own, but, in all the different scenarios – in fact, precisely because they were so different – the Naval Staff still saw the Invincibles and their task forces as crucial, even if the risks that they would face would be high.

And at least one influential part of the Royal Navy was emphasising the need to demonstrate in clear terms the will and ability of the West to use the North Atlantic. In 1980, the then Director of Naval Plans, Captain John 'Sandy' Woodward, saw the pressing need to reinvigorate the naval scene to enhance Western deterrence, and also had a clear idea of what that meant.[5]

Woodward argued that the significant rise in the Soviet naval threat in the previous five years had shown its global intent, and that this had only been confirmed by the invasion of Afghanistan. As a result, the US Navy was going to be increasingly stretched and distracted elsewhere. So there would have to be a greater European effort at sea. And that included the Royal Navy, which would have to bear the brunt in any conflict in the eastern Atlantic.

Of course, it is ambitious and self-confident nations which really value sea power. And, just at this time, neither the United States nor Britain was either of these. The Americans were still licking their wounds from Vietnam and Watergate, and Britain had domestic troubles to contend with.

Admiral Lewin's guarded optimism of 1978 had proved unfounded. Far from having put the dark economic days behind it, Britain had descended into the industrial relations gloom of the public workers strikes of 'the winter of discontent'. To say that Britain's economic slide had continued would have been an understatement. The country was reaching a crisis point in terms of its political and economic outlook.

Also at this point, the period of relatively warm East-West détente had given way to colder ideological war once again. Added to the country's economic woes, that seemed to serve only to sharpen the domestic political divisions over the proper place of defence and defence spending – let alone pretensions of maritime power – in the preoccupations of a medium-sized European country that seemed to be running rapidly out of money.

Paradoxically, there were some short-term benefits in all this for the Navy. In the run-up to the 1979 general election, the Labour government agreed a clutch of new warship orders, no doubt in the hope of brightening the employment prospects in what would be some decidedly marginal constituencies. But, on 3 May 1979, the election itself swept in a new Conservative government under Margaret Thatcher.

That might have appeared for many to have settled the argument on defence, since the Conservatives had won the election on a platform of strengthening the armed forces. The new government quickly confirmed its commitment to the recent NATO goal of increasing defence spending annually by three per cent in real terms. There was also an early move to improve personnel pay, which helped staunch the outflow of people that the services had been suffering lately. But it was a honeymoon that would not last.

HMS *Invincible*, whose existence had been ushered in by a Labour government, which had been ordered under a Conservative one, had been launched under another Labour administration, would finally find herself entering Royal Navy service under the Conservatives. It was nearly a year after the Conservative Party had taken office when the ship made her Portsmouth debut. Pretty soon, her Royal Navy acceptance trials were under way. There was a poignant visit to Plymouth, where *Invincible* passed close to the rather forlorn, decommissioned, and now almost derelict carrier *Ark Royal*. On 19 May 1980 came the first touch down on her deck by a Sea Harrier. And there were the first, modest foreign port visits, to Ostend and Lisbon.

But, whatever the programme of work, or the political and economic backdrop, the main event to which the crew of *Invincible* was now looking forward was the ceremonial highlight of the ship's introduction into the Royal Navy: commissioning day. It was a particularly challenging moment for Brian Goodson. In his first conversation with Mike Livesay when he had joined the ship as supply officer, the captain had asked him to take on the job of organizing the commissioning ceremony. And this would be no ordinary commissioning. It would be in the presence of The Queen, who had launched the ship three years previously.

The first thing Goodson did was to head for Buckingham Palace, for a discussion with The Queen's private secretary. To the supply officer's relief, his broad instruction was to ignore the torrent of advice with which he was certain to be deluged from all quarters, to trust to his instincts, and know that The Queen's private office would soon make it clear if it thought that any of the arrangements being planned were not likely to be acceptable. Sure enough, the advice was soon cascading in. And most of it was happily ignored.

The day of the ceremony dawned: 11 July 1980, alongside at Portsmouth. The main ceremonial would take place in the ship's hangar. And, while *Invincible*'s hangar was not the largest ever, it did stand a full three decks high. So it was an impressive venue nonetheless. Indeed, with the nearly 2,000 guests congregated fore and aft around the VIP area and the guard of honour, and with bright awnings draped along its side, it took on the appearance and atmosphere almost of a great military–industrial cathedral. The ship herself was dressed overall.

The moment arrived. The Captain greeted The Queen as she came aboard, and ushered her and the Duke of Edinburgh into the hangar. There was a short ceremony and the honour guard went through its drill unscathed, to the relief of Lieutenant Commander Malcolm Fuller, an air controller but the guard commander for the day, ceremonial sword and all. There were prayers, and of course a commissioning cake in the shape of the ship.

It all seemed to be going very well. But Brian Goodson was worried. By the time The Queen arrived in the wardroom for lunch, the programme –

uncharacteristically both for Buckingham Palace and the Royal Navy – was about half an hour behind schedule. It put the grand finale of the visit in jeopardy. As a surprise for the Royal Party and the rest of the guests, it had been arranged that a flight of Sea Harriers would swoop over the ship just at the moment The Queen departed down the gangway.

The wardroom staff tried to hurry things along while avoiding indecent haste. Still, lunch was going to end late. Goodson's concern mounted. He hurried away from lunch early and headed for the upper deck. His heart sank when he saw the aircraft forming up in the distance out over Spithead, far too early. But just at the last minute, they broke away. He need not have worried. The air controllers up in flying control, 'Flyco', next to the bridge, were aware of the situation, and had arranged relays of people to ensure that they knew exactly what was going on. They timed it to perfection, so the Sea Harriers roared overhead just as The Queen was halfway down the gangway.

For Tony Hallett, it was the greatest naval occasion that he had ever attended, and an appropriate way to usher in a new dawn for the Navy. For *Invincible*, it had been a good start.

CHAPTER SEVEN

Under the White Ensign

Neil Rankin had been a Fleet Air Arm pilot. His first carrier had been the old *Ark Royal*. He had flown Scimitars. The Americans had joked that only the British could build an aircraft so big and so powerful that only flew subsonic. But he was one of those Fleet Air Arm evangelists for naval aviation. When the CVA-01 decision had been announced, he had handed in his resignation, believing – as many did – that there was no future for flying in the Royal Navy. He was prevailed upon to change his mind. Now he was sitting on his perch high up in the cramped space of Flyco, looking down on *Invincible's* flight deck as a Sea Harrier was manoeuvred after landing. It was winter in the Western Approaches and *Invincible* was carrying out her first extensive trials with the aircraft. Rankin was Commander (Air) – or 'Wings' – responsible for flight operations aboard the ship.

Before joining *Invincible*, Commander Rankin had completed an assignment with the US Navy, helping to evaluate its still-born sea control ship. He was not surprised that the idea had got nowhere in a navy that still had a huge force of full-size carriers. He regarded the sea control ship as 'a fudge'. Now, as he looked down on that flight deck scene from the insulated hum and buzz of Flyco, he was not sure that *Invincible* was much better.

Like most naval aviators, he regarded *Invincible* very much as second-best to the old carriers. While the designers had made allowances for V/STOL aircraft, she was really conceived with helicopters in mind, and that would always compromise her operation of the Sea Harrier, itself a compromised aircraft. But thank goodness for it, he thought. The Navy and the Fleet Air Arm had been given another chance. He had a reputation for getting things done. And, like most of those aboard, he was determined that this new ship, and the new ideas she represented, would be made to work as well as possible. It had been a great moment when she had first welcomed aircraft aboard. Now he and his team were going to set to work to help prove the concept, to develop and establish the procedures that would begin to turn her into an efficient naval unit and prototype of a new type of aircraft-carrying ship. They would work out ways around those limitations and compromises that they saw.

Her operational air group had been settled at nine Sea King helicopters and five Sea Harriers. *Ark Royal*, in her final days, had operated a dozen supersonic

Phantoms, fourteen of the lumbering, sturdy Buccaneer bombers, four ancient, whirring Gannet AEW aircraft, and six Sea Kings of her own. It was quite a different proposition.

There was an early setback. A Sea Harrier clipped the ship's flight deck on a flypast. The pilot ejected safely. But the precious aircraft was lost, and there were few enough of them around at the time.

All the time, though, the ship's company was feeling its way forward. Neil Rankin and some of the carrier veterans aboard were surprised at how many of the old lessons of aircraft operations had been so quickly forgotten as the previous carrier force had run down. It was a gap of less than two years between when the old *Ark Royal* had finally decommissioned and the first Sea Harriers went to sea. But it had been a long, slow, painful decline as *Ark Royal* had struggled on through most of the 1970s. Now many lessons were having to be re-learned.

Similar thoughts went through the mind of Malcolm Fuller. He had served in HMS *Eagle* on her final commission in the Mediterranean and the Far East between 1970 and 1972. For him, as an air traffic and fighter controller, being part of that great ship's last hurrah, as she bowed out in style as a fully worked-up Fleet carrier, was a memorable experience. But the anticipation when he had been preparing to join *Invincible* had also been high, as he waited to set eyes on this vessel about which he had heard so much for so long. And when he saw her for the first time in Barrow, he was not disappointed. Now, in the midst of her exhaustive trials, some of the gaps were showing – for example, no close-in radar to help control the aircraft.

The weapons engineering officer, Commander Anthony Wolstenholme, was another man in two minds. He was getting his hands on a lot of the best equipment that the Navy had to offer. But was it good enough? The radars that they did have aboard were the latest models in the British Fleet, like the brand-new, long-range Type 1022. It was a big advance on the previous model, the Type 965, which had looked like an iron-work bedstead. But Tony Wolstenholme had studied more closely than most what the opposition had at its disposal. He had learned Russian thanks to the Navy, and had been sent to the British embassy in Moscow as assistant naval attaché in 1970. He had lasted only fifteen months before becoming one of the victims in the mass tit-for-tat diplomatic expulsions that the British and Soviet governments carried out at that time. But he had kept an eye on Soviet naval technology, and was impressed with what he saw.

Another young officer who was not totally enamoured with the technological wizardry aboard *Invincible* was Lieutenant Anthony Robinson, another of the ship's air direction officers. And that was because he had had a chance to work at close hand not with the Russians, but the Americans. And, to him, the Type 1022 simply showed how far the country that had pioneered radar had fallen behind the best that the United States had to offer.

Tony Wolstenholme was also firmly in the camp of those who thought that *Invincible* was seriously under-armed in terms of her shipboard defences. Quite simply, that one Sea Dart missile launcher in the bows, however good the system was, looked terribly lonely.

So, this all looked like more evidence that the Royal Navy – which had long given up the race in terms of size – was struggling to keep up with the technological pace of the two other fleets against which it most measured itself. But *Invincible*, like the rest of the Fleet, worked hard to make up in the skill and ingenuity of those aboard what she lacked in outright firepower.

At the end of April 1981, the designers Arthur Honnor and David Andrews would present their paper on *Invincible* to the Royal Institute of Naval Architects in London. It was an important occasion. After all, *Invincible* was the prototype of a new generation of ships. Andrews himself would later go on to be professor of naval architecture at University College, London.

Present at that gathering was Mike Livesay. Also there was another man who would play a significant part in *Invincible*'s early life, Captain Jeremy Black, Royal Navy.

Livesay had been enjoying the challenge of getting to know his new command. She was, he admitted, with her shallow draft and tall sides, quite a handful at slow speeds in harbour, especially with a wind blowing. But, out at sea where she belonged, she had been something close to a revelation to handle. She was fast and agile in a way that no aircraft carrier had a right to be. Again, the thought came to mind that she was like an overgrown frigate. Livesay felt that she could dodge a torpedo if she had to.

At the end of March, the ship was heading back to Portsmouth from a trip to the Mediterranean and the French naval port of Toulon. While at Toulon, she had performed one of her party tricks in front of the French Navy, launching Sea Harriers while alongside the jetty – something a conventional carrier with its aircraft would not have contemplated. The French did not seem that impressed. But now *Invincible* was passing through the Straits of Gibraltar, building up speed for a full power trial as she headed into a long, steep Atlantic swell. These were some of the worst conditions that she had faced. As she reached maximum speed, Livesay was hunched intently in the captain's chair, looking out from the high bridge windows, trying to see how she performed. He noticed a little light spray over the bows. He smiled contentedly. She was riding well, and would clearly be a very dry and stable platform for flying even in difficult conditions.

He knew his vessel's limitations too. She was not a fleet carrier in the old sense, and never would be. But *Invincible* did, he believed, meet the Navy's requirements. She was, in his view, a success. However, even as she was powering north towards her home port, decisions were unfolding in Whitehall which would cast a grey cloud over her future.

Any positive thoughts that the chiefs of staff may have had at the election of a Conservative government on a platform of strong defence had quickly evaporated. There was certainly not going to be any extra money over and above what had been planned. The best that the chiefs could console themselves with was that any cuts may not be as deep as might otherwise have occurred. But it was not much consolation, especially in the light of the expectations that had earlier been raised. Defence may have fared better than some other government departments. But it soon became clear that the Treasury's view of a three per cent real annual growth rate was different from the chiefs'. Margaret Thatcher discovered more quickly than she would have liked that her twin ambitions of strong defence and a strong economy were coming into sharp conflict. On neither front was the reality matching the election rhetoric.

In these circumstances, the increases in service pay were squeezing the equipment budgets even more. For the First Sea Lord, Admiral Sir Henry Leach, it appeared to be another of the many paradoxes in the tense relationship between politics and defence: it seemed that the previous Labour Government had been stoking the Ministry of Defence's equipment budget at the expense of the people in uniform, and now the Conservatives appeared to be putting people ahead of equipment.

To add to what would turn out to be a tidal wave of looming trouble, the new Conservative government was about to commit itself to a new generation of nuclear deterrent based on the American Trident submarine-launched ballistic missile. It was not just that nuclear weapons were becoming an ever more divisive political issue, as the anti-nuclear lobby gained new momentum. Whatever the long-term cost and operational benefits of plumping for Trident compared to the alternatives – and they were very considerable – the initial price-tag for the new weapons and the submarines to carry them was going to be very high.

To add further to the growing difficulties, with a general economic slump developing, firms were rushing through defence contracts more quickly than expected to keep their workforces busy, compounding a mounting cash crisis. The pressure was on the Ministry of Defence to cut more deeply. And the frustrations and frictions between the Prime Minister and her Defence Secretary, Francis Pym, were growing. During the second half of 1980, various cuts, savings, and economies were imposed, including on running costs. Fuel budgets were cut. Even *Invincible*, supposedly the new pride of the Fleet and a brand new ship that had to be proved, was affected. Mike Livesay had to fight hard to get permission and fuel for anything but the shortest of voyages. But, in terms of cuts, Pym would go no further, and even threatened resignation. He staved off the Treasury axe, but only temporarily.

While there may have been some quiet admiration among the chiefs for Francis Pym's staunchness in Cabinet, there was also a grim suspicion that another serious reckoning could not be avoided. In January 1981, Francis Pym was moved.

The carrier that never was. An artist's impression of CVA-01 which was cancelled by Denis Healey in February 1966. The decision gave birth to HMS *Invincible*. (Crown Copyright/Imperial War Museum FL10199)

The hull of *Invincible* dominates the slipway at the Vickers shipyard at Barrow-in-Furness just prior to launch. (BAe Systems)

PREPARED BY MANAGER TECHNICAL ILLUSTRATOR POOLS BATH

Last of the line. December 1978, and a poignant final homecoming to Devonport for HMS *Ark Royal*, the very last of the Royal Navy's traditional fixed-wing aircraft carriers.
(Crown Copyright/MoD)

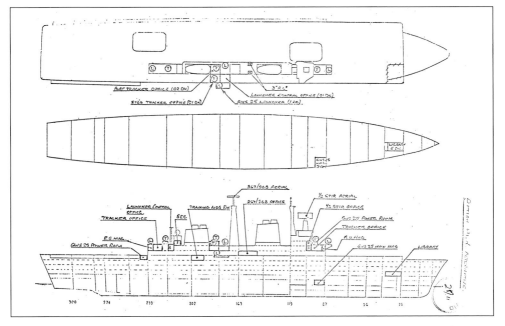

Even before *Invincible* entered service, a study was under way on improvements to the class. In this sketch from the study, T is for tracker, and L is for launcher for the GWS 25 Sea Wolf missiles which would have been dotted round the island superstructure. They would have replaced the Sea Dart missile system, the area for which would have been plated over in this scheme to extend the flight deck. (National Archive, Kew)

Amid cheering crowds, HMS *Invincible* leads the major elements of the Falklands task force out of Portsmouth on their way to the South Atlantic. (Crown Copyright/Imperial War Museum FKD 207)

HMS *Invincible* on operations in the South Atlantic, preparing to launch two Sea Harriers. (Crown Copyright/Imperial War Museum FKD537)

Following the end of hostilities, Captain Jeremy Black anchors *Invincible* in the Falklands, close to where her predecessor had anchored sixty-seven years previously. (Crown Copyright/Imperial War Museum FKD2598)

'Hacking the shad'. A Sea Harrier of 801 naval air squadron escorts a Soviet Tu-95 Bear-D long-range maritime reconnaissance and targeting aircraft. This was the role for which it was primarily envisaged, and on which the case for buying the aircraft was founded. The 'N' on the Sea Harrier's tail indicates the squadron's assignment to HMS *Invincible*. (Crown Copyright/MoD)

HMS *Invincible* at anchor in the Gulf in early 1998. Her flight deck is crowded with sixteen jets – eight Sea Harriers and eight RAF Harrier GR.7s – and a Sea King helciopter. (Crown Copyright/MoD)

Size matters. HMS *Illustrious* in company with the giant US aircraft carrier USS *John C Stennis*, also in the Gulf. (Crown Copyright/MoD)

HMS *Illustrious* operating off the eastern United States in 2007, with an air group of US Marine Corps Harriers aboard. The ship is also about to be visited by the revolutionary and controversial V-22 Osprey tilt-rotor aircraft. Many in the Royal Navy would like to see the V-22 form part of future British carrier air groups as well. (Crown Copyright/MoD)

HMS *Invincible* takes pride of place at the international fleet review to mark the 200th anniversary of the Battle of Trafalgar in 2005. Next in line are the American amphibious helicopter carrier USS *Saipan* and the French nuclear-powered aircraft carrier FS *Charles De Gaulle*. This was *Invincible*'s last outing in the public eye.
(Crown Copyright/MoD)

The shape of things to come? A computer-generated image of the giant CVF, the first of which was given the name HMS *Queen Elizabeth,* and which has been the focus of even more protracted debate than CVA-01 was in the 1960s. The depiction also shows an air group of JSF/JCA fighters, and a Merlin helicopter. (Thales UK)

And in came John Nott from the Department of Trade. It fell to him to announce some of the results of the previously-agreed economies, including the early retirement, for the second time, of the ageing carrier HMS *Bulwark*.

The chiefs did not seem to know what exactly to expect from the new man. They did not know much about him at all, but what they did know did not seem to augur well. He had been a soldier, in the Gurkhas. But the rest of his background – as a merchant banker, and in the key economics departments of the Treasury under the previous Heath government and as Trade Secretary under Thatcher – probably had them uneasy from the outset. To the chiefs, on first acquaintance, he seemed a rather cold and analytical character. Above all, though, there was the obvious assumption that he had been brought in by Margaret Thatcher to wield the axe that Francis Pym would not.

Nott's own views, too, were mixed. He was clearly honoured to be taking on what was a key department, especially for the Conservatives. His background as a former soldier reinforced that. But his more recent experience in government, trying to grapple with the dire state of the country's economic affairs, influenced him more. He quickly became focused on the fact that defence costs were rising much faster even than the general galloping rate of inflation – a long-term phenomenon that he felt was a profound issue, the consequences of which needed to be tackled. He arrived at the Ministry of Defence not only with a freeze on most spending in place, but also with a feeling that the chiefs of staff did not really seem to grasp the economic realities outside their own world of defence, or even the inevitable consequences of those within it. As far as he was concerned, the chiefs had a 'pie in the sky' notion of how much money would be available to them over the next ten years. Instinctively, it seems, he saw the armed forces and the men at their head with some suspicion as a closed, mutually-supportive club of vested interests. Whether or not he walked into the Ministry of Defence believing another defence review was necessary, it soon became clear that – for various reasons – there was no other way.

The broader strategic picture was highly charged. There had been enough concern among the political establishments of NATO about trends in the East-West balance of power that the Alliance had painfully agreed to real increases in defence spending. But delivering those was another matter altogether. Across Europe, the popular consensus on defence was fraying badly. NATO's decision in 1979 to deploy cruise and Pershing nuclear-tipped missiles as part of a response to Soviet deployments of SS-20 intermediate-range missiles only added to the strains. Transatlantic frictions were mounting. The US Congress was again grumbling about Alliance burden-sharing – or, in other words, a European lack of it. The mood of crisis had been stoked by the Soviet invasion of Afghanistan in December 1979. Nine months later, the eruption of war between Iraq and an Iran fresh from its Islamic revolution raised concerns further. Two months after that, in November 1980, the election of President Ronald Reagan – promising a more radical and confrontational approach to dealing with the Soviet Union – seemed set only to increase tensions and those transatlantic frictions further still.

Among the senior civil servants in the Ministry of Defence, there was anticipation of a crunch to come – or rather, yet another crunch. A high-level group known as the Defence Programme Working Party looked at options. It wondered whether – given the level to which conflicting pressures of resources and commitments had now reached – the time had come to make a historic choice. The cuts that had come before had stripped away most of the country's global presence, and shaved away at the fringes of NATO commitments. But there was nothing left on that front. If the ideal of balanced forces at adequate levels could no longer be sustained, maybe it was time finally to decide between a continental and a maritime strategy.

And there, the balance of opinion among the civil servants seemed to be against a maritime choice. The prevailing view was that the ultimate necessities, if everything else had to go, were the nuclear deterrent and the presence in Germany. Such was the extent to which the continental commitment had taken hold. For the Navy, of course, such thoughts were anathema. Surely, if relative economic weakness was the driver, it made no sense in terms of long-term national interest to continue to pour money into a forward commitment that others were better placed to fulfil, at the expense of naval forces that more directly affected the country's own survival and made up a far greater proportion of NATO forces at sea than British troops did the Alliance front line in Europe.

Any strategic debate, though, was immediately trumped by politics. As Mrs Thatcher and her ministers tried to square the circle of contradictions that their different ambitions had created, they too – briefly – tried to grapple with some fundamentals. The Cabinet's Overseas and Defence Committee was presented with a paper by the Foreign Secretary, Lord Carrington, and Francis Pym in his last weeks as Defence Secretary. It argued for reform of NATO that would, in the long term, see member states moving towards greater specialization of roles.[1] For Britain, again, the obvious choice would have been between a maritime or continental role. But it came to nothing because, at the time, it looked just too difficult politically. It was clearly not going to be viewed in a positive light by other members of NATO, notably the West Germans.

So, when Thatcher, Nott, and Carrington met in February 1981, the shape of the prospective review was already becoming pretty clear. The defence budget, Nott felt, was bursting at the seams. Even if he was ready to look at the costs of the nuclear deterrent, Margaret Thatcher was not, so that was not on the table. There was little scope, given the political decisions already made, for cuts in Europe. An overriding concern in Margaret Thatcher's mind was not to give the new President or the US Congress any more reasons to pack up any of the US commitments in Europe, and thus precipitate an unravelling of NATO.

Home defence was not going to yield savings, either. It had already been stripped to the bone. So there seemed to be only one area for making potential savings: the maritime commitment.

John Nott professed an affection for the Navy, based on a long family association with it. His view, though, was that the strategic, political, and economic imperatives at the time dictated only one logical course of action. He would express exasperation at the Naval Staff and how it responded, describing it as 'incoherent', and 'an intellectual desert'.[2]

Many of the admirals would scoff at the idea that John Nott was simply being guided by his head rather than his heart. For many in the Navy, he would come to be seen as the Conservatives' version of Denis Healey – indeed, even more of a villain in many ways. To the more sympathetic, the comparison was not unflattering – Nott may not have been the political figure that Healey was, but both men seemed to have an intellectual drive to understand the issues at hand, and to make tough decisions if they had to.

CHAPTER EIGHT

No Way Forward

If ever there was a clash of personalities in all the arguments and wrangles that there had been down the years, it was here and now, between the Defence Secretary and the First Sea Lord. To John Nott, Sir Henry Leach was the archetypal Nelsonian admiral, who would no doubt have been in his element on the deck of a ship in battle, but who was essentially a throwback, unbending in his view of the Navy and its place in the world – frankly, the worst kind of admiral. To the First Sea Lord, John Nott was equally the worst combination, both a politician and the archetypal cold, calculating, impervious accountant.

Certainly, Henry Leach had the Navy in his blood. From the moment he was born in 1923, his father, John, a naval officer himself, was in no doubt that his son would join the Navy. And so it was.

Henry Leach was still a Dartmouth cadet when the Second World War broke out. His first ship would have been the brand new battleship HMS *Prince Of Wales*. But, when his father was appointed the ship's commanding officer, that had to change. John Leach would be *Prince Of Wales*' captain throughout her short, tempestuous career. He would be on the bridge when she duelled the German battleship *Bismarck* in the Denmark Strait, and would watch in disbelief when the battle-cruiser *Hood* exploded before his eyes. He and his ship would convey Winston Churchill to his secret rendezvous with President Franklin D Roosevelt off Newfoundland in August 1941, at which the two leaders would agree the Atlantic Charter that would form the foundation of the post-war international system. Churchill and Leach Senior obviously hit it off. 'I took a great liking to our captain, Leach,' the Prime Minister wrote. 'A charming and lovable man and all that a British sailor should be.'[1]

But Churchill would also be instrumental in the decision that sealed Captain Leach's fate. Father and son were to meet four months later in far-off Singapore. It would be their last encounter. *Prince Of Wales* and the elderly battle-cruiser *Repulse* had arrived as Force Z, a highly-publicized show of force in the Far East, amid growing concerns about the threat from Japan. The group should have included the aircraft carrier *Indomitable*, to provide air cover, but she had been damaged after running aground in the West Indies, and no replacement was available. Whether her presence would have decisively altered the fate of Force Z will never be known. Captain Leach and hundreds of others were lost when *Prince Of Wales* and *Repulse* succumbed to a Japanese air onslaught. It was a terrible personal loss for young Henry. He would later rationalize the whole operation as 'a classic example of political expediency leading to the misapplication of too little force too late'.[2]

Henry Leach was to play a small part in Royal Navy history himself before the war was over. By now a young lieutenant, he was in charge of the four 14-inch guns of 'A' turret aboard the battleship *Duke Of York*, a sister ship to *Prince Of Wales*, when she encountered the German battle-cruiser *Scharnhorst* on that dark, cold, stormy Boxing Day of 1943, and pounded her to destruction in the last such big-gun surface action by a British battleship.

Thirty-eight years later, he was now standing at the summit of the naval establishment. Henry Leach certainly had an old-fashioned sense of what was right and proper, as well as a very clear-cut perception of what was right and wrong. He also had, to some, a rather stiff and forbidding air, and the bearing of a man out of his time. Others certainly saw a gentleman of the old school, and someone of great courtesy and charm, and they respected his deep attachment to his Service and his fighting spirit, even in the context of the corridors of Whitehall. Most of those who knew him well had a deep affection for him and what he represented. And he had enormous experience on his side.

The frustrations of the two chief protagonists in this tussle were soon bubbling over.

Nott was frustrated at what he saw as the refusal of the Naval Staff, led by Leach, to co-operate. Henry Leach was angry that John Nott appeared to have his mind made up, and would refuse to listen. And the First Sea Lord was not going to do the Defence Secretary's dirty work for him. Each was clearly dismissive, and even disdainful, of the other's methods and mind-set.

In this angry atmosphere, the chiefs of staff seemed unable to reach any kind of consensus position. None of them were eager to co-operate with the new Defence Secretary, or saw much military justification for further defence cuts. Some of the old inter-service antagonisms, especially between the Navy and the RAF, bubbled to the surface. But it seemed pretty clear pretty soon that it was the Navy that was most in the line of fire. That was where John Nott saw that he had room for political manoeuvre, and it was the Navy's budget that seemed most overblown.

When he did not get the responses that he was looking for from the services, John Nott turned to his own civil servants and scientific advisers. And to him and his team, the Navy's views of strategy, and how an East-West conflict might unfold, were out of step with how the rest of NATO saw things. It had come as a shock to Nott when he had arrived at the Ministry of Defence to discover how thin the Alliance's defensive line on the Central Front was, and in particular how few days it would take before its stockpiles of ammunition in Europe would be exhausted and it would face the prospect of having to 'go nuclear' to stem a Warsaw Pact tide of advance, raising huge doubts about the transatlantic reinforcement issue.

Henry Leach and his fellow admirals were faced with the same challenge as a generation of predecessors. The Navy argument, of course, was that the war would not necessarily be short, indeed that wars rarely follow a predicted course, and that to prepare only for a short conflict would critically weaken the West and undermine its options and its chances of maintaining an effective deterrence strategy. It would, in effect, be to plan for defeat.

The other, related argument was a more technical one, over how best to organize any kind of maritime defence. In this regard, Henry Leach's irritation was directed as much at John Nott's chief scientific adviser, Sir Ronald Mason, as it was at the Defence Secretary himself. Mason did not minimize the Soviet maritime challenge. On the contrary, his view was that, such was the scale of the Soviet submarine, missile, and air threats in the north-eastern Atlantic now, that the Navy's cherished ASW task forces centred on ships like *Invincible* would essentially be sitting ducks in the face of what would be a hail of Soviet weaponry. The better option was a barrier defence of the GIUK gap with more emphasis on submarines and land-based maritime patrol aircraft like the RAF's Nimrod, and more money for better torpedoes, since it was doubtful that the Navy's current weapons could even hit the Russians' deepest-diving submarines.

In Nott's mind, the thrust of his review was clear. The Army and the RAF would have to bear some cuts, but the bulk would fall on the Navy. It would mark a strategic shift. The maritime commitment was, in effect, to be demoted in the country's list of defence priorities. This and Ronald Mason's scientific analysis would be the basis for a significant cut in the Navy's surface fleet, the ending of the mid-life modernization programme, and this permitted also big savings in dockyard support. And one of the carriers would have to go. That was the way that the financial numbers would be made to add up. And, in John Nott's view, with fewer refits, the actual available numbers of ships would not fall as much as the overall figures suggested.

Nott's own thoughts had crystallized during a visit to the United States in March. He and his key staff stopped off in Bermuda on the way back. It was there that they began drafting the document that would be the foundation for his review, and it would become infamous in naval circles at the time as the 'Bermudagram'. The final document, just ten pages long, was dated 16 March 1981.

Essentially, it revealed the Defence Secretary's hand and thinking. It declared that the ideas contained in it 'may seem radical but taken as a whole they are designed to be a source of future <u>strength</u> [emphasis in the original] to defence. We are all agreed that we cannot go on as we are.'

But it was all set in the conventional Whitehall and NATO mind-set on the strategy for handling an East-West conflict. And thus it was what most of the Navy had feared. Although there was much bitter argument to come, what was set down in outline here was what would emerge in public three months later. There were adjustments for the RAF, and some reductions for the Army 'which will just permit the Brussels Treaty strengths to be fulfilled'.

As for Britain's maritime effort in the eastern Atlantic and the Channel, 'that should concentrate on the deployment and protection of ballistic missile submarines with free access to their bases, the security of our continental reinforcement ports and, in conjunction with the United States Navy, the disruption of Soviet maritime activity with the aim of containing it north of the Greenland-Iceland-UK gap. This will have to be at the expense of UK effort in the direct protection of reinforcement shipping …'

There should, the memo went on, 'be a sharp change of direction in our surface ship plans reflecting the switch away from direct defence and the protected convoy.' There was not yet the firm intention to sell one of the Invincibles, but a clear hint that they were no longer at the heart of John Nott's vision of the future, but were seen more as part of 'an imaginative and positive look at our naval role outside the Eastern Atlantic and Channel in peacetime including, for example, limited deployment of the new Invincible class ships, in a wider role alongside the United States Navy.' The Royal Marine Commandos would be retained, but 'no provision is to be made for specialist amphibious shipping'.

John Nott and his civil servants would always insist that they had taken great account of the Navy's arguments, but they had been encouraged by chinks in its armour. During that March visit to the United States , Nott returned convinced that the US Navy had left the Royal Navy behind in its view of how the defence of shipping across the Atlantic would be conducted. The Americans' view, at least as far as John Nott's civil servants saw it, was that there would be fewer convoys, and therefore less need for convoy escorts.

And then there were the perceived differences within the Royal Navy's own senior ranks. Nott and his staff saw a marked difference in outlook between most of the admirals in Whitehall and the leadership at the Navy's operational headquarters in Northwood. They believed that the then C-in-C Fleet, Admiral Sir John Fieldhouse, himself a submariner, was more sympathetic to the barrier defence case, and the greater emphasis on submarines and maritime patrol aircraft. If a choice had to be made for the sake of saving money, then that was the one that he would make, even if he would not say so in public.

Fieldhouse was known to love his submarines. But he would also complain later, as First Sea Lord, about 'sea blindness', an inability to understand the importance of maritime affairs in modern Britain, and especially in Whitehall. And he would be an active proponent of the need to maintain an 'out-of-area' capability beyond NATO, for which he saw great need for big aviation ships like the Invincibles.

However, another who confessed some sympathy for the arguments was Fieldhouse's predecessor at Northwood, Admiral Eberle, who had gone on to be the Commander-in-Chief, Naval Home Command. Earlier, in the mid

1970s, he had been the flag officer in charge of carriers and amphibious ships, when the Royal Navy still had the old *Ark Royal*, and so could contribute a proper strike carrier group to NATO. But he had doubts about NATO's whole maritime approach at this time, and wondered if carriers were more of a liability than an asset, especially the British ones. He was more concerned about the anti-submarine effort, and the GIUK Gap, than the carriers.[3] And there were others, too, who looked at the Navy and worried that it was trying to do too much, and felt that something had to go.

For Henry Leach, it was a maddening irony that the Navy was being accused of backward and closed thinking, when to him it was clearly the scale of the British military contribution on the Central Front, agreed thirty years previously, that was the anachronism and anomaly. But it was enshrined in a treaty, and the government had rejected the idea of attempting to tamper with it as part of a wider NATO reform. In his minutes and memorandums, which he sent all the way up to 10 Downing Street, he tried to press home what he saw as the magnitude of the implications of what was being proposed: a historic unbalancing of the Royal Navy that would significantly reduce both Britain's and NATO's military options and would seriously lower the nuclear threshold in Europe.

He decided that he had to seek a meeting with Margaret Thatcher, which was his prerogative as a Chief of Staff. After some delays, an appointment was agreed. John Nott suggested that the First Sea Lord should go alone. But Henry Leach, while appreciating the thought behind the suggestion, insisted that the Defence Secretary should be there too.

Margaret Thatcher received the two men rather coldly, Henry Leach felt. The First Sea Lord put forward his proposition, that what was really needed was a redeployment of the British Army of the Rhine. He also argued that the thrust of John Nott's proposals had been rushed, and that the alternatives had not been properly considered.

It was to no avail. On 25 June 1981, John Nott published his defence white paper, officially designated Cmnd 8288, and entitled 'The Way Forward'. In terms of detail, only two instead of three of the new Invincible-class carriers would be kept in service, with a greater emphasis on their possible usefulness for out-of-area operations beyond NATO. The number of operational destroyers and frigates would come down from around sixty-five to forty-two, with a further eight in reserve. The two amphibious assault ships would go. And, among a list of other seemingly peripheral savings, the ice patrol ship HMS *Endurance* would be withdrawn. Chatham dockyard was to be closed, and Portsmouth run down. The Navy's manpower would be cut by between 8,000 and 10,000. Much was made of the fact that the number of nuclear-powered Fleet submarines would continue to rise to a total of seventeen, although that was just one above the existing plan.

It was, by any measure, a very significant pruning. The nod towards an out-of-area role was the smallest of small consolations. Henry Leach was seething. But what would he do?

As the Nott review unfolded, the Navy Minister, Keith Speed, had become increasingly uneasy and frustrated, not least because he felt that he was being excluded from much of the deliberation. When, at a constituency meeting, he made a speech which seemed at odds with the policy that was evolving, he was asked to resign. When he refused, Margaret Thatcher dismissed him. He was given a hero's send-off by the Navy department at the Ministry of Defence, and was personally escorted from the building for the last time by the First Sea Lord. He would be the last Navy Minister. Margaret Thatcher would scrap the post, and those for the other single services as well.

Should Henry Leach resign? He had fought, but he had lost. He was conscious that David Luce's resignation fifteen years earlier had caused barely a ripple in the body politic. Times, and people's attention, he thought, had moved on again since then. Leach believed that, if he had resigned, even if the entire Admiralty Board had gone with him, and he thought it might, it would have been a futile gesture. Equally importantly, he felt that resignations were for matters of honour, personal indiscretions or failures, and not for professional disagreements.

One enigma in all of this was the position of the then Chief of the Defence Staff, Admiral of the Fleet Sir Terence Lewin. He was respected on both the civilian and uniformed sides of Whitehall. He was in a difficult position, since the Chief of the Defence Staff had little real bureaucratic clout at this time, and yet the other chiefs were clearly at odds with each other and with their ministerial boss. Some of John Nott's advisers would hint that Lewin was probably more sympathetic to their predicament and their proposals than Henry Leach had been. But Lewin had been one of the architects of the concept of the Navy that these new measures were calling into question. Some in the Navy clearly felt that he could have done more to support the Naval Staff.

Might things have been different if there had been someone wilier and more willing than Henry Leach to play the political game? It might have made a marginal difference. But the overall strategic, political, and economic parameters had been largely set. If money had to be saved, it had to come from somewhere, and there seemed – in John Nott's view – to be only one place where it could come from. The thrust of John Nott's thinking would probably have been the same, whoever the First Sea Lord or the Admiralty Board had been at the time. And the same differences of perspective within the Navy would have been there to be exploited whoever was the First Sea Lord. Nott and his advisers clearly saw these differences as a weakness. But no institution like the Navy is a monolith. The Conservative government at the time was certainly not either. There has always, in that sense, been more than one Royal Navy, just as there is more than one US Navy.

The fact is that there were very different philosophies and outlooks at work here. John Nott saw the role of the Navy, at this time in history, in a very specific and narrow way. For admirals like Henry Leach – and probably Terence Lewin as well – the whole point of the Navy, and the value of maritime power to a country like Britain, was about something completely different. It was about keeping political and military options open, in both the NATO context and beyond, not narrowing or even closing them, as they believed the Nott formula did.

Perhaps the timing, again, was against everyone concerned. Just as the Navy was being forced to change course again, developments and events elsewhere were propelling maritime thinking in a different direction. In the United States, in February 1981, just a month after John Nott became Defence Secretary, the combative John Lehman took office as Ronald Reagan's Navy Secretary. He would quickly begin to question the assumptions about how much, or how little, sea power could contribute to the Western defence of Europe. He would describe the barrier defences of the GIUK Gap as 'a sort of maritime Maginot Line', as the Americans began to fashion a new, more aggressive US maritime strategy. It was perhaps the most eye-catching element of the Reagan build-up that was getting under way, not least the idea of turning the US fleet back into a 600-ship navy after a long decline of its own. The plan to reactivate and modernize four Second World War battleships was probably the most striking statement of intent.

But it was not just on the maritime front that things were moving. Just as John Nott was making his own judgements and calculations, army strategists and theorists in the United States were putting together a new concept that would become known as Air-Land Battle 2000. It formally emerged in March 1981, in the midst of the British review. In a few years it would be approved as a NATO doctrine called Follow-On Force Attack (FOFA). The idea was that the revolutions taking place in intelligence, surveillance, and targeting technology would allow the West to counter a Soviet attack with deep strikes at the enemy's legions of reinforcements – the follow-on forces. That way, the theory went, NATO could decisively slow down a Soviet advance. Crucially for NATO's navies, even in a purely Central Front scenario, that would buy time for the Alliance's own transatlantic reinforcements to become a much more critical part of the East-West military equation.

Of course, the Reagan build-up – and the new forward US maritime strategy in particular – sparked their own controversies. The issue of the vulnerability of surface ships was also being at least as hotly debated in US defence circles as it was in British ones. And Ronald Reagan was not embarking on a plan for a 600-ship navy at the expense of the other US armed forces. He was putting more money into all of them. That was a level, and breadth, of commitment that Britain just could not contemplate. But it was still telling that, on each side of the Atlantic, the political establishments in London and Washington looked at the same problems of Western defence, and came up with radically different approaches with dramatically different effects. The United States was, of course a superpower, while Britain was still in the doldrums, politically and economically.

If the Naval Staff had been able to grasp some of this, it might have made a difference. As it was, the generalized case for British maritime power, as espoused by the Navy, did not seem to cut much more ice with John Nott than it had with Denis Healey.

And perhaps the Navy had lost its way somewhat as well, at least as far as actually putting its own vision into practice was concerned. If so, that had happened over a period in the 1970s, not just during the rushed few weeks in the spring and summer of 1981 when John Nott was putting his review together. It laid the Navy more open to the charge that its vision was not affordable, and could not be sustained by a country like Britain.

The Navy had embraced the concept of a largely defensive, ASW, NATO-orientated fleet to a great extent, plus enough spare capacity to retain some level of world-wide capability. If it had embraced some of the other options to deliver it earlier on, it might have had a more robust case to put to the Nott team, and thus lessened the blow. Cheaper helicopter carriers, for example, to supplement the Invincibles and get more of the crucial Sea Kings to sea might have made more sense than holding on to the Navy's older, bigger, obsolescent destroyers. And maybe it should have embraced one of those cheaper frigate designs earlier and more eagerly. The warnings were already there, in the price tag of the Type 22s and the programme of gutting and filleting the Leanders at two-thirds the cost of a new ship.

It might have addressed the vulnerability issue more urgently and more flexibly as well. As all the world's navies took stock of the shock destruction of the *Eilat*, the Royal Navy's particular focus had been on the fact that the missiles which sank her had been fired by relatively small Egyptian patrol boats. So its main response was to arm its ship-borne helicopters with missiles of their own, in the hope that they could take on such patrol boats before they got in range. In terms of the wider anti-ship missile threat, the Navy was putting most its eggs in the very expensive basket of the Sea Wolf anti-missile missile. But it would never be able to afford to equip all its ships with this weapon.

However, a group of engineers in the United States decided that their response would be to marry an old idea with some new technology. They took a modern version of the Gatling gun, attached it to its own, very precise radar, and called it the Vulcan-Phalanx. It produced a weapon that could, with great accuracy, hose the air with shells in the path of oncoming missiles. The first experimental weapon was produced in 1973. It looked rather unassuming. Some would liken it to a Dalek from the Doctor Who television series, others to the dustbin-like robot, R2-D2, in the Star Wars films. But tests seemed to confirm its potency. By 1978, production had been agreed, and a US Navy warship was fitted with a first full system in 1980.

Tony Wolstenholme had pushed hard to have it fitted to *Invincible*. But, at this stage, Royal Navy interest seemed low. It certainly did not figure in the options that the working group finally considered when improvements were being studied for the third Invincible-class carrier, *Ark Royal*, while she was being built. It would have meant spending money, of course, but perhaps a digestible amount if there could have been savings elsewhere – perhaps even some of the savings that John Nott would impose, but in the context of a fleet more palatable to the admirals, and more capable overall.

CHAPTER NINE

For Sale

On Tuesday, 2 June 1981, Queen Elizabeth the Queen Mother had launched the new *Ark Royal*, the third Invincible-class carrier, at the Swan Hunter shipyard at Wallsend on the Tyne. She had performed the same ceremony for the previous *Ark Royal* thirty-one years before.

But the Defence Secretary, John Nott, had already put a dampener on proceedings. His review was reaching its climax. Speculation, rumour, and leaks about big cuts in the Navy were already in wide circulation. In a bad-tempered debate in the House of Commons two weeks before the launch, Nott had said of *Ark Royal* as she waited to thunder down the slipway: 'I do not think she would have been ordered if we were making the decision today'.

And, sure enough, three weeks after the new ship had taken to the water for the first time, Nott announced the decision, as part of his review, that only two of the three Invincibles would be kept in service. But which two?

The name ship of the class, *Invincible* herself, had been nearly a year in trials already. At the beginning of March, the ship and her crew had suffered a tragic setback, when two of her Sea Kings, while performing manoeuvres around the carrier in misty conditions in the Channel, had collided in mid-air. Five crewmen were lost. The effect on the ship's company was devastating. A pall and a silence fell over *Invincible*. That evening, Malcolm Fuller sat gloomily in Neil Rankin's cabin as the two searched for answers as to how it could have happened. Captain Livesay made a poignant broadcast to the ship's company. His message was that, if the lives of those lost were to be honoured, the ship had to press on, to make a success of what they had been striving to achieve. The ship held a memorial service the following Sunday. But it also did bounce back.

As time had passed, Neil Rankin – Wings – had warmed to the task of making the most of *Invincible* and her assets. After the lengthy trials, she had finally got her own Sea Harrier squadron, No 801, with its commanding officer, Nigel 'Sharkey' Ward. He had flown supersonic Phantoms from the deck of the old *Ark Royal*. Now he was anxious to demonstrate the qualities and prove the capabilities of the Sea Harrier.

801 squadron had only five Sea Harriers aboard *Invincible*. But Rankin soon learned that the ship could do a lot in short bursts. Indeed, thanks to the

heroics of the maintainers and the air crews, she was able to keep more aircraft in the air for longer than seemed reasonable. In that respect, she was embarrassing some of the American carriers and their squadrons. During one NATO exercise, she was able to keep an aircraft on combat air patrol continuously for five days.

One advantage that the Sea Harrier pilots had soon discovered was that the combination of *Invincible*'s Ski-jump ramp and the aircraft's V/STOL characteristics meant that they could continue flying in conditions that would probably defeat even the biggest of conventional carriers. In heavy weather, a carrier's flight deck would be pitching thirty-forty feet at each end, making conventional launches, and especially landings, extremely dicey, if not impractical. But the Ski-jump gave an added safety margin on take-off. And, on return, a Sea Harrier could simply come to a hover alongside the ship, midway along its length where the pitching was at a minimum, and then edge sideways and down to land safely on the flight deck. So, again, in certain conditions, *Invincible* was finding that her Sea Harriers were embarrassing the US Navy's fighters in air interceptions.

The Americans were also becoming mightily impressed by the anti-submarine performance of the ship's Sea King helicopters. It was all helping to boost morale again. Within the inevitable limits of her design, and the numbers of aircraft that she had, the crew was making her work.

And yet, the crew's growing enthusiasm for *Invincible* was still not shared by everyone in the Navy. Despite all the battles that had been fought to get her and her Sea Harriers, some still saw her as little more than a glorified cruiser, rather than a worthy flagship for the Fleet. But the reports that *Invincible,* and especially her Sea Harriers, were starting to meet or exceed expectations started to filter back to the admirals on the Naval Staff in Whitehall. The mood began to shift. Unfortunately for the Naval Staff, and especially the First Sea Lord, Sir Henry Leach, that only added to the poignancy of the Navy's position. Here was concrete evidence not only of *Invincible*'s worth, but also of the flaws to the kind of operational analysis that had discounted the value of the Sea Harrier.

When it had been announced that the Navy would be allowed to keep only two of its new carriers, it was widely assumed that a buyer would be sought for *Ark Royal* while she was still being built. But when a potential customer emerged in the shape of the Royal Australian Navy, the problem immediately arose that the Australians wanted to take delivery some two years before *Ark Royal* would be finished. So the focus quickly switched to *Invincible*. And, pretty soon, *Invincible* found herself playing host to an Australian Navy inspection team. Many on board could not believe that, just when their hard work seemed to have shown that *Invincible* and what she stood for worked, she was to be sold off.

As might be expected of any prospective buyers, the Australians had some issues. There was the vibration question. They also wanted to know how easy it would be to modify the ship to carry more fuel, for the longer ranges that they wanted. But, generally, they seemed to like what they saw.

It was all too much for the First Sea Lord. When John Nott asked him to meet an Australian delegation, he told them bluntly that, as far as he was concerned, *Invincible* was a great success, was an important part of the Royal Navy's future, and was not for sale. The episode did nothing to help the atmosphere between the Chief of the Naval Staff and the Secretary of State.

But it was also indicative of how wide the chasm was between the perspectives of the two men and what they represented. Henry Leach seemed simply not to accept that *Invincible* was going to be sold. He continued to try to persuade John Nott to change his mind. In October, he wrote to the Defence Secretary, again arguing that the proposed sale made no sense, either militarily or financially. *Invincible* was just beginning to show her military value, he said. He regarded the 175 million pounds being asked for her as a 'knock-down sale price', and said that she was being let go 'virtually for a song'.[1] He suggested that maybe she could simply be kept at reduced cost in reserve. Perhaps as a delaying tactic, he hinted that, at the very least, the sale should be put off, since it would take time for the Navy to reshape itself with new submarines and frigates to try to fill the capability gaps that her departure would leave behind.

However, there seemed to be little new in these arguments, as far as John Nott and his advisers were concerned. Indeed, far from regarding *Invincible* as a valuable, shiny new asset for the Navy, many of them still saw her as an expensive, vulnerable white elephant that probably would not last five minutes in an all-out fight with Soviet forces in the Norwegian Sea or the northeast Atlantic.

Still, Henry Leach would not let go, and sought a meeting with John Nott. The move was to lead to another bizarre episode.

It was late on a Thursday in November 1981, and the First Sea Lord arrived at the Defence Secretary's office for an appointment to find John Nott preparing to hurry away to his constituency in the West Country. He had no time for a meeting. To John Nott, there was nothing more to say on the subject of *Invincible*. To Henry Leach, this was unacceptable, and he announced that he would pursue the Defence Secretary to Cornwall if he had to in order to sort the matter out. Whether John Nott thought he was serious or not, he left.

But the admiral was both angry and serious. He summoned John Nott's private secretary, David Omand, and told him that – one way or another – he was going after him. The civil servant tried to persuade him that nothing could be done about *Invincible*. 'It's over,' he said. 'There's nothing to be done'.[2]

But the First Sea Lord was determined. Omand reluctantly agreed to try to arrange something. And so it was that, the following morning, the two men headed for Paddington Station to catch a train to the West Country.

It was an ill-starred expedition. It had been snowing. The train timetables were in a shambles. The journey proceeded at an agonizing pace, and the train got later and later. In their first-class compartment, Leach and Omand tried to pass the time, chatting cheerfully, and even exchanging each other's briefs and rehearsing the argument to come. Eventually they arrived at the chosen venue for the meeting, an early nineteenth century mock-medieval country house called Caerhays Castle, the home of a prominent West Country Conservative, set in a valley outside St Austell. It was already late, dark, bleak, and bitterly cold. John Nott greeted them at the door and ushered them into the warm. The host's hospitality and dinner delayed matters further. But eventually Nott and Leach retired to another room for a dramatic fire-lit showdown. They talked for about an hour with no meeting of minds. Henry Leach had to catch the last train back to London. So John Nott agreed to drive to the station with the admiral.

As they continued to argue, the First Sea Lord offered to find the 175-million-pound price tag for *Invincible* with savings elsewhere in the Navy budget, even though he made the offer resentfully, believing that the Fleet would, in effect, be paying twice for *Invincible*. But John Nott would not accept that anyway. As, finally, they stood in the freezing cold on the platform at St Austell station at what was, by now, well after midnight, Henry Leach asked the minister for his decision. But John Nott said that he would telephone the Ministry of Defence in the morning to give his answer. He did. The decision stood.

All this time, the negotiations had been continuing with the Australians and a sales contract had been agreed. It might have been an agreement for a second-hand car. The price was, indeed, 175 million pounds, plus seven-point-two million for spares and stores, with a ten per cent deposit to be paid within thirty days of signing or – interestingly in view of subsequent events – 1 April 1982, whichever was later. Handover was scheduled for 30 September 1983, unless *Invincible*'s sister ship, HMS *Illustrious*, still had not been completed by then, in which case the handover would be held back until 31 March 1984 at the latest.[3]

In fact, although nobody knew it at the time, the contract would never be signed. Henry Leach had tried one last, desperate gambit, warning that The Queen would have to be informed of the sale, since she had launched the ship. Like all his other arguments, it made no difference.[4]

Like Henry Leach, but for very different reasons, senior officials in the Treasury were concerned about the price, and still wondered why the newer *Ark Royal* could not be sold, thus raising more money. A complication in choosing *Invincible* was that, to keep a force-level of two carriers until HMS *Ark Royal* arrived, as was the government's declared policy, the elderly HMS *Hermes* would have to be kept in service instead of *Invincible* alongside *Illustrious*, at an estimated extra cost of thirty million pounds. So the net revenue to the Treasury from the sale would be only about 145 million pounds. As one senior Ministry of Defence official pointed out, that could still buy one brand-new nuclear-powered Fleet submarine. Henry Leach's view remained that, however fine such a vessel might be, it would not begin to make up for the breadth of abilities that the Navy would be losing with the sale of *Invincible*.[5]

In late February 1982, the deal was finally confirmed and announced. Among a flood of regretful signals sent to the ship was one from the C-in-C Fleet, Admiral Sir John Fieldhouse, one of the senior officers whom John Nott and his aides felt had been sympathetic to their prescription for the Navy. Fieldhouse wrote: 'Despite the long warning time, I know the decision on *Invincible*'s future has come as a sad shock to you, as it has to us all. My faith in your ship, your ship's company and embarked squadrons, remains unshaken. The running on of *Hermes* and the retention of your sister ships show that the importance of your role is widely acknowledged. I know that throughout the remainder of your challenging and varied programme you will continue to operate to the very high standard you have already set yourselves. There is a lot of water to flow under your bridge yet'.

HMS *Invincible* came under the direct responsibility of the Flag Officer, Third Flotilla, Vice Admiral John Cox. He had been a key ally of Captain Livesay's as he had battled for resources and priorities to turn his ship from an untried and unfamiliar concept into an effective fighting unit. His dismay was also clear, as he signalled: 'What do I say? What can I say? The decision that has just been announced, albeit not a total surprise, hurts badly'.

The Navy, and Henry Leach, did win one concession from John Nott. A visit was arranged for him to the amphibious assault ship, HMS *Fearless*, off Portland. She and her sister ship, *Intrepid*, had both been earmarked for disposal. The First Sea Lord called *Fearless*' captain personally, and told him that, 'short of killing somebody'[6], he and his ship's company had to pull out all the stops because the future of the two vessels depended on it. For once, luck was on the Navy's side. The sea was calm, the sun shone, and everything worked. John Nott came away impressed, and acknowledged that it had been mistake to decide to scrap the ships. They were reprieved. It was yet another example of how the Navy was able, just, to hold on to something that would prove to be of great value, and keep a capability going that would become a key ingredient in the Fleet's long-term future.

On *Invincible*, crew members who had made up that first happy band of the ship's company had begun to disperse to new jobs. Among the recent departures had been the first commanding officer, Michael Livesay, who had had such an impact on the ship and her crew. His successor was another extraordinary character, and an exceptional commanding officer, but it fell to him to come to terms with the sale of the ship, and how to handle it.

Jeremy Black had joined the Navy in the summer of 1946. He had been a sub-lieutenant and then a lieutenant aboard the Navy's last battleship, HMS *Vanguard*. He was a gunnery officer aboard the aircraft carrier, HMS *Victorious*, in the Far East. He had commanded a couple of destroyers, including the big guided-missile destroyer HMS *Fife*, with a crew of over 500. Even so, his first impression of *Invincible* was similar to that of many others who had gone before, that she was huge.

Black had been working at the Ministry of Defence, and was looking forward to another spell at sea. As a senior captain by now, he had considerable hopes. Indeed, he had expressed interest in command of either *Invincible* or *Hermes*, Britain's only two aircraft carriers by then. He was delighted to be told that it would be *Invincible*. He took command on 5 January 1982. He slipped on board at ten o'clock that morning. By midday he was in charge.

Black had almost left the Navy once early in his career when he had faced a court martial in Singapore. Not knowing anyone, and desperate, he had decided to go in search of a fellow gunnery officer to defend him. Thus, he found himself knocking on the door of a certain young captain, Henry Leach. They had never met before. But Leach agreed to take on the case, and proceeded to work tirelessly on it. Black was acquitted of all but the most minor of the charges. Black was to hold Leach in the highest esteem and affection ever after.

Now, as he surveyed his new command, he was impressed by her size, but was also immediately struck that she seemed a very fine ship, and that her ship's company had an air of confidence about it. He began to reflect on why that might be. She was new. She was novel. She was unique in the Fleet. She had been a great success in her trials and her first few months of operational service. But it was more than just confidence. There was, he noted, 'that wonderful spirit which is instantly detectable in a happy ship'.[7]

That spirit might have taken a knock with the news that she was to be sold. The crew was upset. But Captain Black was equally struck that morale did not take the dip that he had feared. People, it seemed, wanted to get on with the job, to go out with a bang rather than a whimper.

And it was a busy time still. There were exercises off Scotland and Norway. With thick snow covering her flight deck, she practised for the first time her potential role as a Commando carrier, with assault helicopters and Royal Marines aboard. But she was back in Portsmouth by late March, with her air group and crew dispersed for Easter leave.

It was four o'clock in the morning on Friday, 2 April 1982, when the telephone started ringing at the Black family home. This was a large, comfortable cottage-style farm house on the outskirts of the village of Durley, near Southampton, with broad lawns and beautiful views out over the fields and rolling countryside of Hampshire. It was an ideal place to relax. And that is what Jeremy Black had been doing with his family after the hectic and challenging first three months that he had had in charge of *Invincible*.

Black and his wife were fast sleep. As he stirred himself to the sound of the ringing phone, the captain was ready to be angry with this intrusion and whoever was on the other end of the line. His mood, and his state of alert, underwent a rapid transformation. It was the ship. At 0227, the C-in-C Fleet had signalled *Invincible, Hermes*, and a number of others ships to come to four hours notice to sail by noon the following day.

The commanding officer ordered a general recall, and asked what the fuss was about. He was told that there was some trouble brewing in the Falklands. Black issued a few more instructions. Already running through his mind was the thought that it would be a daunting task reassembling the hundreds of crew members who were currently scattered around the country, across Europe, and even as far as the United States. Then he decided to snatch a few hours more sleep before heading into the dockyard.

He realized that things were going to get very busy.

In the long-running history of the dispute between Britain and Argentina over the sovereignty of the Falklands Islands, there had been periods of diplomatic tension before. And there was, of course, the fact that the Falklands had also been the scene of a notable naval battle in the First World War, involving the previous HMS *Invincible*.

That *Invincible* had been sent to the South Atlantic with her sister ship, *Inflexible*, under Vice Admiral Sturdee following the Battle of Coronel, off Chile, at the beginning of November 1914. In that encounter, a group of British cruisers had been overcome by a crack squadron of German armoured cruisers under Vice Admiral Count Maximillian Von Spee. *Invincible* and her squadron were coaling at the Falklands on the morning of 8 December when Von Spee's squadron suddenly appeared, apparently intent on attacking the islands. The tables were turned. The British battle-cruisers put to sea and, in a running battle, the superior British firepower destroyed the German squadron, and Admiral Von Spee went down with his ship.

For some of those now contemplating events in the Falklands in the spring of 1982, there was the memory of a much more recent, minor flurry of naval activity concerning the islands, in late 1977, while the previous Labour Government was still in office. David Owen, who had been the young and energetic Navy Minister who had helped push through the concept of the through-deck cruiser, was now a very young Foreign Secretary. The Labour Government was about to embark on new negotiations with Argentina on the Falkland Islands. But the previous eighteen months had been a tense period in Anglo-Argentine relations, with a number of incidents, including the firing of warning shots at a British survey ship, and an Argentine landing on a remote island of the Falklands archipelago, South Thule.

With this in mind, his Navy background, and a particular respect for the power of the Navy's nuclear-powered submarines, Owen had requested the secret despatch of an SSN to the South Atlantic, just in case. The First Sea Lord then was Admiral Sir Terence Lewin. He and the Naval Staff were concerned that an SSN on its own was a very blunt instrument – it could do nothing, or it could sink a ship with a torpedo, but it had none of the intermediate levers of traditional gunboat diplomacy at its disposal and so, in the view of the Navy professionals, it would not be very effective as a deterrent. There would also be problems in communicating at such distance with a submerged submarine.

The Naval Staff argued that, if a force was to be sent, it should be balanced. There should be a couple of destroyers or frigates, plus support ships. Such a force would also help with the communications issue. Here again was another example of the different perceptions between those inside the Navy and outside it of what sea power was, how it worked, and how it could and should be used. But the priority for most of the government was that this deployment should remain secret until such time as it might actually be needed, in order not to upset the negotiations in advance. David Owen at least knew what naval towns were like, and how rumours spread, and he feared that news of the despatch of surface ships would leak out.

But the small group was indeed despatched, and the secret held. The submarine HMS *Dreadnought* was joined by the frigates *Alacrity* and *Phoebe,* a tanker, and a stores and ammunition ship. The idea was that the submarine would deploy close to the Falklands, while the surface ships would remain well out into the South Atlantic – about a thousand miles from the islands. It was felt that then, if they were detected, that might actually be an advantage – it would be regarded as 'non-provocative preparedness'.

There is still some dispute about whether the Argentine Navy got a hint of what was going on. But the episode came and went. So what lessons were to be drawn? Later, it would be argued that, if such 'non-provocative preparedness' had been attempted in 1982, there may never have been an Argentine invasion. The fact that it was not certain whether the ships in 1977 were ever detected, and they were certainly not declared at the time, meant that their real deterrent value was never tested.

David Owen and Terence Lewin would later have a very public disagreement over the nature and meaning of the rules of engagement (RoEs) for the force. As Owen suggested, they clearly did anticipate the possibility of an attempted invasion. The official military perspective was that the main concern was Argentine interference with British shipping, rather than invasion. There were considerable military doubts about whether such a small British force could really have deterred a determined Argentine move to take the islands.

The Lewin view was that the real deterrence lay in Britain's overall naval capabilities at the time – the age-old 'fleet in being' argument. The fact was that, in 1977, the Royal Navy still had a full-size aircraft carrier, the old *Ark Royal*, which could have become the centrepiece of any task force for the South Atlantic. Her Phantoms and Gannet AEW aircraft would have provided a genuine air defence umbrella, while her Buccaneers had a very obvious ability, if needed, to launch sizeable strike missions, including possibly against the Argentine mainland. As far as Lewin was concerned, that latent capability was one reason why no-one has ever heard of the 1977 Falklands War. Four-and-a-half years later, *Ark Royal* had gone, and however Buenos Aires may have interpreted all the other political signals emanating from London over that intervening period and change of government, the Royal Navy's ability to muster a fully-capable force to retake the Falkland Islands was more open to doubt, at least from an outsider's point of view, than it had been. Deterrence failed.

By 1982, the mixture of tensions over the Falkland Islands had become more volatile. The military government in Buenos Aires under General Leopoldo Galtieri was more desperate, and the attitudes of the British Government seemed more ambiguous. The Nott review, and in particular the planned sale of HMS *Invincible* and the decommissioning of the ice patrol ship HMS *Endurance*, seemed to signal reduced interest in maritime affairs generally, and in the South Atlantic in particular.

Endurance was a modest, German-built cargo ship, originally called the *Anita Dan*, and launched in 1956. She had been strengthened to operate in ice and was bought by the Ministry of Defence in 1967. Her conversion to military use had included fitting a flight deck and hangar for two small helicopters, and adding two small 20-mm machine guns. And that, in terms of her military potential, was it. But the symbolism of her presence in the South Atlantic was not really doubted. The dispute for years between the Ministry of Defence and the Foreign Office was whether it was worth the cost of running her, and who should pay for it. She had seemed for a while to be living on borrowed time.

In London, the messages of unease being sent back from the South Atlantic by *Endurance*'s commanding officer, Captain Nicholas Barker, in late 1981 and early 1982, were often heavily discounted. Nick Barker was seen as a person dedicated to preserving his ship and its role.

And there was other evidence of the very contradictory nature of Anglo-Argentine relations, particularly between the two navies. In the autumn of 1981, the Argentine Navy's magnificent sail training ship, the *Libertad*, the largest of its type in the world, had moored off Greenwich on an official visit, and Sir Henry Leach was invited to go aboard for an inspection. When he arrived, he saw that the ship had arranged a huge welcome, with sailors manning the masts and yards, and a ceremonial guard on the quarterdeck. Leach thanked them for the honour that they had done him, and then enjoyed a most convivial lunch with several of the officers.

By March 1982, general unease over the situation in the South Atlantic was mounting. In the last week, serious thinking about contingencies and the earmarking of ships for possible deployment to the South Atlantic finally began. An SSN was ordered south, and then a second. The C-in-C Fleet, John Fieldhouse, visited Gibraltar to observe the large flotilla of Navy warships on exercise there. He conferred about possible plans with the man in charge of the exercise, Sandy Woodward, now a Rear Admiral.

Wednesdays were normally not meeting days for the service chiefs, who tried to use them to get out of London to visit units and establishments around the country. So it was on Wednesday, 31 March 1982. Henry Leach had been in Portsmouth. He arrived back at the Ministry of Defence in the early evening to find an intelligence report and a number of briefs. The intelligence report suggested that an Argentine landing seemed likely on about 2 April. The others suggested that this period of tension was potentially no more serious than others that had gone before, and that no further naval deployments were either necessary or desirable.

The First Sea Lord was very concerned. He felt that the advice before him was contradictory. His other chief reaction was, 'what the hell was the point of having a navy if you don't use it for this sort of thing'?[8] He decided that he must seek out the Defence Secretary. While there had been some preparatory thinking on naval contingencies, he needed political approval to take things further, and in particular to start assembling a task force.

But John Nott was not in his office. Having discovered that he was in the House of Commons, Henry Leach jumped into his car and headed in that direction. He was still in his First Sea Lord's uniform from his visit to Portsmouth. Despite this, he could not get past the imposing policeman on duty in the Central Lobby, who was not in the least bit ruffled by the sight of the Chief of the Naval Staff demanding an immediate interview with the Defence Secretary. So Leach sat on a bench while efforts were made to locate John Nott.

Henry Leach was rescued first by one of the party whips, and taken to the whips' office. While he was waiting, somebody thrust a whisky into his hand, for which he was grateful, and which he felt he rather needed. He chatted amicably for about fifteen minutes, but did not feel – for security reasons – that he could really say why he so urgently needed to see John Nott. Eventually word came that the Defence Secretary was with the Prime Minister in her room, and he was asked to go up.

The character of the meeting changed dramatically with the First Sea Lord's arrival. The thrust of the discussions up to that point had been how to get the Americans to intervene. There had been little talk of military options, except perhaps sending an extra submarine. Leach himself was somewhat stunned by the atmosphere in the Prime Minister's room. There seemed, he felt, to be a lack of ideas, a void. When Margaret Thatcher asked him for his view, he said that little could be done to forestall or defend against an invasion now, and recapturing the islands would require a very considerable naval task force.

He was asked about air cover, and he said that he believed that the Navy had just enough Sea Harriers, but that it would clearly be a risky operation. But he insisted that he could assemble the necessary task force in forty-eight hours.

Margaret Thatcher asked if it could really do the job. Henry Leach replied that not only could it do the job, but it should. 'Why do you say that?' the Prime Minister asked. 'Because if we do not,' Leach responded, 'or we pussyfoot in our actions and do not achieve complete success, in another few months we shall be living in a different country whose word counts for little'.[9]

The First Sea Lord was very clear and decisive. That was his character. It was a critical intervention. And he was made for the moment. John Nott was amazed, and not a little sceptical. He had had more than a year of bitter skirmishing with Henry Leach. The two of them did not get on at all. What the Defence Secretary did not know at the time was the amount of preparatory work and thinking that the Navy had been doing in the previous few days. In any event, it seemed to impress the Prime Minister. Henry Leach managed to convince her that the operation would be feasible, if hazardous. He left the meeting with the authority that he had sought to prepare a task force. There would be scepticism in other parts of the Ministry of Defence. But the die had been cast.

CHAPTER TEN

Invincible At War

After his surprise phone call and a few more snatched hours of sleep, Captain Jeremy Black headed into Portsmouth and his ship. A huge operation was getting under way to prepare *Invincible* for action. And the same scene was being repeated around the dockyard, on *Hermes* and a number of other ships. All sorts of health and safety regulations were broken in order to get *Invincible* fuelled and loaded with ammunition at the same time. Sailors from other ships and dockyard workers were all lending a hand.

Jeremy Black was having various meetings with his admiral and fellow commanders. It looked for a while as if *Invincible* would be made flagship for the task force. But, after some discussion, it was agreed that *Hermes* – which had had a recent upgrade of her communications equipment, and had more accommodation for an admiral's staff – would have the flagship role. Jeremy Black, secretly, was relieved. Quite apart from the thought of any admiral breathing down his neck, he had known Sandy Woodward all his professional life. They had been at Dartmouth together. Black knew the admiral had a fearsome intelligence, but he knew his prickly side as well.

In the thick of all the preparations was the ship's second-in-command, Dermot Rhodes. But he faced a terrible dilemma. He had been selected for promotion to captain and had been assigned to a NATO staff job in Naples. He was due to leave, and his relief to take over in *Invincible*, on the Monday. But it rapidly became apparent that the ship would be sailing for the Falklands on that day. What should he do?

Rhodes had a meeting with the captain. The ship was fully worked-up. And Rhodes did not think it would come to war. After all, 8,000 miles is a very long way. There would be plenty of time for the politicians to sort things out. And he had had the experience, in the 1970s, of rushing to get a frigate out of reserve with a scratch crew to help maintain the Royal Navy operation to support British trawlers against Icelandic gunboats in the Cod War, only for the dispute to be settled just as his ship was ready to sail. He knew, on this occasion, that his relief was fully trained and ready. So he and the captain decided that the changeover would go ahead.

As part of the preparations, a strengthened Sea Harrier squadron of eight aircraft had come aboard on Sunday afternoon, under the command of

Sharkey Ward. *Hermes*, with her bigger hangar and flight deck, would take twelve. But that was still only twenty aircraft in all.

On the Monday morning, last-minute stores were still being loaded, and would continue to be landed by helicopter even after the ship sailed. Departure was set for 10.15. Jeremy Black woke up and was working in his cabin until about five minutes before *Invincible* was due to slip her moorings. That was his normal routine for leaving harbour. It was only when he left his cabin for the bridge, and caught glimpses out of the portholes and passageway openings in the side of the ship, that he began to appreciate the scene all around. He had made many departures from Portsmouth in his career. But this was something quite different. There were the crowds, the flags, the sailors lining the decks of the other ships in harbour.

It was a magnificent sailing, with a Sea Harrier perched theatrically at the end of the Ski-jump ramp, Sea Kings on prominent display aft, and the ship's company lining the decks. If ever there was a modern-day example of gunboat diplomacy, designed to stir a nation and the let the other side know what it had got itself into, this dramatic, highly-choreographed departure was it, with first *Invincible* and then *Hermes* groaning even more under the weight of the aircraft on her flight deck.

Dermot Rhodes, who had been such an integral part of turning *Invincible* into the ship that she had become, left her in the morning just before she departed. He walked out on to Southsea beach to watch her sail off. It was, he later realized, the worst decision that he ever made.

Most of that first band of officers, the first 'Invincibles', who had seen her through her final stages of construction and early life were now well and truly dispersed to other jobs in the Navy. Their reactions to what was now unfolding took different forms. Tony Hallett had been promoted and was now serving at the Fleet headquarters at Northwood. With his intimate knowledge of the ship, he called and asked if he could be reassigned to her. The answer was 'no'.

Tony Wolstenholme, the first weapons engineer officer, had been close at hand and heavily involved in getting her and the other ships ready to sail south. He was now on the staff of the flag officer at Portsmouth. Helping *Invincible*'s preparations was a daunting task in itself. *Hermes*, the future flagship, had just taken a battering in gruelling NATO exercises in the Norwegian Sea, and was really in no fit state to sail. Her superstructure was covered in scaffolding. But she had to be ready, and she was.

And yet, as he watched those departures, so charged with emotion, he was filled with apprehension. His had been among the voices raising doubts about *Invincible*'s ability in her present state to look after herself in a fight.

Another witness to those events, standing on the opposite shore on the Isle of Wight, was another man filled with a mixture of emotions. Captain Jock Slater had been appointed as the first commanding officer of the second Invincible-class ship, HMS *Illustrious*, which was still being completed at the Swan Hunter yard on the Tyne. She was due to be commissioned in October, and to become operational some time in the following year. Captain Slater had been spending a weekend on the Isle of Wight with his wife and two sons as the momentous events were unfolding, and the feverish activity was taking place across the water. He stood and watched the great ships sail. And he felt awful. But he knew that he would do everything possible – and he knew that the pressure would be on – to get *Illustrious* ready as quickly as possible. At that stage, nobody really knew what would happen, and she might be desperately needed.

Jeremy Black soon had a problem on his hands. It was just two o'clock in the afternoon following departure, still not far off the Isle of Wight, when the marine engineering officer came to him to say that a gearbox coupling would need changing, work that would normally dictate a period in the dockyard. The commanding officer's heart sank. Frantic signals were despatched. Would the ship have to turn back? In fact, *Invincible* continued slowly on her way on just one of her two propeller shafts, as the desperate search began for a replacement three-ton coupling, and the operation got under way to get it to the ship. Eventually, the new coupling was delivered aboard somewhere in the Western Approaches by an RAF Chinook helicopter, with a Navy Sea King to guide it through the fog which had descended. The task then was to get it down to the machinery space, and to carry out the changeover – something that had never been done before at sea. *Invincible* crept along with one shaft locked and between ten and twelve degrees of rudder on as the delicate surgery was completed.

At the same time, her squadrons and crew had already begun the business of practising for war. Easter Sunday, 11 April, found *Invincible* off the West African coast, and there was a lull in the operational activity to give the crew time to relax with some deck hockey and sunbathing. Captain Black reflected that it seemed difficult to believe, in such an atmosphere, that they were sailing potentially towards hostilities. 'Having said that,' he recorded in his journal, 'there is an air of apprehension abroad, hardly a soul has seen any form of action, and no-one has seen the type of action which could be before us, replete with missile-armed aircraft and ships, and modern submarines'.[1]

Still, *Invincible* made quite a sight when she steamed into view off Ascension Island on a bright morning on 16 April to join the advance group of task force ships which had been waiting. One member of the task force who was impressed was Ian Forbes, operations officer on the destroyer HMS *Glamorgan*. Like many in the Fleet, Forbes had heard a lot about *Invincible*, but had never seen her before, since she had been off on trials so much of the time. He knew that much rested on how effective a role she would be able to play in whatever transpired further south. It was reassuring to see her Sea Harriers screaming overhead.

There were two days off Ascension Island, re-storing and regrouping, and the passage south continued. The preparations, tensions, and anticipation began to mount. The task force now comprised the ships that had left from the

United Kingdom and the group of ships from Gibraltar, with Admiral Woodward as the task force commander. Jeremy Black was designated anti-air warfare commander for the group. One thing he and his team focused on as they approached the Falklands was how to decoy Exocet anti-ship missiles using chaff.

The fact was that the Royal Navy and the other services were about to attempt something which more than fifteen years of official policy had decreed the country would never again undertake: an opposed landing, outside the range of land-based air cover, without allies. As Jeremy Black had noted, nobody really had any experience in modern naval warfare of this type. Some in the task force may have had a complacent faith in the abilities of some of their weapons, like the new Sea Wolf missiles on a handful of the ships. Supposedly, it could shoot down a 4.5-in shell in flight. Others in the Navy, though, were acutely aware of the shortcomings in the task force's capabilities. The questions were how effective would they be in papering over those gaps, and how skilful would the opposition be in finding them?

As *Invincible* prepared to enter the total exclusion zone (TEZ) declared by Britain around the Falklands, she practised 'goalkeeper' drill with the Sea Wolf-armed frigate HMS *Brilliant* – the escort would stay close to the carrier, and between her and the expected direction of any threat, in the hope that the frigate's weapons would be able to intercept any low-level attack, since *Invincible* had no actual weapons of her own to defeat such an attack. It was, perhaps, a sobering exercise. And yet Jeremy Black noted at the time: 'no-one on board is in any doubt that we will have to fight, and now that doubt is removed, they are calm, relaxed, cheerful, and ready'.[2]

Jeremy Black had, in the commander of 801 Naval Air Squadron, Sharkey Ward, perhaps the most forceful and experienced exponent of the Sea Harrier's abilities that there was. He was constantly trying to impress on anyone who would listen the real potential of the aircraft, which went far beyond simply 'hacking the shad'. And yet it remained an untried weapon. As the ships sailed deeper into those remote, inhospitable seas, a lot of people on the task force were feeling exposed and vulnerable.

HMS *Invincible* entered the TEZ on 1 May, and hostilities commenced. As he braced himself for what lay ahead, Jeremy Black confessed to himself that he had no idea whether he would have any aircraft left by nightfall.

In fact, the early skirmishes favoured the British. And, on 2 May, news came in to the task force that the Argentine cruiser *General Belgrano* had been sunk by the SSN, HMS *Conqueror*. There was cheering in *Invincible*'s wardroom. But Argentina quickly exacted revenge, when an air-launched Exocet missile devastated the destroyer, HMS *Sheffield*, two days later. It was a huge shock. Captain Black had just been sitting down to write about how his confidence in the task force's ability to deal with the air threat had been growing, when it was shattered again.

The reverberations reached all the way back to the United Kingdom. Henry Leach watched the news sweep through Whitehall like a hurricane. For the first time, it seemed, people realized that the country was truly at war, and lives were being lost. There was, Leach thought, something close to panic. Leach, like the Chief of the Defence Staff, Terence Lewin, was a naval officer whose experience stretched back to the Second World War. They understood about, and had witnessed, the sacrifices that had to be made to achieve ends in war. The First Sea Lord had estimated that the Navy could lose up to half-a-dozen destroyers and frigates, and was prepared to accept up to double that number. Destroyers and frigates could be replaced, albeit at a cost, including in lives. The key was the carriers, and the calculations were complicated. They depended on the stage at which the war had reached when one or both of them might have been put out of action or sunk. But it was clear to Leach that, if both were taken out before the landing, that would have involved having to call off the entire operation.

The shockwaves from *Sheffield* spread much further, indeed around the world, reigniting the whole debate about the vulnerability of surface ships in the age of precision anti-ship missiles. Beyond Britain, the effects were felt nowhere more so than in Washington. There the Reagan administration was in the early stages of its planned naval build-up, with a lot of emphasis on big surface ships, and was facing considerable scepticism in the US Congress.

The US Navy Secretary, John Lehman, the chief architect of the build-up, had actually just arrived on a visit to London, and saw at first-hand the fallout in Whitehall from the disabling of HMS *Sheffield*. He and his boss, the US Defence Secretary, Caspar Weinberger, had received pessimistic Pentagon briefings about the chances of British success in the South Atlantic. For him, though he dearly loved the Royal Navy, the events off the Falklands had a clear-cut message. The British, he believed, had come 'face-to-face with the limitations of their fleet and the consequences of their anti-naval budget-cutting of the previous fifteen years … no big carriers, AEW, supersonic interceptors, cruise missile defences, 3-D radars'.

As far as John Lehman was concerned, this all added up to a vindication of his 600-ship, carrier-based plan. The critics drew very different conclusions. The Royal Navy may not be the US Navy, but the Exocet was a 'firecracker' compared to the weaponry that the Soviet forces had at their disposal. US Navy carrier task forces would be just as vulnerable as the British in an East-West confrontation in the north Norwegian Sea.

Despite the pessimism in the Pentagon over Britain's chances, and the overall ambivalence early on in the Reagan administration over what was going on, both Weinberger and Lehman were hugely supportive of the British. The early despatch of US stocks of the latest version of the Sidewinder missile, the AIM-9L, to equip the Sea Harrier, was one example. Weinberger even offered the British an American carrier, although the British never really pursued the option, not believing it to be either operationally viable or likely to get past the White House itself.

There was one glaring, and well-known, defensive handicap with which the Royal Navy was having to contend. As in many other fields, it had been one of the pioneers of AEW, the ability to put a long-range radar aloft in an aircraft, to give extra warning-time of an attack, and then to direct defences to take care of it. It was far ahead of the RAF in this area, for example. The decision to phase out the conventional carriers left a question-mark over how and whether that capability could be provided. The need was not forgotten. The studies of the Future Fleet Working Party, in the immediate wake of CVA-01's cancellation, made regular references to a requirement for an AEW helicopter as part of the Fleet. There were design studies. The Naval Staff was also aware that the United States had actually experimented with a Sea King helicopter carrying a radar in a collapsible installation beneath its fuselage. But, with the concentration on NATO, and the assumption that land-based AEW would be available, the requirement slipped down the list of priorities. With the battles to get *Invincible* herself, then the Sea Harrier, and then a major new programme for a replacement for the Sea King helicopter, it never seemed to be the right time to press for an AEW helicopter.

Suddenly, the need was urgent. And the race was on to turn those previous studies into a reality as quickly as possible. In the meantime, the Navy improvised. It deployed the SSNs that it had in the South Atlantic in a screen just outside the twelve-mile limit of Argentina's territorial waters. From there, they observed and reported when air raids took off from the mainland. It was rudimentary and imprecise, but it provided a valuable forty-five minutes of warning.

The other major concern for the British regarding the air threat was the lack of options to go on the offensive. There were serious worries that air superiority was far from being achieved ahead of the landing that was planned actually to retake the Falklands. And part of the problem was that the Argentines were not joining the air battle on the scale that had been hoped, so that the British were not achieving the levels of attrition with their Sea Harriers and missile defences that they had planned. The question was what else could be done to force the issue.

Attacking Argentina's mainland air bases might have been an option, albeit with huge political sensitivity attached. But the British did not have the wherewithal to pursue that option. For all their exploits, *Invincible*, *Hermes*, and their Sea Harriers could not substitute for the lack of a real strike carrier and mount long-range bombing missions against the mainland. The RAF had, with great effort, launched raids on the Falklands with a couple of antique Vulcan bombers that were themselves about to be retired. But it did not seem viable to use them against the mainland either.

As for the Vulcan raids on the Falklands itself, some in the Royal Navy felt that they were the RAF trying to muscle in on the operation. The likes of

Sharkey Ward argued that the Sea Harriers could have done the job much more effectively. The vast resources that were expended on the Vulcan missions in terms of air-to-air refuelling tankers and other support compared to the actual damage caused – just one bomb on Stanley runway – seemed to some in the Fleet Air Arm to vindicate all their doubts about how realistic the RAF's claims were in the 1960s about what it could and could not do to project air power around the world and protect the Fleet, the claims that had put paid to CVA-01. Still, the Vulcan attacks were a considerable propaganda coup as well as great feats of flying, and they probably did make the Argentine Air Force wonder and worry whether its home bases might themselves be attacked.

As another initiative, Jeremy Black and those with him aboard *Invincible* suggested moving further west, with escort ships to act as pickets, operating among the many smaller islands to try to reduce the threat from Exocet attack. But Admiral Woodward turned the idea down on the grounds that it would represent too high a risk. His decision to try to keep the carriers as far as possible out of harm's way would come to be resented by some others in the task force, not least troops ashore, and would lead to some frictions and awkwardness among the crew on *Invincible*. But the carriers were so crucial that the decision was understandable.

In the event, *Invincible* did make a dash west to launch a helicopter for a reconnaissance mission on the mainland for a planned special forces raid. But bad weather intervened, and the helicopter came down in Chile short of its target, with some embarrassing subsequent publicity. The raid itself never took place. Later, after the landing, and under cover of darkness, *Invincible* made another push west, launching Sea Harriers to probe the Argentines' mainland air defences. But they did not respond.

On 21 May, the Royal Navy and the assembled landing force ran a gauntlet in San Carlos Water to get the troops ashore. The escort ships suffered badly. The land campaign would also be a grim, gruelling, and hard-fought campaign. There would be tragic setbacks, the deadliest being the Bluff Cove bombing of the two landing ships carrying Welsh Guards. But, once the British forces had established themselves ashore, the balance of power shifted crucially in their favour.

Invincible herself had a number of particular alarms. Early on, two Sea Harriers were lost, apparently in a mid-air collision in cloud. As well as a blow to the ship, it was a significant reduction in the task force's air defences at the time. After the landing, on 25 May, the Argentines mounted a determined attack on the carrier force with air-launched Exocet missiles. Ian Forbes watched in mounting alarm on a radar screen in HMS *Glamorgan*'s operation room as the raid unfolded. The ship was just two miles from *Invincible* at the time. He watched the two Exocets veer away from the carrier towards the frigate *Ambuscade*, but they were decoyed by her chaff, only to slam into and destroy the large container ship *Atlantic Conveyor*. That was damaging enough, since she was still loaded with vital stores, including Chinook transport helicopters, for the landing force. Twelve crew died, including the ship's revered master, Captain Ian North. But at least she had offloaded her cargo of Harrier reinforcements. And her loss was not as grave as the sinking of one of the carriers would have been.

During that attack, *Invincible* had fired a spectacular salvo of Sea Dart missiles. In the ship's operation room, the missile controller saw a contact moving on his radar screen which he thought was an enemy aircraft. He called the commanding officer. Black rushed over and watched the contact himself over the missile controller's shoulder, and agreed that it was a potential contact. So the ship unleashed six missiles in quick succession. But, whatever it was, it seems to have been a spurious contact. It may have been the radar echo from the cloud of chaff fired by *Hermes* to divert the incoming Exocets.

Five days later, the Argentines mounted a last air-launched Exocet attack on the task force. Based on estimates of the group's position using tracks of Harrier movements from radars based on the Falklands, the Argentines pressed home the attack. In fact, the Sea Harrier pilots had been deliberately employing deception tactics, flying at low level after launching from the carriers, and only climbing into the view of the Argentines' radar some time after that. So the estimated position of the task force was some thirty miles out. The attackers identified a target, but it was the frigate *Avenger*, and the Exocet was decoyed away and was either shot down or flew into the sea. Four more aircraft followed up to attack with conventional bombs, two were brought down, and the other two missed their target. This was all a great relief to Jeremy Black as, at just that moment, and for the only time in the war, both the missile control radars for his Sea Dart system failed. He was also, for once, without his 'goalkeeper' frigate. He would have been defenceless. In fact, the Argentines believed that they had hit *Invincible*, and continued to claim so for some time after the incident.

But perhaps the most hair-raising moment for Captain Black was when he believed he had been fired on with torpedoes by an Argentine submarine. He took furious evasive action, and then launched his helicopters to try to locate the suspected submarine. They found nothing, and the incident was dismissed by the rest of the task force. But he would later read a newspaper report that claimed a submarine attack on the task force on the day the episode took place.

All the while, as the battle took its course in the South Atlantic, back in the United Kingdom, as well as looking on anxiously as a nation, great efforts were under way to support the war effort, and if necessary to sustain it over a long period. Reinforcements of weapons and warships were on their way. And, critically, every effort was being made to accelerate the completion of HMS *Illustrious*.

Jock Slater had been thrilled when he got the news that he had been appointed to command *Illustrious*. Apart from the fact that she had a hugely evocative and famous name, synonymous with heroic carrier action in the

Second World War, there was also a family connection. Slater's great-uncle was Admiral of the Fleet Sir Andrew Cunningham, who had been Commander-in-Chief of the Mediterranean Fleet at the time when slow, antiquated Swordfish torpedo bi-planes – 'Stringbags' as they were affectionately known since they were held together with wire and canvas – had launched the first-ever attack of its type from the flight deck of the previous *Illustrious* against the Italian fleet in harbour at Taranto in November 1940. It was a devastating blow against Italy's battleships, which changed the balance of naval power in the Mediterranean at a stroke, and was the precursor to Japan's attack on Pearl Harbour.

Having watched the task force sail away, Slater got quickly back to work. The efforts by the workers on the Tyne, spurred by a tide of patriotism, had been remarkable. Just a couple of weeks after the task force's departure, Captain Slater got in touch with Fleet headquarters at Northwood and suggested that the ship could be sent south with the planned Harrier and helicopter reinforcements. But Admiral Fieldhouse turned him down. It was not clear how long the conflict would last and, if it stretched into the southern Atlantic winter, *Illustrious* would be needed at full strength to relieve either *Invincible* or *Hermes*. So, her preparations continued, and the reinforcements were sent south in the ill-fated *Atlantic Conveyor*.

Illustrious did suffer some serious problems with equipment. But she was accepted into Royal Navy service on 18 June, just three days after the Argentine surrender, but well ahead of the original timetable. As evidence of the haste involved, a workman was still painting the centre line of the flight deck runway as the handover took place. But still the pressure was on. It was not clear if the ceasefire would hold. Uniquely, two days later, the ship's company held a commissioning ceremony on the way to Portsmouth and her accelerated acceptance trials and operational work-up.

Illustrious had to borrow RAF Harriers for her work-up, as there were no Sea Harriers to spare. As well as being a new ship, she had received some rush modifications as a result of the early lessons from the south Atlantic. Among the most significant of these were two of the new Vulcan-Phalanx radar-controlled Gatling guns, hurriedly purchased from the United States. Captain Slater knew nothing about these until he returned to the Swan Hunter yard one Monday morning and found two holes drilled in his new flight deck and forecastle. When he enquired, he was told they were for the Vulcan-Phalanx guns.

Originally, the installations were going to be fully automatic. But the captain insisted on having a fail-safe switch in the operations room. He did not want these new, untried weapons spraying hundreds of shells across the flight deck with loaded Sea Harriers parked there. Still, he was impressed enough with the first trials in the Western Approaches. The first towed target, at sea level to simulate an Exocet, was obliterated. Captain Slater, on the bridge to observe the test, saw bits of it flying over his head to land in the sea beyond. He was certainly satisfied. It gave him great confidence as he contemplated the voyage south, although this did highlight one criticism of the Vulcan-Phalanx – that debris from a destroyed incoming missile could still have enough forward momentum to fly on and do damage to the target ship.

The other great advantage that *Illustrious* would have as she sailed south was the result of that crash programme to fill the AEW gap. Within days of *Sheffield*'s destruction, work had begun to convert two Sea King helicopters to carry the powerful Searchwater radar, a version of which was already fitted to the RAF's Nimrod patrol aircraft. Some of the earlier studies were dusted off and by early August – in other words, in less than three months – the two aircraft were ready. Some shook their heads at the ungainly appearance of these machines – with the radar in an inflatable and retractable dome attached to the starboard side of the fuselage, they looked a bit like old ladies with handbags under their arms. But they would become indispensable, and they were ready to embark on *Illustrious*.

Even so, Captain Slater knew that he had a considerable challenge ahead. Many of his ship's company were disappointed that they would be too late to see action. In fact, it was less certain than that. There had been a surrender and ceasefire. But was that really the end of it? So Jock Slater had the job of motivating his crew and preparing his ship for war, when apparently the war was over.

For Jeremy Black on *Invincible*, the task was subtly different. In the aftermath of the surrender, there was a respite for *Invincible*. She sailed north for some maintenance and rest for her crew. There was not much relief for the engine room staff, however, as they performed another first – changing one of *Invincible*'s main Olympus engines while still at sea.

And soon she was heading south again. As the rest of the task force, including the carrier *Hermes*, rust-streaked and betraying both her age and her origins in the Second World War, sailed for home, *Invincible* faced another two months on station until *Illustrious* arrived to relieve her, and longer still before she got home herself. 'We face a great challenge,' Black wrote in his journal, 'to keep this ship efficient and its morale high with a further three months before we return to the United Kingdom, and without the impetus of war, but with the awful weather of the southern winter'.[4]

One thing that helped was that, quite soon, rumours began to circulate that the ship's sale to Australia was going to be cancelled. The very first HMS *Invincible* was a prize captured from the French. Steeped as he was in the traditions of his service, Jeremy Black reflected in his journal on 17 July: 'It would be a great achievement to have won a ship in battle'.[5] Two days later, he had. Confirmation came through: the sale of *Invincible* was off.

CHAPTER ELEVEN

What Lessons?

*I*nvincible had survived, in more ways than one. Other ships had not, nor many members of their crews. Very few of the warships had emerged from the conflict in the South Atlantic completely unscathed.

As hostilities ended, Tony Wolstenholme flew down to Ascension Island to meet and survey some of these battered task force vessels on their way home. It would be his job to start patching them up when they returned to Portsmouth. It was a sobering experience, as he contemplated what might have been.

There was HMS *Glasgow*, which had seen a 1,000-lb bomb smash into her side amidships, crash right across the engine room, and emerge the other side without exploding. And HMS *Antrim*, under fierce attack in San Carlos Water on the first day of the landing to retake the Falklands, had been hit by another bomb which had crashed into the stern by the flash doors for her Sea Slug missile magazine, and into the magazine itself. But, again, it did not explode. The magazine complex for the large, ungainly missiles ran right along the centre of the ship. Had that bomb gone off, Wolstenholme thought, it would have been like HMS *Hood* in the Second World War, when her main magazines ignited and blew her to pieces virtually in an instant.

Down south, after a remarkable and – since the Second World War – probably unique few weeks since leaving the builder's yard, HMS *Illustrious* finally arrived on 27 August to relieve her elder sister. Jock Slater had already been enjoying the advantages of his new and improved ship and her aircraft. With one of the new AEW Sea Kings aloft, he had first spotted *Invincible* over 200 miles away. Indeed, *Illustrious* was crammed with aircraft – ten Sea Harriers in all, and eleven Sea King helicopters, including the two new AEW machines, Sea King 'Whiskeys' as they came to be known. Slater had the new Vulcan-Phalanx as well. His ship represented what many, including Tony Wolstenholme, felt that the Invincibles should have been like from the outset – with more weapons, more aircraft, and that crucial AEW capability. He certainly had a range of new abilities that Jeremy Black and the rest of the task force would dearly have loved back at the beginning of May.

Maybe it was that thought that prompted a moment of exuberance as Jock Slater bid farewell to Jeremy Black and *Invincible*. In the Navy's best traditions of bold seamanship, with a flourish – and with the admiral in charge sailing off at a safe distance towards the horizon – Slater steered *Illustrious* on a high-speed steam-past of *Invincible* with both ships' companies waving and cheering. It certainly raised Jeremy Black's eyebrows on *Invincible*'s bridge. For its part, again in true Navy style, the crew of *Invincible* had a little jab back at the new arrival, brandishing a banner on the flight deck which read: "Welcome back *Hermes*, nice paint job".

It would still be nearly three more weeks, on 17 September, before *Invincible* made her triumphant return to Portsmouth. The Queen embarked by barge, to renew her association with the ship, and for a private reunion with her second son, Prince Andrew, who had been a Sea King pilot on board during the conflict. The First Sea Lord, Henry Leach, was aboard as well. *Invincible* had been at sea continuously for 166 days, then a record for an aircraft carrier. *Illustrious* would also notch up 100 days herself.

The joyous homecomings, and the national euphoria and relief over the victory, added an extra layer of emotion as the debates got under way over the lessons to be learned. Many people were still coming to terms with the fact that they had seen pictures that they had not expected, of Royal Navy warships burning and sinking. In fact, the arguments over the Nott review had been reopened while the fighting was still going on. In so many different ways, it had been a damned close-run thing. But what did that tell people about the significance of what had taken place?

There were many heroes among the sailors, aircrew, and troops. The inanimate heroes without which the operation could probably never even have been contemplated were undoubtedly the Sea Harrier, the AIM-9L Sidewinder missile which it carried, and the Ski-jump ramp from which it was launched. Some seasoned Fleet Air Arm pilots would concede in whispered tones that, even if the old *Ark Royal* and her Phantoms and Buccaneers had still been available, she might have struggled to fly her aircraft in the kinds of conditions with which the Sea Harriers were often confronted in those bleak South Atlantic waters.

Invincible was at one point operating ten Sea Harriers – twice her normal complement – as well as her helicopters. But dear old *Hermes* ended up with more than double that number of Sea Harriers and RAF Harriers, a tribute to her greater appetite as a pure carrier both for more aircraft and their weapons. It was something of an irony given that, for all those battling years in the 1960s, she was the weak link in the Navy's carrier case, because of her relatively small size and supposedly limited aircraft capacity.

It was significant that the two glaring gaps in the task force's defences, the presence of which might have made a very considerable difference to the scale of the damage and casualties suffered by the Fleet, were very specific. And they were quite easy and not very expensive to remedy. They were the lack of AEW, and of sophisticated close-in gun systems. The former could be excused to a large extent because, in the NATO context, AEW cover would have been available from US carriers or land-based aircraft. But it was still an omission, given that the Navy and the government had supposedly planned for and endorsed a fleet that could operate out of area. The absence of close-in guns was another matter, and even more relevant for the Alliance battle as any beyond the NATO region.

John Nott had already bowed to the new political mood. He had quietly dropped the sale of *Invincible*. The more detailed official conclusions about the significance of the Falklands campaign were still being debated when Admiral of the Fleet Sir Henry Leach bid an emotional farewell to the Ministry of Defence in early December 1982, with a mass of dark blue uniforms at the North Door to give him a rousing send-off. It was a measure of the affection that the Navy felt for Leach that, years later, in 2004, it would name its new Fleet headquarters building in Portsmouth the Sir Henry Leach Building.

In the middle of the month, the government's post-Falklands defence white paper was published. The Defence Secretary would continue to insist that his basic analysis remained sound. 'The many useful lessons we have learned from the Falklands Campaign,' the document said, 'do not invalidate the policy we have adopted following last year's defence programme review'.[1]

The white paper also rather pointedly observed that, following the conflict, 'we shall now be devoting substantially more resources to defence than had been previously planned'.[2] In other words, if there were to be any changes of plans, it was only because the pot of money had got bigger and changed the equation.

Dropping the sale of *Invincible* meant that the Navy would be able to look forward to keeping three such ships after all. So there would be a good chance that it would have two rather than just one operational most of the time, which had been the argument all along for the cost-effectiveness of the three-ship programme. Each of the carriers would be equipped with three of the new AEW helicopters. They would also all get the new close-in gun defences, as would the Type 42 destroyers.

The Navy's radars would be improved. The plan was still that the overall number of destroyers and frigates would drop to fifty, but the idea that eight of them would be kept in reserve was forgotten. What was more, the Navy was allowed to replace the warships which had been sunk with much-improved, bigger versions of its new Type 22 frigates. The final batch of these would be the first Royal Navy warships in a very long time that would begin to look as if they were really bristling with weapons. They would take on something of the appearance, and be able to mirror in modern times some of the capabilities of the cruisers of old, just as the ship that had been described as a cruiser for so long had turned out to make a passable impression of an aircraft carrier.

The white paper was right in a sense, there was no sea change in attitudes in Whitehall. In terms of resources, there was rebalancing for a while. Out-of-area operations acquired a new and permanent focus, and the Navy was the chief beneficiary of that. But the extra money from the Falklands war chest, and from the pledge to NATO to increase annual spending, would run out in the middle of the decade. Worries and questions about the numbers of destroyers and frigates would be back by the end of the 1980s. It was a further breathing space for the Navy, and perhaps the most that could have been expected.

But beneath the surface, something more had changed. The way in which, and the speed with which, the Navy in particular had responded to the Falklands, and how it had fought and prevailed in a modern missile-age encounter, helped reconnect it with the public consciousness. Here was a real and vivid demonstration of what the possession of maritime power was all about, that was not just confined to the particulars of a single, seemingly anomalous colonial dispute in the far-off South Atlantic. It was simply a reminder of what a navy, and particularly the Royal Navy, could do, even when its main job was meant to be hunting Soviet submarines in the northeast Atlantic.

It was also a display of naval determination that was surely not lost on other observers, and for that reason probably had an unquantifiable ripple effect on the wider strategic picture at what was a crucial period of transition in East-West tensions. Two years previously Sandy Woodward, when he was Director of Naval Plans, had written of the demonstrative effect on the potential adversary of maintaining and even bolstering the West's maritime defence, and by implication the risks of economizing on the naval front. At the time, such thoughts may have been discounted too far in other parts of the Ministry of Defence, where the preoccupation was worrying about the reaction of Britain's own allies to making economies anywhere else. Perhaps, in worrying about the impact on NATO cohesion of cuts to Britain's continental commitment, insufficient weight was given to the impact of cuts in naval forces, on either General Galtieri or the Kremlin.

The conflict also came at a critical time for Britain, and was a vital boost to national morale, almost a return from the dead in terms of self-esteem and international standing. It had seemed to slay some of the ghosts of Suez, whether that was a good thing or not. The services generally, but most visibly the Navy, had played a part in cementing Margaret Thatcher's place in history. But for the springboard of victory in the South Atlantic, economic traumas at home might well have seen her government voted out of office after just one term. For better or worse, but for the Navy, the world might not still be talking about Thatcherism.

The Falklands was a reminder of how useful maritime power could be when crises erupt far away. But it was also a display of how effective the Royal Navy could be closer to home. The deficiencies in the south Atlantic were plain to see, but so too the remedies. Neither side in the Whitehall battle over the Navy's future the year before had got it right. But, then, without experience of a war at sea for thirty-five years, lessons needed to be re-learned.

Britain probably ended up with a navy closer to the one that it should have had.

The Falklands additions in equipment and weapons would make a critical difference to the credibility and effectiveness of the Fleet both in the NATO domain and further afield. Ironically, given how crucial it was to the success of the campaign, the one area which was to remain relatively weak, and would steadily get more so over the years, was that of amphibious shipping. John Nott had reprieved the two assault ships, *Fearless* and *Intrepid*, before the Falklands crisis erupted. But there was only a promise, and no concrete sign, of any replacements.

In this connection, the retention of *Invincible* was doubly significant, since that meant an extra carrier which could play the part of a Commando ship if needed. And that fact was about to take on greater importance, as the protection and reinforcement of NATO's northern flank by amphibious forces was about to take on an increased significance in the Alliance's evolving maritime strategy.

On her return from the Falklands, *Invincible* herself spent a much-deserved break of nearly four months in dockyard hands in Portsmouth. Among other things, she received two of the same Vulcan-Phalanx gun systems that had been fitted to *Illustrious*.

After that, it was a return to a more normal routine. There were trials, and then it was across the Atlantic for exercises and a deployment to the Caribbean. It was while there in February 1983 that Jeremy Black's promotion to Rear Admiral came through, and he left the ship in Barbados. She sailed back across the Atlantic for more manoeuvres off Gibraltar – the very same series of exercises that had, the year before, been the launching pad for many of the warships that sailed south to the Falklands. And then it was north for more exercises which tested her secondary role as a Commando carrier once again.

Meanwhile, the Navy's two other carriers – *Hermes* and *Illustrious* – were also gearing up for major NATO exercises that would practise exactly those scenarios of naval warfare in the North Atlantic that had been so contentious two years earlier. At the end of May, *Hermes* would set off from the sprawling US naval base at Norfolk, Virginia. This time she was not the main flagship, but a supporting act in a multinational task force headed by the 87,000-ton carrier USS *John F Kennedy*. They were rehearsing the manoeuvre that would, in a time of East-West crisis, bring the US Navy's carrier battle groups across the Atlantic, to take up a holding position near the Azores, before heading north.

As the ships moved round to the southeast of the Azores, another assembly of warships set sail from Portugal's ancient port capital of Lisbon. This was the group that included HMS *Illustrious*, but again she was playing junior partner to – and chief anti-submarine cover for – the French aircraft carrier *Foch*. The two groups would rendezvous and then spread out northeast into the Bay of Biscay and towards the Western Approaches, to carry out exercises in the protection of shipping, while aircraft from the USS *John F Kennedy* carried out simulated strike missions deep into southern Germany.

Already, in the wake of the Falklands, and with a new dynamic force in Washington, NATO's naval thinking was shifting. When John Lehman took office as US Navy Secretary under Ronald Reagan in February 1981, he came face-to-face with what he regarded as an 'entrenched anti-naval orthodoxy' in the Pentagon, especially among the civilian staff. He came to be associated with the implementation of the new US maritime strategy, for which he was such a strident advocate, but which had been forming in the minds of senior US Navy officers and in naval staff studies for some time.

Most controversially, it was envisaged as a forward strategy, and a key focus was the new emphasis on pushing US and NATO naval forces north beyond the GIUK Gap into the teeth of the Soviet maritime defences, to take them on in their bases and bastions in and around the Kola Peninsula.

It was an expensive proposition. There was the banner headline of a 600-ship navy, as the means to fulfil the strategy. More specifically, it would require more investment in the priciest items of US maritime power, the nuclear-powered aircraft carriers and the hugely-capable Aegis air defence system aboard escorting cruisers that provided a radar and missile umbrella for the US carrier battle groups. The critics would argue that the United States was playing into the Soviets' hands, and that not only was it risky but also potentially provocative and destabilizing. It was in fact pushing against a Soviet military, economic, and political façade that was beginning to show the first signs of crumbling.

HMS *Hermes* was now rapidly approaching her retirement from the Royal Navy. *Invincible*, on the other hand, had had a new lease of life. And she also found her way into the headlines again.

In the Falklands Campaign, HMS *Invincible* had been one of a number of warships to sail to the South Atlantic with nuclear depth charges aboard. When ministers became aware of this, there were considerable alarms, but it was felt that trying to remove them would mean unacceptable delays to the deployment of the task force. They were eventually returned to the United Kingdom, but some only after the fighting had finished.

The Falklands effect and the renewed interest in out-of-area operations saw the resumption of Far East deployments, to practise the ability to project power and influence. On 1 September 1983, *Invincible* set off from Portsmouth on her first such deployment, with her old captain, Jeremy Black, embarked as the flag officer. Indeed, it was the most significant Far East deployment by the Royal Navy for some time. *Invincible*, however, had to make do with a minimum air group of five Sea Harriers and eight Sea King ASW helicopters – there were no extra jets available, or any of the Sea King AEW machines.

By November, the ship was heading to Australia. It was always going to be a poignant series of port calls there. In other circumstances, it would have been at about this time that *Invincible* would have been arriving under another name and other colours as the latest addition to the Royal Australian Navy.

The ship had got as far as Sydney when strange noises on one of the shafts started to cause concern. Admiral Black was not unfamiliar with the problem of mechanical grumblings from the ship's machinery spaces. But he was less familiar with the political grumblings which ensued. The Australian Government said that it could not allow the ship to go into dry-dock to investigate the problem unless it received an assurance that there were no nuclear weapons aboard.

In fact, after the experience of the Falklands, *Invincible* had left her nuclear depth charges behind before she sailed from Portsmouth. But Britain operated a 'neither confirm nor deny' policy. So there was an impasse. It was decided that *Invincible* would head to Singapore for dry-docking. Although there seemed to be a late change of heart by the Australians, the British stuck to the Singapore option. But media interest in the ship's predicament in the Far East was increased when the Japanese Government decided that it could not accept a visit from a British warship which might be carrying nuclear weapons, so that planned part of the itinerary was also scrapped. Moreover, the work in Singapore clearly had not cured the shaft problem, so she returned home early for more investigations and repairs to be carried out.

By now, the last of the Invincibles was nearing completion, and with it a plan that the Naval Staff had been clinging to for nearly fifteen years. *Ark Royal* would have a somewhat different appearance to her two elder sisters. The working group which had looked into improvements in her design early on had rejected most of them on the grounds that they would delay the ship too much. The Falklands changed the equation. There was the improved, much more prominent twelve-degree Ski-jump ramp, which was also extended forward in order not to interfere with the Sea Dart missile and so as not to encroach on the available parking and helicopter operating space on the flight deck. She would receive three instead of two of the new Vulcan-Phalanx guns, and they would be fitted in special emplacements at the bow and stern, and on a platform added to the side of the island superstructure.

Invincible and *Ark Royal* would meet at sea for the first time in October 1984, when the latter sailed out of the Tyne at the start of her builder's sea trials. *Ark Royal* made her debut in Portsmouth to quite a fanfare of attention on 1 July 1985. Completing the triumvirate of first commanding officers for the class was Captain James Weatherall. On her flight deck as she eased in towards her berth at the Middle Slip Jetty were a Sea Harrier and, near the stern, an ancient Swordfish torpedo plane, as flown by her predecessor but one, the third *Ark Royal*, which had performed heroically in the early part of the Second World War before being sunk off Gibraltar in November 1941.

Another faint echo of the past was that, with her various modifications, and the extra platforms and sponsons for new weapons, she had lost some of the clean, uncluttered character that *Invincible* had had when she first appeared. She looked just a little bit more like the carriers of old. And, to some of the traditionalists, she was the better for it. But she still had her Royal Navy acceptance trials ahead, and it would be nearly another year before all her extra weaponry was fitted.

The other sister, *Illustrious*, then hit the headlines for the wrong reasons. At the beginning of April 1986, she left Portsmouth at the head of the most ambitious deployment – with the exception of the Falklands task force – for over a decade. The group would be away for eight months, and would circle the globe. But *Illustrious* was only a day out of port when disaster struck. There was an explosion, the sound of alarms throughout the ship, and a sudden inferno in one of the starboard machinery spaces. A sheet of flame belched from one of the ship's funnels. The fire was brought under control, but *Illustrious* had to limp back to port. It would be more than two months before she could rejoin the deployment.

While this was going on, *Invincible* bowed out for what was going to be her first major refit at Devonport Dockyard. The price of the refit would be more than two-thirds the original building cost of the ship, 120 million pounds. It would last two-and-a-half years. But she would emerge with a major improvement in her capabilities.

Invincible arrived at Devonport in May 1986. For a year, she languished almost dormant, with little work being carried out, as the dockyard concentrated on refurbishing her old task force fleet-mate, HMS *Hermes*, for sale to and service in the Indian Navy as the INS *Viraat*. In May 1987, the formal handover and renaming ceremony took place. And, in July, the INS *Viraat* finally sailed away.

So the dockyard set to the task in earnest of transforming *Invincible*. There was a massive effort to service and repair her equipment and machinery. But, more importantly, there were very considerable changes to be made, many mirroring those already seen in *Ark Royal*. The old Ski-jump ramp was dismantled, and a new, larger, extended one was built, with a twelve-degree incline like *Ark Royal*'s. She was given a new 3-D radar, and much more advanced sonar, again as in *Ark Royal*. There were three new radar-controlled, close-in gun systems, but this time they were the Dutch Goalkeeper design, as opposed to the Vulcan-Phalanx. The operations room was upgraded.

But, most significantly, there was another big step on the path to making her a more effective aircraft carrier. Many of the changes were the result of experience from the Falklands. *Invincible* would emerge with the ability, routinely, to operate a force of twenty-one aircraft or more – a far cry now from that initial target of nine helicopters. Some of the ship's fuel tanks were converted to be able to carry more aviation fuel. At last, *Invincible*'s magazine capacity was increased, and provision was made for her to be able to handle the new Sea Eagle anti-ship missile, which could be carried by the Sea Harriers, and which greatly improved her firepower.

By now, the Navy had also set in train development of a Mark Two version of the Sea Harrier, to make up for the deficiencies of the original aircraft that were exposed in the Falklands. There would be a new, more advanced radar, and longer range, radar-guided missiles in place of the short-range, heat-seeking Sidewinders. The Navy saw it as a vital programme, to try to push out that outer layer of defence as the likely air threat increased. To the huge satisfaction of Fleet Air Arm pilots, it was also taking the Sea Harrier even further away from that rudimentary 'hack the shad' role that was its origin.

Still, the Sea Harrier FRS.2, as it was being called, was a long time coming. It had been announced in the year after the Falklands. It would not see service until the 1990s.

All the changes to *Invincible* meant the need to find room for more people aboard – an extra 120 places in all. So a new mess deck was squeezed into the space under the new ramp, rather unfortunately for those who would be occupying it. And a mezzanine deck with more officer accommodation was built out into the aft end of the hangar. Life would definitely feel more crowded aboard.

Other navies were by now following the Royal Navy's example in taking V/STOL aircraft to sea in a new generation of mini-carriers. The Italian Navy commissioned the 14,000-ton *Giuseppe Garibaldi* in September 1985, although she would not get her own Harriers for another four years. The Spanish Navy adapted the US sea control ship design to produce the *Principe de Asturias*, with a twelve-degree Ski-jump ramp. She had been laid down in 1979 but would not actually enter service until 1988. The Italians and the Spanish would buy US versions of the Harrier for their ships. The Indian Navy became the only export customer for the Sea Harrier, to operate from the newly-acquired *Viraat*.

Invincible finally went to sea again near the end of 1988. And, all the time that she had been in dockyard hands, the world beyond had been changing.

The services, and in particular the Navy, continued to enjoy a certain Falklands afterglow. But, by the late 1980s, the questions about overstretch and under-funding were resurfacing. There were complaints of a 'defence review by stealth'. Specifically, the Government's commitment to maintain a destroyer and frigate of 'about fifty' was wearing thinner and thinner. It was looking more like 'about forty-six or forty-seven'. The Navy was still thinking about a new Commando carrier, but getting nowhere. The idea of a new cheap frigate, or an even more modest corvette, had typically been squeezed out of consideration to preserve the Type 23 programme. The gathering pace of the Trident programme was adding to the stresses on the defence budget.

These facts were all adding to the strain on the Royal Navy as it got to grips with the implications of the new US-led forward maritime strategy. It was still expected to try to take the lead in 'holding the ring', until the US carrier battle groups could arrive, and to push north into the Norwegian Sea into the teeth of Soviet forces. The NATO plan would be to take on the Soviet Navy in its northern bastions and bases, and seek bastions of its own among Norway's fjords.

On the face of it, the adversary hardly looked any less daunting; new ships and new submarines armed with formidable weapons like the SS-N-19 anti-ship missile, which gloried in the NATO codename 'Shipwreck'. The sceptics ashore, and some of the gloomier intelligence assessments, questioned whether the Royal Navy had any weaponry that could touch these opponents, and wondered whether all that it was practising was a futile if heroic headlong rush to destruction.

But, for some of the practitioners, out in the grey expanse of the Atlantic and the icy waters north of the British Isles, the perspective was perhaps rather different, as they grappled with their task. One of those taking a leading role in this developing drama was Julian Oswald, who by the mid 1980s was the Flag Officer Third Flotilla, the commander at sea of the Navy's main anti-submarine force, based on one or more of the Invincibles. In the new, more determined jargon of the forward maritime strategy, this would be known as the NATO ASW Strike Force.

The first task was getting the main Striking Fleet, the US carrier battle groups, across from the United States. That presented its own problems just in terms of natural hazards. The route went through some of the most challenging waters from an acoustic and anti-submarine point of view. It is known as the north wall of the Gulf Stream, where warm waters meet the cold water of the Atlantic. But it was the job of Oswald and his force to move ahead of the US carriers to try to ensure that, as they came through, they were not going to be troubled by Soviet submarines.

It was certainly hard work in conditions that tended to favour the attacker. But, as the exercises progressed over the years, the Royal Navy learned more about the acoustics and the environment, and how to use its new towed-array escort ships. And Julian Oswald realized that the West was beginning to spot cracks in the Soviets' capabilities, of which the catastrophic losses of a couple of their nuclear-powered submarines in accidents during this time were only the most visible sign. He would later be stunned by the hollowness of most of the Soviet Union's naval forces on a visit to the Black Sea as First Sea Lord in 1991. He witnessed the shambles of a gunnery exercise and wondered how the West had frightened itself to such an extent for so long, and not spotted the weaknesses.

Still, in the mid 1980s, there was no doubt in Oswald's mind that the Navy was putting its head in the Soviet noose. Or that it would need the support of those American carriers as they thundered north. But the other thought in Oswald's mind was, what impact was all this having on the Soviet mind? He felt that perhaps the Soviet forces would have been impressed.

The culmination of these manoeuvres probably came with Exercise Teamwork 88. By then, Admiral Oswald was C-in-C Fleet. The British flagship was HMS *Illustrious*. And, on the staff of the new flag officer aboard the carrier was Ian Forbes.

Those on board *Illustrious* as they headed north in the opening stages of Teamwork 88 were fully conscious of how exposed they would be in a real crisis. Even when the American carriers arrived and moved north themselves, it would be *Illustrious'* job and that of the force around to stay 150 miles ahead, screening the carriers, which were meant to be part of the air umbrella in their turn. But they would still feel very remote.

But, as the exercise took *Illustrious* and the American carriers in amongst the fjords of Norway at NATO's northern tip, there was a strong sense that the pendulum in the arguments – and the balance of pressures on the opposing sides – had finally swung.

Forbes and his colleagues still worried that they did not have as many ships as they would have liked. But this was now the era of 'area' ASW operations, with the whole network of towed arrays, submarines, aircraft, and carrier-borne helicopters.

There would undoubtedly have been losses. But, as Forbes considered the Soviet Northern Fleet forces, they looked to him to be very much a one-shot system, with little recourse to reloading their batteries of anti-ship missiles once they were at sea and in action.

That could be deadly enough, of course, in this guided-missile era. But the situation presented serious dilemmas to Soviet commanders. Should they use their main batteries against the likes of *Illustrious* and her escorts? Or should they hold their fire, until the American carrier battle groups were properly in the cross-hairs? But how effective would that be against what would be at least three carriers, their massed air groups and escorts? Would that be too late? And what should be kept in reserve to defend their bastions and home bases if the NATO forces should survive and break through to continue the fight? To Forbes, it seemed to be NATO that was finally posing the critical questions to its opponents.

Even as the exercise planners pored over the results and digested the lessons of Teamwork 88, events on the broader political and diplomatic stage were beginning to move in a significant way. The arrival on the scene of Mikhail Gorbachov as Soviet leader, the first hints and suggestions that there was the possibility once more of accommodation and compromise, and the first breakthroughs since the era of détente on the arms control front, had in some ways only sharpened the arguments in NATO on how to respond, how far to go and how flexible to be in dealing with Moscow.

Suddenly, though, as 1989 unfolded, the prospect of the imminent collapse of the communist system began to seem very real. The Solidarity movement won elections in Poland. Hungary opened its borders to Austria. A tide of refugees from East Germany began to flow. Almost unthinkably, mounting protests in East Germany saw the fall of the long-time leader, Erich Honecker.

On 10 November 1989, people began to pull down the Berlin Wall. It was the real start of the unravelling of a system, and of the Cold War.

The arguments have been endless as to what the key catalysts were in this process. Was it a growing realisation in Moscow that the economic system there was approaching breaking-point? Was it the stridency and apparent inflexibility of the likes of Ronald Reagan and Margaret Thatcher in their dealings with the Soviet Union during the early 1980s? How much did the way the nuclear debates in Europe resolved themselves convince the Kremlin of the need to find a different way? Did the Reagan bombshell in 1983 of beginning work on a missile defence shield, the Strategic Defence Initiative or 'Star Wars', finally convince the Soviet leadership that it could no longer afford to compete with the US military-industrial complex?

Did the lessons from the South Atlantic reach all the way back to the Kremlin? And how much did the gauntlet that was thrown down by the new US maritime strategy, and the way NATO sought to put it into effect, add to the growing burdens of the Soviet military establishment? There must be a plausible case that they did have a significant effect, and that the cascade of events throughout the 1980s provided further evidence of the enduring strategic impact of maritime forces and capabilities.

CHAPTER TWELVE

Carrier Comeback

More than two decades had passed since the Healey defence review had appeared to snuff out the prospect of any long-term future for fixed-wing flying from Royal Navy ships at sea. But patiently at first, then surreptitiously and perhaps craftily, and in the end doggedly, determinedly, and maybe luckily, the Navy had kept the art alive. And, in so doing, it had kept open the option for Britain to exercise a level of maritime power and influence that it would otherwise have foregone completely. The question once again, though, was what would the future hold now that all the established defence and security assumptions were apparently being discarded and new ones defined and written?

For *Invincible*, back in service after her long modernization, life resumed with more NATO exercises and port visits. But, all around, the certainties of the Cold War were vanishing. After the decades of a frozen political landscape in Europe, the events were breathtaking in their speed. With a timescale measured in weeks and months, the edifice of Soviet control in Eastern Europe crumbled. But the effects of all this were far from clear.

It might have seemed like unadulterated good news for the Royal Navy. At last, surely, the tyranny of the Central Front had been broken, and Britain would be free to pursue a maritime strategy again. But the justification for much of the current Fleet, the battle against the Soviet submarines in the eastern Atlantic, was also evaporating. And if, by one bound, the Navy was free from the Central Front, none of the services was free from that unchanging impulse to save money. The political imperative to seek a 'peace dividend' was already asserting itself. The cautious would warn of the risks of an unknown future, but public opinion just would not sustain defence spending at existing levels when the rationale for that spending was disintegrating before everyone's eyes.

In fact, there was a dilemma for the Naval Staff. There would still be much hedge-betting. Were the changes irreversible? Could Russia return to its bad old ways? If so, with forces in Europe at lower levels, would that not increase the significance of potential transatlantic reinforcement by sea should an East-West crisis re-emerge? Or should the Navy start focusing again on wider horizons? In fact, it tried to do both.

There was a new Defence Secretary, Tom King, in office for just a few months before the Wall came down. Affable and confident, but at times also domineering, he was not a deep thinker on defence, but was – from the services' perspective – a bit of a meddler when it came to detail. But to him fell the task of taking the first tentative look at the post-Cold-War world from the Ministry of Defence's perspective.

Tom King would quickly predict that the chief complaint that critics would make of his 'Options for Change' review in 1990 would be that he had not cut enough. But the very title of the review underlined the imponderables that existed. Staff in the individual services would complain that the review would be too centralized, that too many options for change would actually not be considered, and that the process would look backwards as much as it looked forward: the template of forces was not changed much, just shrunk.

At the helm of the Navy now was Julian Oswald. He was mild-mannered and thoughtful. He was not really from a naval family, although his father had been a naval officer. Having leapt at the chance to go to Dartmouth as a boy of thirteen to avoid Latin, he would turn out to be one of the most intelligent First Sea Lords of modern times.

As for the idea that the chief complaint against 'Options for Change' being that it did not cut enough, Oswald's view was that it took a large enough bite out of all the services. The results of the review were unveiled at the end of July 1990. The process of German reunification was well under way. But it would not formally take place until October. The Warsaw Pact would not formally dissolve until July 1991, and the Soviet Union itself would not disappear until December of that year. The direction of political travel may have been pretty clear. The full ramifications of it were not.

The cuts clearly fell most heavily on the Army. Its presence in Germany would be cut by half. Likewise, the number of RAF bases in Germany would be reduced from four to two. But the Navy faced some further hefty reductions as well: another cut in destroyer and frigate numbers to 'around 40' over the next five years, but more painfully a reduction in submarines, with the SSNs chopped down from sixteen to twelve, and the number of conventionally-powered submarines reduced from ten to four.

But, in Julian Oswald's eyes, there was at least one glimmer of hope. He had always been a great champion of the Royal Marines. They had overcome countless threats to their survival in the previous twenty years. They had reinvented themselves as elite arctic troops for NATO's northern flank. And, paradoxically, they had proved their value and their valour at the other end of the world, in the South Atlantic. But, as the Navy had scrimped and saved through the 1980s, the plans for new amphibious ships from which they could operate were being forever postponed. The ships that they had were wearing out, and with them the Royal Marines' skills as truly seaborne soldiers.

As long as their main theatre of operations was going to be just a short voyage away across the North Sea, that did not matter so much, perhaps. In the future, it would. The Chief of the Naval Staff already felt that this capability would be a central part of the Navy's future. His priority was a new helicopter carrier – the Navy's first-ever custom-built Landing Platform Helicopter (LPH) in the jargon, a successor to the Commando ships that had been rather shabby conversions of old aircraft carriers. The LPH had been talked about for so long, but Sir Julian detected the first signs that it might just be possible to turn it into a reality.

Through all the arguments, the twists and turns, the frustrations of the last generation-and-a-half since the end of the Second World War, naval officers in the Ministry of Defence – whenever they had the chance – had always pounded away at the message that governments had to 'expect the unexpected'. And, of course, the Navy's reasoning was that, for that imprecise but apparently inevitable contingency, the inherent flexibility of maritime power would always find some sort of utility. And barely had the ink dried on 'Options for Change', than the unexpected happened, just as it had done with the Falklands.

After all the anguish of the withdrawal from East of Suez, and especially from the Gulf, it seemed that the Navy had hardly left for any time at all. In September 1980, the brutal new leader of Iraq, Saddam Hussein, decided to capitalize on the upheavals in Iran following the Islamic revolution there, and provoked a war with his neighbour. Far from Iraq achieving the rapid humiliation of Iran that Saddam Hussein intended, there would be eight terrible years of human wave offensives and chemical attacks, and hundred of thousands of casualties.

Within weeks of the outbreak of hostilities, the Royal Navy had established what would become known as the Armilla Patrol, to keep a watch on threats to shipping in the strategic Gulf waterway. The patrol, too, would endure. The attacks on shipping presented the greatest risk that the fighting would spill over. But the steadily mounting international naval presence, the growing Western efforts to protect the vital oil shipments, and especially some one-sided skirmishes between the Americans and the Iranians, would ultimately be important factors in persuading Tehran to accept a ceasefire in 1988. The Royal Navy may have been only a small player compared to the Americans, but it was there for the long haul. And those years in the 1980s, patrolling in the gruelling, shimmering heat of those strategic waterways, provided another example of the endurance and impact of maritime power over the long run.

At that time, for the West, Saddam Hussein had been the lesser of two evils, and a bulwark against the spread of Islamic revolution. But, when the Kuwaitis showed what seemed to Baghdad to be insufficient gratitude for Iraq's war efforts, and asked for the return of the money that they had loaned it, the Iraqi leader was not amused. On 2 August 1990, exactly a week after Tom King had announced the results of his defence review to the House of Commons, elite Republican Guard units of the Iraqi army swept into Kuwait, setting in train a looming international confrontation with Saddam Hussein.

The other accident of timing, unfortunately for Saddam Hussein, was that Margaret Thatcher was in the United States when the invasion happened, and was famously on hand to stiffen the resolve of the US President, George H W Bush. Less than four months later, she would be gone, ousted by her own party after eleven years in office. But still, over succeeding weeks and months, an international coalition was formed first to deter further Iraqi advances into Saudi Arabia, and then to reverse the occupation of Kuwait – as Operation Desert Shield transformed into Operation Desert Storm. Britain would be a major player in that coalition, and would ultimately commit 45,000 personnel to the enterprise.

The naval contribution would be a sizeable one. But, unlike in the Falklands, the Royal Navy's role would not grab the headlines. It kept an eye on the long sea routes that were crucial to the massive international war machine that was built up in the deserts of Saudi Arabia. But a threat to them never materialized. And everyone's attention was quickly grabbed by the blitz of the air war, the grainy fascination of gun-camera videos, and the bravura of the man running it all, US Army General 'Stormin' Norman Schwarzkopf.

The US Navy would be at the leading edge of the fight, with its six full-size strike carriers and volleys of cruise missiles. The Royal Navy had to be content with a supporting role, and the important but unglamorous mission of mine clearance. One of its destroyers, HMS *Gloucester*, did score a notable first, shooting down an anti-ship missile aimed at an American battleship. Missile-armed Royal Navy Lynx helicopters also caused havoc among the few Iraqi vessels that ventured out. The big frustration for the Navy was a battle fought mainly along the corridors in Whitehall.

HMS *Ark Royal* had departed from Portsmouth in the middle of October, and got as far as Gibraltar. While she was there, a change of command took place. Captain John Brigstocke, on his promotion to rear admiral, was replaced by Neil Rankin, who had been the first Wings on *Invincible* ten years previously.

It was a case of many happy returns for Rankin in a number of ways. The old *Ark Royal* had been his first carrier at the outset of his career as a naval aviator. Now, as he surveyed his new command, he could see the strides that had been made in the practice of operating the Invincibles since his time at the dawn of their era. He particularly noted the better Ski-jump ramp, the better accommodation, and more space. It was not quite night and day, he thought, but it was pretty close.

But he and the rest of the ship's company would be confronted with mixed signals on whether and where *Ark Royal* would be deployed in this gathering Gulf storm. Finally, early in the New Year, as the drumbeat towards actual conflict got louder, she sailed for the eastern Mediterranean. Admiral Brigstocke returned as the flag officer in charge, and was eager to get in on the action. Captain Rankin, too, expected that *Ark Royal* would sail on through the Suez Canal, the Red Sea, and into the Gulf.

There was a very good case for having *Ark Royal*, with all her command capabilities, in the Gulf. But there was also a suspicion that the Navy just wanted to get more in on the act. Tom King was not having it. The episode would in turn leave a bad taste in the Navy's mouth, and a feeling that it was deliberately being kept as much on the sidelines as possible.

Ark Royal did find a role, but on the periphery of the action. She took over the command and control of the coalition naval forces in the eastern Mediterranean, providing protection for the clutch of US warships that were launching cruise missiles into Iraq from there, as well as maintaining surveillance over what were still seen as rather vulnerable supply lines. In this way, *Ark Royal* released another American carrier to head through into the Red Sea. It was still intensive, demanding work. She remained at a high state of readiness, and flew many air defence missions with her squadron of Sea Harriers. But Rankin and his crew still wanted to get closer to the action, and he was disappointed when they could not.

The decisiveness of Operation Desert Storm, and the fact that such a huge international coalition had been assembled under the umbrella of a UN mandate, led to enthusiastic talk of a 'new world order'. Such notions would prove to be short-lived; the international stage soon began to resemble a new world of disorder, with nobody really willing to take the lead in sorting things out. An early US stab at humanitarian intervention in Somalia would quickly run into the debacle of 'Black Hawk Down' and an ignominious withdrawal.

There were the beginnings of the tortuous Balkans tragedy, and the first stirrings of a popular sense that 'something must be done'. But, at this stage, the British government, like others, was recoiling from any temptation to get involved, let alone to embrace a broad new policy of interventionism. It was an unsteady policy platform for the services as they tried to contemplate the future.

The Gulf War certainly had not deflected the government from its pursuit of the peace dividend. There was a dawning realization in the services that they would have to set out a positive new case for themselves. The Army's incentive was that it knew unequivocally that its previous *raison d'etre* was ending. But a residual commitment lingered in Europe, and it would be partially sustained as a Balkans commitment did begin to emerge – at least some of its garrisons in Germany would be turned into 'reaction forces'. The RAF could bathe in its Desert Storm exploits, which had given new force to the arguments that air power was now truly a war-winning tool.

The Navy might have been in danger of complacently believing that now, surely, its time had come again, and politicians would come to realize the true value of a flexible and mobile maritime capability in an uncertain world, that the time of maritime forces had finally returned. Some on the Naval Staff, though, felt that was not enough.

Meanwhile, HMS *Invincible* was heading east. One thing that the Navy was clearly determined to do was to demonstrate once again the extent of its reach, and if possible to drive home the message that it had a modern relevance and was not just another voyage down memory lane. In May 1992, the ship sailed away from the grey, squally conditions of home waters at the head of a six-ship task force bound for a six-and-a-half-month deployment to the Far East.

At the heart of this expedition, dubbed Orient 92, were two very different men, but each in their own way dedicated to what they felt the Navy now stood for. In charge was John Brigstocke, who had now put the frustration of Operation Desert Storm behind him. An able commander, he was intelligent but intense, ambitious and an eloquent advocate of the Navy's modern *raison d'etre*. This deployment, he clearly believed, had nothing to do with the colonial past, and everything to do with being ready to deal with modern-day concerns like threats to oil supplies and support for allies.

Invincible's commanding officer, now Captain Fabian Malbon, was quiet and laid-back. He was a man with the traditional enthusiasms of a naval officer – a deep attachment, of course, to his family, but also to the Navy, the sea, and a thirty-three-foot sailing cruiser. And his casual style seemed like a breath of fresh air to those who served with him.

This deployment would also present a very modern challenge for him as a commanding officer. It would certainly be a powerful confirmation for him of how the Navy had changed since he had joined it twenty-seven years previously.

The Navy, like the other services, was finding it increasingly difficult to recruit enough of the right sort of men to crew its ships. So, after much anguished debate, reluctance, and soul-searching on the Naval Staff, and some prodding from ministers, the Navy took the momentous decision to accept women at sea. So Fabian Malbon was the first captain of a Royal Navy aircraft carrier, or indeed of any British capital ship, to embark on a long deployment like this with a mixed crew aboard. *Invincible*, as well as having to squeeze many more crew members aboard than originally planned, now had to cater for the fact that among them were 80 women sailors as well.

There would be grumbling and discontent and not a few discipline problems as the Navy came to terms with the change. It added another dimension to the task facing every commanding officer at sea. It would change the character of life at sea, and the atmosphere aboard the Navy's ships. But this was a transformation that the Navy simply had to make if it was to continue to be effective in the modern age.

Another man with a particular challenge on this deployment was Captain John Lippiett, the commanding officer of HMS *Norfolk*. He had taken over from the ship's first commanding officer, Jonathon Band. She was the newest operational frigate in the Navy, and the first of the Type 23 Duke class. Her design had emerged after the arguments of the late 1970s and early 1980s on the right size and shape of the Navy's future warship, and the trade-off between quality and quantity. Her presence on this deployment also represented yet another paradox in the modern story of the Royal Navy.

For much of the time when it was trying to adapt to the role of an ASW fleet focused on NATO, the Navy had to rely on ships that were a hangover from its colonial policeman days. The Type 23s, on the other hand, had been designed more than any other previous class of escort for the very specific Cold War task of modern anti-submarine war against the Soviet Navy in the northeast Atlantic, and as a vehicle for using a towed-array sonar. But they were just starting to arrive on the scene when that requirement itself disappeared beneath the waves. At least, thanks to the lessons of the Falklands, the Type 23s were much more like general-purpose frigates than they would otherwise have been.

Now it would be the job of Captain Lippiett and his crew to see how HMS *Norfolk* and her sisters would be able to perform on the broad oceans, on the kind of long deployment far from home for which they were not really designed but which could turn out to be one of the Navy's main priorities once again. The fact that the ship's company itself was far smaller than those in previous generations of frigates was part of the challenge.

Thanks to the efforts of John Lippiett and his crew on Orient 92, the Navy would convince itself that these Cold War warriors were perfectly suitable for the age-old tasks of traditional cruisers and frigates as well. The Navy would build sixteen of them altogether, the last not entering service until more than ten years after the Berlin Wall had come down. They would become the backbone of the Fleet, and perform sterling service in many ways. But some shook their heads, and thought that – yet again – the Naval Staff clung on to a design in hand when it should have started to think about constructing something simpler, more cost-effective, and more appropriate to the changed world scene.

As the ships, officers, and crews of Orient 92 made their meandering way out to the Far East and back, the news headlines were of continuing tensions with Iraq and growing worries about events in the Balkans. For Admiral Brigstocke and his staff, there was the nagging question of whether the task group might be called on to deal with a real contingency.

Neither of these crises actually boiled over while the ships remained on their deployment. But the public pressure to take a hand in the Balkans was growing. The United States was not ready to get involved on the ground. However, as the stories of violence and atrocities continued to emerge, the UN Security Council authorised the deployment of a UN protection force (UNPROFOR), first to Croatia and, as concerns grew over the situation in Bosnia-Hercegovina, to Sarajevo airport and then to protect humanitarian aid convoys.

The British government despatched troops to join UNPROFOR in October 1992. But it also wanted further back-up for the force, without adding to the number of troops on the ground. So, early in 1993, the decision was taken to deploy a naval task group to the Adriatic centred on an aircraft carrier. *Invincible*'s sister ship, *Ark Royal*, was the first of the carriers to deploy, under the command of Captain Jeremy Blackham. As the Balkans agony continued, the next few years would see all three of the carriers carry out this Adriatic deployment, and it would evolve significantly over time.

Jeremy Blackham received his instructions on 8 January 1993. He was to proceed to the Adriatic with a small task force and be ready for action by 26 January, to support the British UN troops and, if the situation on the ground really turned sour, to assist in pulling them out.

After some hurried preparations, *Ark Royal* set sail from Portsmouth on 14 January. Blackham would have with him in the Adriatic a small force including a destroyer, a frigate, and three Royal Fleet Auxiliary (RFA) support ships. Crucially, one of those was the 28,000-ton RFA *Argus*, a helicopter training ship, which would serve as a sort of troop carrier, with a detachment of light artillery weapons, some 400 troops, and a host of associated support vehicles, ready to be landed if the need arose.

For *Ark Royal* herself, it was hardly business as usual either. Aboard were eight Sea Harriers and three Sea King AEW helicopters. But in place of her normal anti-submarine squadron was a force of eight Sea King troop-carrying helicopters. Half-a-dozen ASW machines were scattered among the RFAs in the force, just in case. This would be another step in the evolution of these ships which had started their lives as cruisers, and along a path which might, just might, take the Royal Navy full-circle in its relationship with the aircraft carrier.

Some sceptics wondered why a carrier was needed when there were NATO air bases so close in Italy. But a carrier and its task force were that much more flexible, and available, closer to hand and able to react more quickly if things turned nasty on the ground. To Blackham, what he and his flotilla of ships were embarking on was a classic 'poise' operation, which had been an enduring strength of naval forces down the ages. Unlike the costly, politically sensitive, potentially provocative, and diplomatically fraught option of despatching even more ground troops, guns, and land-based air power, the Navy could stand ready, for as long as it took, as a visible statement of serious intent, but without raising the level of risk or the political stakes unnecessarily.

Using the Navy in this way left more options open for longer. In Blackham's view, this was a task that was both ancient and modern, and would become the most likely form of naval operation again in the future. Unfortunately for the crews concerned, and perhaps not least for the pilots of the Sea Harriers, 'poise' translated into another age-old naval tradition, familiar to the crews of the storm-tossed sailing ships that had kept Britain safe from Napoleonic invasion. It was that of mounting frustration and even boredom when nothing in the way of significant action materialized.

The Navy was also now in something of a Catch-22 situation. *Ark Royal's* commanding officer saw this dash to the Adriatic as demonstrating once again the flexibility inherent in a ship like his, large enough to take on a whole group of aircraft to perform a variety of possible missions. But there was a very real snag. The Navy had already squeezed much more out of the Invincibles than some in the Naval Staff had probably ever expected. They were showing what valuable political and diplomatic tools they could be. But, if the situation required serious amounts of firepower, they were still just too small. The Invincibles offered a window onto what might be possible again. But the Navy, with these ships, would largely be consigned to the sidelines or a supporting role when really major air power was required.

Back in Whitehall, Julian Oswald retired as First Sea Lord in March. But he had a couple of parting shots before he left. He paid his last call on the Defence Secretary, now Malcolm Rifkind. The minister asked the admiral if he had a parting thought. 'Yes,' said Sir Julian, in his reflective way. 'If I were to leave you with one idea, it would be the need to go ahead and order the LPH.'[1]

For Julian Oswald, that one move would be a critical step towards fashioning a fleet for the future, creating a centrepiece for the return to a genuinely effective amphibious capability for the unstable world ahead. The LPH – the new helicopter and Commando carrier – would fill a gap that had existed for about twenty years. The plans had faltered. Shipyards had been asked to bid to build such a ship, but the project had lapsed. However, within months of Sir Julian Oswald's departure, Malcolm Rifkind would indeed agree to order the ship, which would be HMS *Ocean*. The contract was placed a couple of months after Julian Oswald departed, and she would finally enter in September 1998.

The Navy had cut many corners to try to get her. Her price tag was just 150 million pounds, not much more than the cost of a frigate at the time for a vessel that weighed in at over 20,000 tons.

Just a few weeks before he stepped down, at a lecture in Cambridge, the First Sea Lord had taken as a theme the deterrent value of naval forces, in a conventional rather than a nuclear sense. In a world in which the threat of an East-West nuclear confrontation had receded, but the dangers of limited crises looked to be on the rise, it seemed like fertile ground on which the Navy could plant a post-Cold-War case. It would become an emerging theme, although not without resistance from elsewhere within the Ministry of Defence, where the concept of conventional deterrence was seen as potentially complicating and undercutting the case for retaining the ultimate deterrent, Polaris, and its successor, Trident.

Conventional deterrence was taken one step further when ministers began to contemplate openly the concept of coercion – the limited application of force to have a specific effect, for instance to make a potential troublemaker think twice. The idea would become associated with the Navy's bid to buy a limited number of Tomahawk cruise missiles for some of its SSNs, that would for the first time give the submarines the kind of potential that had been envisaged for them for thirty years.

There may have been an ingrained cultural hostility in the Navy to setting down a doctrine. But everyone else was doing it. The political thrust, in the wake of the Gulf War experience, emphasized the joint approach between the services. The Navy needed to join in, or risked being left out.

Still, naval thinking remained cautious. Jock Slater, now the C-in-C Fleet, established his credentials early on as an advocate of 'jointness': 'I am in absolutely no doubt that joint operations will be the cornerstone of any future conflict.'[2] But he, like others, was still hedging his bets, defending the size and shape of the existing fleet on the grounds that there were new threats at sea, from the proliferation of conventionally-powered submarines and sea skimming missiles.

There was continued emphasis on the balanced fleet, and the enduring attributes of naval forces − of flexibility and mobility − even as the types of missions envisaged began to change, to include counter-terrorism and disaster relief, peacekeeping, and all the way up to hostilities, possibly involving a 'national task force'.[3]

Late in 1993, a key document entitled 'UK Maritime Power − A Change in Emphasis', heralded the main shift in thinking from a preoccupation with sea control towards amphibious operations and the support of land forces, with a focus on that area of water between the shore and the deep sea that has become known as the littoral. It might have made some Nelsonian navalists wince. But, at about this time, the US Navy and Marine Corps were also producing their 'From The Sea' doctrine of force projection. One thing Royal Navy thinking was already highlighting was that, in this new uncertain age, maintaining close transatlantic ties would become increasingly difficult, and Britain's naval forces could play a key role in achieving that.

The Navy also did not flinch from trotting out its old axiom 'expect the unexpected'. It did shy way from the term 'gunboat diplomacy', for obvious reasons. Others did not, and asserted that its value was as sure as ever when a time of trouble and of frequent and fractious disputes seemed so obviously ahead.

The impetus continued with the production of a broad doctrine paper, BR 1806, in 1995,[4] on the way to the more focused thinking on the maritime contribution to joint operations, which really enshrined power projection as the Navy's primary role after providing the strategic deterrent. Those at the top of the Navy would make no apology for accepting that its central conventional task would be in support of events and operations ashore. The Navy should certainly press to play a prominent part, but should not claim for itself more than was reasonable. Apart from anything else, there were limits to what it could offer with the hardware it currently had, not least its compromised carriers and the lack still of a dedicated helicopter carrier for the Royal Marines. But there were certainly some of the old school who would feel that the Navy was selling itself short, just at the moment when it should be pressing its case hardest.

At the beginning of August 1993, *Invincible* took over from *Ark Royal* for her first stint on the Adriatic patrol. Very soon, Captain Fabian Malbon found himself entertaining some unusual guests. The two international mediators on the Balkans, the former Navy Minister and Foreign Secretary, Lord Owen, and the Norwegian former Defence and Foreign Minister, Thorvald Stoltenberg, convened peace talks. *Invincible*, cruising offshore, was the chosen venue.

It was a memorable moment for Owen as he flew aboard by helicopter. This was the ship whose design and justification had taken up so much of his time and effort when he had been at the Ministry of Defence over two decades before.

The parties huddled for eight hours of talks in *Invincible's* wardroom. A tentative agreement would emerge that would be known as 'the *Invincible* package'. But it would founder, and the fighting went on.

Invincible handed back responsibility for the Adriatic mission to *Ark Royal* early in the New Year. As the violence on the ground worsened, the United Nations, now joined by NATO, was being driven gradually to ratchet up the pressure. The British carrier presence was now only a small cog in a large NATO machine enforcing a no-fly zone and supporting UN peacekeepers. But, as the tensions mounted, one of *Ark Royal's* Sea Harriers was shot down as the pilot tried to protect UN troops near the town of Goradze. He ejected and was recovered safely.

In April 1995, Captain Ian Forbes took command of *Invincible* just before her third appearance on the Adriatic mission. It had become a repetitive and unrelenting task, cruising up and down the 'launch line', flying daily air patrols. The ship had the new version of the Sea Harrier, now called the FA.2. But events in Bosnia were coming to a head. The Bosnian Serbs had overrun the UN 'safe area' of Srebrenica in July, and were threatening others. This led NATO to threaten a campaign of air strikes, Operation Deliberate Force, against Bosnian Serb targets. The actual trigger, though, at the end of August, was a devastating mortar attack on a market in the Bosnian capital, Sarajevo, that killed over forty and injured scores more.

Operation Deliberate Force would be the first sustained military action in NATO's history. It would be a big test for *Invincible*, and there would be much riding on how she performed. But her eight Sea Harriers were fighters, they were not really bombers. They could deliver laser-guided bombs, and Forbes made sure that they had practised hard, but there were limits to their capabilities. Because of those limits, the aircraft could not be allocated the most precise targets that NATO had identified.

Invincible had withdrawn from the Adriatic to undertake a port visit and some rest and recreation in Palma, Mallorca, when the crisis suddenly escalated. Forbes himself was on the golf course when the call came to return to duty. *Invincible* sailed within hours. The speed of her departure meant that she would leave some 200 of her crew behind. But Forbes had taken precautions, and made sure that he had the key personnel for air operations with him. Then it was a 25-knot dash to be on station at the appointed moment. She was, and would launch her first mission of four Sea Harriers to strike their allotted target, a warehouse on the outskirts of Sarajevo.

Operation Deliberate Force would last three weeks. *Invincible's* operational tempo would settle at two missions a day, of four aircraft each. That was hard work. There were constant reminders that she had not really been designed as a strike carrier. Struggling to get enough bombs from the magazines to the aircraft, and arming them, was a significant challenge all by itself.

And *Invincible's* contribution was hardly decisive in the context of the whole campaign. NATO had some 270 aircraft of various types at its disposal, which flew 3,500 missions in all. The Adriatic itself was crowded. As well as *Invincible*, there were two American carriers and a French one. And the RAF could also point out that twelve of its Harriers were happily flying from an air base in Italy. Operation Deliberate Force was hardly a cast-iron case for the carrier.

Of course, it had always been the Navy's contention that friendly host nations would not always be available: that had been the situation in the Falklands, and it would be again, as the world became even more unpredictable, and the number of potential friendly footholds got smaller and smaller. The Navy view was that, even in the unpromising Adriatic, right under NATO's nose, the carriers had demonstrated their added flexibility, often sailing out of bad weather to keep flying while aircraft ashore remained grounded.

Ian Forbes knew that *Invincible's* contribution, counted in sorties and bombs, had not been huge. Some of her limitations had been exposed again. But, after a very long gap, what she had done in those three weeks had surely given renewed credibility and concrete expression to the idea of a Royal Navy carrier in a strike role, projecting power ashore. The question was whether there was enough force in the argument to sustain it for long enough and powerfully enough to turn what was latent and limited in the Invincibles into something on a different scale that could make a much bigger military difference.

Another step on that road took place the following summer. As an experiment, *Invincible* took aboard a detachment of RAF Harrier GR.7s. This was the real bombing version of the aircraft, with more range, payload, and accuracy. It may have been an uneasy first encounter. There had been plenty of RAF pilots who had flown with the Royal Navy over the years. But the cultural divide between the Fleet Air Arm and the RAF had been so wide for so long, the suspicions so deep, and the practices of flying from ships and from the land so different in so many ways. But perhaps the climate was different now.

And elsewhere, in quiet offices in the Ministry of Defence, people were beginning, tentatively, to consider a more distant horizon. *Invincible* was already approaching the half-way point in her planned operational life. It was looking as if she would retire in about 2010. In the Navy, they were daring to think about what might come next.

Initially, the ambition seemed to be to produce an almost direct replacement for *Invincible* and her sisters. The strategic backdrop in the early 1990s remained unclear. The notion still had not taken hold that the Navy's main business in the future would be projecting power ashore, rather than preparing for a full-blown war at sea.

The ship designers started looking at a range of options, and produced some twenty to thirty possible designs, with numbers of aircraft ranging from ten to fifty. The Navy also considered the possibility of keeping the Invincibles going, by stretching them to fit in more aircraft. The ships would be cut in two, and a new section inserted, to carry more planes, ammunition, and other equipment. But the idea looked doubtful and the number of aircraft would hardly increase at all because the new generation of planes would be bigger. Many of the Invincibles' old handicaps would remain. The ships would also get heavier, expanding to about 24,000 tons, but slower.

It looked risky. The state and design of the ships' hulls might make the task a lot more difficult than it at first appeared. And the Navy always seemed to have unhappy experiences every time it tried to carry out a major modernization of its ships. The memories went back to HMS *Victorious* in the 1950s, and the mid-life frigate refits in the 1970s that got the Navy into so much trouble when it came to the Nott review.

It was the Adriatic mission that started to shift the focus. Anti-submarine warfare and air defence became less of a priority, a strike capability more so. The trials with RAF Harriers took on a growing significance. The Navy experimented to see just how many Harriers it could squeeze on to *Invincible* and her sisters. Two dozen was the record, but that created terrible traffic jams on the flight deck, and was not really operationally viable.

There were studies which looked into converting merchant ships. The thought was that they could at least provide a relatively cheap stop-gap which might last for ten years or so. But, given its past habits, the Navy probably did not ever have much enthusiasm for this proposal, which seemed to be dismissed very quickly. The conversions were considered either too slow or could carry too few aircraft.

But there was plenty of thinking and work going on. That was just as well, because the political landscape was about to shift dramatically.

CHAPTER THIRTEEN

The Blair Effect

James Burnell-Nugent had arrived in Spain's ancient port city of Barcelona. A larger-than-life character, confident, some would say overly-so, he fitted in to the mould of those more flamboyant naval officers of the past, brimming with self-belief. A Cambridge graduate, he had spent much of his early career in submarines. But now he was here in Barcelona at the beginning of December 1997 to take over command of one of the Navy's big ships, *Invincible*. It was a confused and confusing time. Tensions were simmering in the Gulf after Saddam Hussein had forced the UN weapons inspectors in his country to leave. The ship, at the time under the command of Captain Roy Clare, had just made a headlong dash across the Atlantic from Barbados at nearly 30 knots, with the prospect of sailing on eastwards. But the politicians seemed to be uncertain what to do next.

Burnell-Nugent himself had not been sure for a while whether he would be taking charge of the helicopter carrier *Ocean* or *Invincible*. He had never set foot on an Invincible-class carrier before. But it was, for him as much as for anyone, a dream command. It was not just the size, but also what he felt a carrier represented as a political and diplomatic tool. And his time in command was to demonstrate that amply.

The Gulf crisis was ebbing and flowing. It looked as if *Invincible* would probably just sail home after all, or maybe linger for a while in Gibraltar. So the new commanding officer had clothes for only a few days away – and a gentle passage back to Portsmouth so that he could get a feel for his new charge. He was optimistic that there might be a stopover in Gibraltar, and if so there might be an invitation to dine with the Governor. So the only item of social attire that he had with him was a dinner jacket. As it turned out, he would not need it. Within a couple of days of departing from Barcelona, he had to break the news to the ship's company that *Invincible* would be staying in the Mediterranean and would not be home for Christmas.

The ship would spend another month sailing up and down the Mediterranean before finally heading on through the Suez Canal and into the Gulf. What then followed was a classic piece of gunboat diplomacy – even if the Navy may have been reluctant to acknowledge it as such.

Invincible had made her first foray into the Gulf just over a year earlier, in November 1996, with Roy Clare in charge. He had taken the ship over from Ian Forbes, while she was at Izmir in Turkey. The two men knew each other well. As always, there was much build-up and preparation to a change of command. But, when it happens, it is always swift. Forbes and Clare had dinner the night before. On the day of the handover, the actual business was completed in fifteen minutes.

The ship knew that she was heading for the Gulf. As such, she would be the first British aircraft carrier to enter the waterway for over thirty-five years. The last time that had happened was in the summer of 1961, when HMS *Victorious* had dashed to the Gulf as part of the British force rushed in to protect the then newly-sovereign state of Kuwait from a threatening Iraq. *Victorious* was relieved by HMS *Centaur*. On that occasion, deterrence and gunboat diplomacy had seemed to work.

There was no specific crisis on this occasion, just the background war of nerves between Saddam Hussein and the West that had gone on since 1991, over UN inspections and the hunt for suspected weapons of mass destruction. There had been flare-ups along the way in the previous few years. There might be another. *Invincible's* mission was to assert Britain's naval presence in the region at what remained an uneasy time, and to gain new experience of operating a carrier in the waterway, which might be of value in the future. It was.

Clare himself was an unusual mixture. He believed in working a ship to its limits; he had felt the Navy had been caught off-guard in its training by the Falklands. He did not believed in enforcing rules inflexibly. But he would let a ship's company know what was expected of it, and deal firmly with those who let him down. When he joined *Invincible*, he knew that she was worked-up and efficient, but also that she had been working hard. So, one of the first things he did, as the ship sailed in the heat and humidity of the Red Sea en route to the Gulf, when there could be no flying operations anyway, was to hold a flight deck barbeque, to get to know the crew.

Clare knew the Gulf well. He had served in the region at almost every stage of his naval career, not bad for an officer who had made his way in the Navy precisely at the time when Britain had supposedly relinquished its East of Suez interest. So he knew the tensions and potential pitfalls of the area. There was the edgy transit through the narrow Straits of Hormuz, under close Iranian surveillance. There was a visit to the Saudi port of Jubail, the first ever by a British carrier, and not an easy run ashore for the crew. The ship also deliberately sailed right up to the north of the Gulf, and anchored off Kuwait City.

And so it was, a year later, that *Invincible* found herself hurrying back in the direction of the Gulf. The ship was visiting Florida, and much of the crew was on leave, when Roy Clare received the order to sail. Once again, there was all the excitement of a rushed departure, and the added difficulty of recalling the crew when the instruction from London had been to keep things low-key. *Invincible* would sail with about a hundred members of her crew missing.

Some had an early opportunity to catch up. The politicians changed their minds again. The urgency reduced, *Invincible* diverted to Barbados. But then the plan changed again. That was how *Invincible* found herself dashing across the Atlantic in five days, encountering heavy weather on the way, and sometimes surfing down the huge waves as the ship rolled and plunged her way across the ocean.

Ian Forbes, meanwhile, had been ordered to rejoin his old ship urgently to take overall control as the flag officer. After he had handed over command to Roy Clare, he had served for nine months as the military adviser to the UN High Representative for Bosnia, Carl Bildt. Now he was back as the admiral in charge of the UK Task Group. He had already paid one return visit to *Invincible* while she was in the United States. This visit would be different.

In the headlong rush, Forbes managed to get aboard *Invincible's* sister ship, *Illustrious*, by helicopter in thick fog off the Cornish coast. The two ships would rendezvous off Gibraltar to transfer stores and the admiral. While all this had been going on, permission had been given to embark nine RAF Harrier GR.7s aboard *Invincible* to provide the bombing effort to support US forces in the Gulf should it come to that. In a massive effort, the aircraft, the support crews, and supplies all came aboard off Gibraltar.

The urgent task now was to mould the ship and the extra aircraft together into an effective force as a quickly as possible. Both immediately embarked on intensive flying training, day and night. And then, suddenly, in the middle of the night, disaster struck. The emergency klaxons aboard *Invincible* sounded. An RAF Harrier had ditched in the pitch darkness.

The pilot was safe. But the hearts of both Clare and Forbes sank. For Clare, it was the second aircraft that the ship had lost while he was in charge. He would get a reputation, he thought. For Ian Forbes, it was the sinking feeling that so much of what the Navy was pinning its hopes on for the future was represented in what *Invincible* was doing now – the response to a crisis, the coming together of the Royal Navy and the RAF to project power and influence, the whole development of a new generation of carriers. Was the concept to fail before it had even been properly tested?

In fact, it was an isolated incident. The ship and the squadrons would quickly get over it. And they would soon be on their way to the Gulf. But not Roy Clare. His time in command was up. There had been some thought that perhaps it would be better to keep the experienced commanding officer, rather than have a changeover now. But it was still unclear how this particular crisis would unfold, and how long it would last. So James Burnell-Nugent took up the reins.

The orders were still confused. First, it looked as if the crisis would blow over. The ship would return to Portsmouth. Then came the instruction to remain in the Mediterranean. That lasted over Christmas. Then, on 16 January, the order was sent to deploy, to conduct air operations over Iraq.

Invincible was joining a force that would ultimately include three US aircraft carriers. So, again, the British contribution to this particular example of coercion looked tiny in comparison. But she was packed with over twenty aircraft, with a squadron each of Royal Navy Sea Harrier FA.2 fighters and RAF Harrier GR.7 bombers, plus Sea King AEW and ASW helicopters. *Invincible*'s complement of aircraft was, in a relatively small way, now echoing the air groups of the old strike carriers of over a generation before.

There were some new aspects to the exercise of maritime leverage, and presenting a high profile to send a message. *Invincible* also took aboard a BBC news crew, including the veteran correspondent Kate Adie, to broadcast the first live television news reports from a carrier while under way. *Invincible*, because of her name, and because of the Falklands, attracted headlines anyway as the crisis developed. And that was useful.

Invincible arrived in the Gulf. Her aircraft would join 'packages' of thirty planes and more in missions over Iraq, as the military pressure mounted, and the threat of real confrontation loomed. Talk of war, of a campaign of air strikes, grew louder.

In the end, the negotiating efforts of the new UN Secretary-General, Kofi Annan, defused the crisis temporarily. *Invincible* handed over to HMS *Illustrious* and sailed quietly away. But the part played by the very public build-up of naval and other forces in the Gulf was widely acknowledged, including by the UN's top diplomat himself. Kofi Annan may have been playing a deft bit of politics there, knowing that the US and British governments needed some crumbs of consolation for the fact that he had somewhat hijacked their own diplomacy.

But two key elements in this drama were that *Invincible* had played a very high-profile part in the first major international crisis for the new British Prime Minister, Tony Blair, and she had done so just at the moment when decisions were being made back in Whitehall on whether the Royal Navy could look forward to a new generation of aircraft carriers. *Invincible* was helping to secure her own legacy.

Britain, in May 1997, had experienced a political sea change. After eighteen years of Conservative government, the Labour Party had swept into office. Tony Blair, who had never previously served in any government, was untried and unknown on the international stage. The imprint that he would leave on the country's foreign, defence, and security policy could hardly have been anticipated at the time.

The new government came in to office with a manifesto pledge to carry out a major review of defence policy. And this was at a time when key decisions were beckoning on the need for new carriers. In fact, this avowedly 'new' Labour administration, or at least its prime minister, appeared determined to depart from the party's most divisive policies of the past, and would set the foreign policy conditions and the political atmosphere more favourably for the Navy's carrier case than at any time in nearly four decades.

Tony Blair would emerge as a conviction politician on international affairs. He would become identified with a creed of liberal interventionism. In part his developing views may have been a reaction to what many had seen as costly hesitations and indecision in the Balkans for most of the 1990s. He would talk of 'the beginnings of a new doctrine of international community'. The existence of states like Britain may no longer be under threat, but now 'our actions are guided by a more subtle blend of mutual self-interest and moral purpose in defending the values we cherish … In the end, values and interests merge.'[1]

Whatever the Prime Minister's motivation, this philosophy would provide the platform for an expeditionary defence policy. It would offer a modern, forward-looking policy agenda around which the Navy could lay its own plans and proposals, instead of having to rely on arguments that appeared to rely as much on the past as the future. At least at this early stage, Tony Blair certainly did the Navy a great favour in the international stance that he adopted. And, for a young prime minister, finding his way in the world and believing strongly that Britain had a significant and active role to play, the appeal of the carrier and the broader maritime case must have seemed strong in return.

It would not remain that way, of course. And to the sceptics, there was little new in this. It was, to the sternest critics, merely the latest incarnation of the prolonged and ultimately debilitating self-deception from which British governments had been suffering since at least 1945.

The government confirmed in The Queen's Speech on 14 May 1997 that it would carry out a Strategic Defence Review (SDR). It was launched two weeks later by the new Defence Secretary, George Robertson.

The man to lead the Navy's case at this time was Jock Slater. He had been in office as First Sea Lord since 1995. He was a seasoned Whitehall warrior. Since his time as HMS *Illustrious*' first commanding officer, as well as being the C-in-C Fleet, he had been Assistant Chief of the Defence Staff (Policy and Nuclear) and Vice Chief of the Defence Staff. He was intelligent, sharp, determined, highly articulate and charismatic, and a very capable pair of hands at the head of the Navy at a crucial time. He was a determined and persuasive advocate. However, the path that he would pursue to try to secure what he believed to be the central elements of the Navy's future would provoke unease among the more traditionalist parts of the naval establishment.

Jock Slater was from a medical rather than a naval family. His father and grandfather had both been eminent neurologists. But there was that illustrious naval relation, his great-uncle, 'Uncle Ned' as he was known in the family. At the time of VE Day, Admiral of the Fleet Sir Andrew Cunningham, First Sea Lord at the time, and a fiery character, had created quite an impression on the seven-year-old Jock when he had taken him in his very big and smart official car with his leading seaman chauffeur to see the fireworks over Edinburgh Castle.

Cunningham was an inspirational figure anyway, one of the country's great war-time commanders, who had wrested control of the Mediterranean from the Italian Navy with some daring actions, like that at Taranto, launched from the then HMS *Illustrious*, the forerunner of the ship that Jock Slater would later command.

Still, it was perhaps the biggest crisis in the Slater household in the post-war years when Jock decided that he wanted to pursue a naval rather than medical career. 'He'll end up as a golf club secretary by the time he's forty,' his father despairingly predicted. Jock Slater joined the Navy in September 1956 just a few weeks after the Suez Crisis had erupted with Egypt's nationalization of the Canal. Unfortunately for him, his father did not live to see him rise to the highest naval office once held by Uncle Ned.

He might have gone further still. In the dying days of the Conservative government, he was the favourite to become the next Chief of the Defence Staff. He had a strong track record in promoting the joint approach in defence. As the Vice Chief, he had been instrumental in setting up the Permanent Joint Headquarters to run future operations.

But some were not convinced. And there did seem to be a tension in Admiral Slater. When he reverted to the 'dark blue' of the Navy as First Sea Lord, he doggedly pressed the case to keep all three Invincible-class carriers in operation, and to push for new big amphibious ships. It harmed his cause. So too did the fact that, at the highest level, the Army was lobbying heavily behind the scenes for its man to take the job. Unfortunately for Slater, he too was a particularly able and effective operator, General Sir Charles Guthrie.

Inevitably, the Navy felt aggrieved when Guthrie got the job. But some pointed out that it then left Admiral Slater in a strong position to promote the Navy's cause without reservation.

Jock Slater and the other chiefs of staff knew that the review was coming. It had, after all, been in the Labour Party's election manifesto. And, in his first encounter with George Robertson, he was very open in saying that he was going to spend a large part of the time from now arguing the case for new aircraft carriers.

The Navy's thinking now was to press for two much larger ships to replace the three Invincibles. Admiral Slater was uneasy about arguing a case for just two ships, but he knew that money would be limited, and the key was for the new generation of ships to be able to deliver a much bigger military punch than the Invincibles.

Officially, the programme was dubbed CVF by now, for Future Carrier. The First Sea Lord and the Defence Secretary would quickly come to refer to the two new ships, jokingly, as HMSs *Tony Blair* and *Gordon Brown*, after the Prime Minister and his powerful Chancellor of the Exchequer.

The question of the carriers would become the single biggest issue in the SDR. In fact, it had been looming for some time now. And, of course, it came with a huge amount of historical and political baggage.

It is also the case that there is just something about aircraft carriers that excites controversy. There is the cost of course. But they also make such a statement about a country and its aspirations in the defence field. With their great flat expanses of flight deck, the bigger ones at least are akin to floating islands; 'four-and-a-half acres of mobile real estate' as the Americans are wont to say of theirs, and very visible launching pads for a nation's firepower that can be stationed off another country's coast.

And, as instruments of war or even just of international leverage, aircraft carriers have become so closely associated with one nation, a superpower, the United States. Somehow, that fact would lend weight to the doubts of some about what Britain was doing even thinking of reviving such a capability. And the ships that were being proposed were certainly going to be a big leap back up in capability.

One thing that the Naval Staff had done early on was to commission a study of all the old papers from the CVA-01 debate, to try to learn the lessons from them. A difference between then and now was the strength of the Navy team this time. Slater had, as his first Assistant Chief of the Naval Staff, Jeremy Blackham. He would be succeeded by Jonathon Band. Between them, a key decision was taken that the Navy would have to enlist the RAF's support for the new ships. As Blackham put it, these had to be presented as 'the RAF's carriers', runways at sea that could take RAF aircraft. Jonathon Band became part of a small team, which was known as 'the quad', of two senior officers each from the Navy and the RAF, to thrash out a united approach to the problems that they faced.

The problem that the Navy faced was that, in the view of officers like Admiral Band, it had become too small to continue to run a separate fixed-wing air force supporting its Sea Harriers. Both of the services would also face a challenge supporting a new generation of aircraft. Between them, the four officers agreed to create a joint Harrier force, which would be a link to a new joint aircraft that could operate from a new generation of aircraft carriers. They also agreed that both land-based and maritime air power would underpin the emerging expeditionary strategy.

Clearly, Admiral Slater felt that the agreement was vital. He was uneasy that there was hostility to the carrier case among the top civil servants in the Ministry of Defence, and that the arguments of the Navy were not being properly communicated to the Defence Secretary. He told George Robertson so.

That was also the catalyst for a document produced in January 1998 that enshrined the agreement between the Royal Navy and the RAF, and was signed by Admiral Slater and the Chief of the Air Staff, Air Chief Marshal Sir

Richard Johns. The admiral would call it 'the historic paper', and it was meant to leave no room for argument.

As Jonathon Band put it, the two services would be trying to 'disprove history'. Of course, it had been tried before: the Navy gambit at the beginning of the 1960s of portraying its carriers as 'national assets'; and the proposed joint aircraft, the still-born P.1154. There were howls of protest from former Fleet Air Arm officers, and talk of 'a dirty deal' and 'a pact with the devil'. The First Sea Lord's response to the accusation that he had got into bed with the RAF and that nothing good would come of it, was simple: 'the RAF has got into bed with me'.

The other great argument was the price that the Navy would pay for the carriers in terms of destroyers, frigates, and submarines. And, again, the First Sea Lord was anxious that the civil servants had been working away behind the Navy's back.

The Navy's shrinking escort force had dwindled further. The figure of 'around forty' escorts at the time of 'Options for Change' was whittled down to thirty-five in another round of savings in 1994, which also saw the Navy lose its last four conventionally-powered submarines. Suddenly, Admiral Slater was presented with a proposal to cut the escort number to twenty-nine, for which he believed there was no rationale. He was very uncomfortable.

At the end of a long discussion with the Defence Secretary and his full team, George Robertson looked at the First Sea Lord and said, 'I'm going to give you three more'.

'You mean thirty-eight?' the admiral asked.

'No, I mean thirty-two,' replied Robertson.

'But that's three less,' retorted the First Sea Lord. 'Twenty-nine was never my figure.'[2]

But thirty-two it would be.

The losses for the Navy from the SDR would include three destroyers and frigates, two SSNs over time, and a clutch of smaller vessels. But Jock Slater felt that those were a price worth paying to get the carriers into the programme, preserve the new amphibious ships that he had previously fought for, and protect the overall nuclear programme. Another coup for the Navy was also the commitment to build twelve advanced new Type 45 air defence destroyers, the long overdue replacements for the increasingly antiquated Type 42s.

Maybe it was the strong advocacy of Jock Slater and his team, or the co-operation that seemed to exist between the services. Maybe it was the way that the Navy had positioned itself earlier in the 1990s, with its new doctrine and shift in focus. Maybe it was the inclination of the incoming government and the new team of defence ministers to embrace the arguments that were deployed. Whatever it was, there was much to the Naval Staff's liking in the tone and thrust of the SDR when the results emerged in July 1998. The First Sea Lord may have been uncomfortable about the numbers question. But the Navy seemed to be central to the new government's thinking on defence in a way that it had not seemed to be for as long as anyone could remember. There was no question in particular but that carriers were at the heart of the review.

In his introduction, George Robertson spoke of a changing and complex world of uncertainty and instability that posed real threats to Britain's security, a world in which 'we must be prepared to go to the crisis, rather than have the crisis come to us'.[3] Here was the justification for the expeditionary strategy that was now explicitly espoused, and which was further underpinned by the affirmation of policy based on values: 'The British are, by instinct, an internationalist people. We believe that as well as defending our rights, we should discharge our responsibilities in the world. We do not want to stand idly by and watch humanitarian disasters or the aggression of dictators go unchecked. We want to give a lead, we want to be a force for good.'

For better or worse, this was a hymn sheet for interventionism. What is more, the SDR argued that power projection was a role for which maritime forces were well suited. The elevation of 'defence diplomacy' to a mission in its own right also seemed to be tailor-made as much for maritime forces as any others. And recent experience had shown that aircraft carriers 'play a key part in peace support, coercion and combat'. Although she was not actually named, even the recent high-profile despatch of HMS *Invincible* to the Gulf was cited as evidence of 'a coercive presence which can contribute to conflict prevention'.[4]

The sceptics would quickly dismiss all this as another misguided attempt to perpetuate an inappropriate British self-image on the world stage, and a transparent effort by the new government to re-establish the Labour Party's credentials at home as 'sound' on defence. On balance, though, the SDR would win good reviews itself as a model of how to get to grips with the problems and questions facing defence establishments around the world. But that would not last. As with much else associated with the Blair years, the gap between the promise and the delivery of the promise would soon begin to show. And the carefully-crafted scenarios set out in the SDR of the kinds of operations that Britain would plan for in the future would also in the end be swept aside in the face of new realities, with huge consequences for the armed forces that would present a new challenge for the Royal Navy.

The confrontation with Iraq had quickly soured again during the summer. In mid December 1998, UN weapons inspectors were withdrawn, and Britain and the United States launched Operation Desert Fox, an intense air and missile campaign lasting three days, aimed at Saddam Hussein's suspected illegal weapons sites. There was much scepticism about the motives and effectiveness of the operation at the time, although it has subsequently been judged to have had a far more profound impact on the Iraqi leader than was then suspected.

None of the Navy's carriers was directly involved, but there was still a requirement to keep the pressure on Baghdad. So *Invincible* was on her way again. She set sail on 9 January. James Burnell-Nugent was still in charge.

Perhaps because of the prevailing mood at the time, and with a sense of history and a desire to capture his moment in charge of one of the Royal Navy's big ships in a special way, he did something quite unusual for what were the dying days of the twentieth century. As the ship stored for possible hostilities, he decided to have his portrait painted. It was a novel experience for *Invincible's* crew members, being told that the captain could not be disturbed because he was sitting for his portrait.

There were no delays this time and *Invincible* arrived in the Gulf at the end of January. There would be no actual bombing missions. But the ship's aircraft supported the much bigger presence of the US Navy aircraft carrier *George Washington* in some aggressive policing of the no-fly zone over southern Iraq, to send a message.

Invincible spent more than two months on Gulf operations. But, as the weeks passed, and the Gulf summer began to loom, the pilots and maintainers began to confront one of the crucial limitations of their aircraft and the Navy's existing carrier capabilities. The planes, designed to wage war for NATO in the temperate or cold skies of northern Europe, began to struggle in the thinner, hotter air of the Gulf as the seasons changed.

In early April, *Invincible* departed the Gulf. But it was not to be a simple passage home. By now, in those European skies, NATO was in fact waging a full-scale air campaign over the breakaway Serbian province of Kosovo. *Invincible* was ordered to divert to the Ionian Sea to bolster the fighter cover for the NATO bombing missions with her Sea Harriers. The aircraft and pilots would mount long sorties, flying at night, to maintain their part of the overall fighter umbrella.

As the size of the NATO air armada continued to mount, *Invincible's* small contribution was no longer necessary. But, as she set a course for Portsmouth, Captain Burnell-Nugent reflected on the story of his year-and-a-half in command. He saw it as an object lesson, in a new and unpredictable strategic environment, in the mobility and adaptability of maritime power, and especially of that part of it which is embodied in the aircraft carrier. Twice now in the Gulf, *Invincible* had acted as a political messenger, a deterrent, and a military enforcer. Within days of leaving the Gulf for the second time, she was an integral part of another military operation in another theatre.

Kosovo would see another important milestone for the Royal Navy, and for Britain's armed forces. HMS *Splendid* would become the first British nuclear-powered submarine to launch Tomahawk cruise missiles in action. It was another significant string to the Navy's bow. For the Royal Navy, it brought closer to realization the enormous potential of these vessels, in which it had invested huge sums and efforts. But it was also ammunition for those who saw nuclear-powered submarines armed with such weapons as an alternative to aircraft carriers as a way of projecting maritime power from the sea to the land.

Invincible had shared duties in the Gulf with her sister ship, HMS *Illustrious*. And, as *Invincible* now disappeared into dockyard hands for another facelift that would see her changed significantly again, *Illustrious* was preparing to take up the challenge and the story in yet another theatre.

Illustrious had already had her latest facelift, which might more appropriately be described as a nose job. Up until now, throughout the lives of these ships, one prominent reminder of the fact that they had started out as hybrids – part cruiser, part carrier – had been the bulky Sea Dart missile system that had been planted so very obviously in the bows, at the forward end of the flight deck.

Even as they were being built, and the first inklings appeared that the balance of their employment would be shifting, designers looked at removing the system. Then, with the focus still on the prospects of a hot war with the massed ranks of Soviet forces, and with the value of the Sea Harrier still uncertain, it was decided that it would be too high an air defence price to pay for the possibility of a small increase in aircraft capability. Now, in the post-Cold-War world, the balance of the argument had changed. *Illustrious* lost her Sea Dart, gained a full-length flight deck to aid air operations, and the magazine space for the missiles was taken up with stowage for aircraft ordnance, to help with what had remained one of the key weaknesses of the ships. *Invincible* was the next to receive the same treatment, and finally *Ark Royal*.

At the beginning of May 2000, *Illustrious* was testing her new facilities in NATO exercises in the Bay of Biscay. In command now was Captain Mark Stanhope, who had taken over just as the modifications to the ship were being completed. For Stanhope, those changes were a critical moment in the evolution of these ships towards the principle role of delivering carrier air power. It was a small change on the face of it, but would make a considerable difference to the way that the ships could operate.

Suddenly, the former British colonial possession of Sierra Leone, on the West African coast, leapt into the consciousness of everyone aboard. The country had been scarred by civil war for most of the 1990s. With UN peacekeepers and the capital, Freetown, seemingly about to be overrun by rebels, the British government had rushed a military force to secure the airport, initially to evacuate civilians. But the operation quickly became more than that – an attempt to use a limited but capable force to try to restore an element of political stability.

Illustrious was the flagship for the NATO exercise, with a mixed force of Sea Harriers and RAF Harriers aboard. But suddenly Captain Stanhope received a call from London asking for an assessment within two hours of whether the ship could deploy jets from where she was over the jungle of Sierra Leone in a show of force. The squadrons quickly did their calculations. It would need a lot of tanker support. There were other technical issues. But it was feasible.

The conclusion was that such an operation was not needed quite so urgently. However, it was decided to withdraw *Illustrious* from the exercise. Captain Stanhope was told to head for Sierra Leone, in the time-honoured phrase, 'with all despatch'. Thus *Illustrious* found herself hurrying south to support the intervention. She steamed 2,500 miles in five days. Having not long completed a full tour of duty in the Gulf, it seemed to be another demonstration of how maritime power, and an aircraft carrier in particular, could swing from one role and mission in one part of the world to another in a relatively short time with the minimum of outside assistance. Eventually the naval group off Sierra Leone would comprise *Illustrious*, the helicopter carrier HMS *Ocean,* three frigates, and supporting RFAs. *Illustrious'* aircraft would conduct a number of patrols to back up the mission. Under the skilful command of Brigadier David Richards ashore, this classic piece of brushfire intervention would have a telling impact on the ground.

It had been a remarkable flurry of activity in the last few years, a level and tempo of operations that was unlike anything that the last couple of decades of the Cold War had seen. There had been the Gulf War, the US debacle in Somalia, the Balkans, Kosovo, and Sierra Leone. This was the context of the SDR, when the unusual and unexpected seemed to be becoming the norm, and the impetus to do something was actually translated into action. But Sierra Leone would come to be seen as the high-point of Blair-style interventionism. Things would quickly get a lot more difficult.

CHAPTER 14

Another Twist

James Burnell-Nugent, now a rear admiral, was sitting in the departure lounge at Heathrow airport, watching the television screens in growing disbelief at the unfolding events in New York and Washington. It was early afternoon, UK time, on 11 September 2001.

Burnell-Nugent had been due to fly out to the United States. It was soon clear that was not going happen. So he decided that the best thing for him to do was to rejoin his flagship, HMS *Illustrious*, then alongside at Malta, but en route to a huge exercise, Saif Sareea, off Oman.

He found a flight for later that evening, had his kit rushed up from Portsmouth, and finally touched down in Malta around midnight. With her alert state raised, *Illustrious* sailed the following morning, as the British government, the chiefs of staff, and Admiral Burnell-Nugent worked out what to do.

It was quickly decided that, while the United States began to weigh its options, the British forces would go ahead with the Oman exercise, not least as a political signal of steadfastness with a critical British ally in a strategic part of the world at an important moment. It would, in any event, be useful training for what might ensue.

But, as *Illustrious* arrived off Oman, it was also an enormously twitchy time for the admiral, his staff, and all those involved in the exercise. Everyone was digesting the implications of what had just happened. And, as well as having to cope with the mock attacks that the exercise would throw up, the whole force was also on guard for the possibility of real suicide attacks from the air, or from dhows sailing in amongst the warships of the assembled naval task group.

And then things got even more complicated. The United States had determined that it would attack Afghanistan, where the Al-Qaeda organization and its leader, Osama Bin Laden, had sanctuary from the Taleban government. A campaign plan to attack Afghanistan was taking shape, and it was clear that elements of the British task group in the exercise would be needed. The two nuclear-powered submarines involved, which were armed with cruise missiles, were quietly spirited away to join a third that had been rushed to the area, and they would participate in the first wave of attacks on Afghan targets. In fact, they would be the only actual strike elements that Britain would contribute to the opening shots in the campaign on 7 October.

The remoteness of Afghanistan meant that the only other public assets that Britain could bring to bear at this stage, albeit that they were valuable in their own way, were some air-to-air tankers and surveillance and reconnaissance aircraft. Here, much more than the Adriatic, and more even than in the Gulf with its sensitive host nations, was a situation where, for Britain to make a real impact at the outset of a coalition operation, nothing but a full-size carrier with real reach and punch would have done. Indeed, for the entire assembled coalition, the initial phase of the operation was predominantly a maritime one.

But the British, and especially the Royal Navy, were still busily trying to work out what else they could do with what they had. As the opening shots in the Afghanistan campaign were fired, and exercise Saif Sareea was moving to its close, speculation mounted in London over what forces from the war games might be switched to the real conflict.

On 26 October, the government announced its decision. *Illustrious* would be re-equipped as a helicopter carrier, the assault ship *Fearless* would also be redeployed with 200 Royal Marines aboard, and the task force for the operation would be completed by a destroyer, a frigate, a continuing submarine presence, and no less than seven RFAs.

James Burnell-Nugent and his personnel, and especially *Illustrious'* commanding officer, Charles Style, had a tense set of conflicting pressures. They had to remain committed to the exercise right to the end, in order not to upset relations with their Omani hosts. But, at the same time, they had to convert *Illustrious* into a helicopter carrier. It was something that had been practised before, but not so far from home. And, to add to the challenge, she would be fitted out to operate Special Forces. So her squadrons and their equipment, stores, and personnel had to be disembarked, and then a force of huge twin-rotor RAF Chinook helicopters, and a whole outfit of Special Forces gear and vehicles, had quietly to be brought aboard.

As Saif Sareea reached its climax, the task force commander had a discreet meeting in the desert with the British Chief of the Defence Staff, Admiral Sir Michael Boyce, and the head of US Central Command, General Tommy Franks, in overall charge of US forces in the region for the Afghan operation. They discussed making Admiral Burnell-Nugent the deputy commander of coalition maritime forces, based in Bahrain.

The admiral duly headed for the Gulf state, but had to spend nearly two weeks mainly sitting in a hotel and keeping in touch with his forces by mobile phone, until the diplomatic hurdles could be overcome and his appointment confirmed. His flagship was in radio silence conducting Special Forces operations off the coast of Pakistan, a section of his staff were still in Oman, and the rest were with him in Bahrain. The approval actually arrived in late November. For the first time since the withdrawal from East of Suez thirty years before, a regional command role for a British admiral was re-established in the Gulf. Admittedly, it would be part of a coalition. But the arrangement would endure, to reflect the increased instability and renewed strategic interest in the region.

The admiral would remain until March, when he handed over to Major General Robert Fry of the Royal Marines. *Illustrious*, too, handed over her role to the helicopter carrier HMS *Ocean*, which would help launch a Royal Marine contingent into Afghanistan.

Within a year, the final showdown with Saddam Hussein was reaching its climax. In the aftermath of the 11 September attacks, the Bush administration had made a decision that the confrontation with the Iraqi leader could not carry on as before. Tony Blair, through a combination of separate conviction and a wish to stay close to and be supportive of the United States, decided to commit British forces to a US mobilization that seemed to be leading inevitably towards another war.

The British build-up would include a significant naval contingent built around HMS *Ark Royal* and HMS *Ocean*, both of them operating essentially in a Commando or helicopter carrier role. For the commanding officer of *Ark Royal*, Captain Alan Massey, it was yet another example of how much times had changed while he had been in the Navy.

Massey had served before in *Ark Royal*, as a warfare officer, in the late 1980s, in what were the dying days of the Cold War, although they did not know it at the time. Then, the emphasis remained very much on anti-submarine warfare. Even when *Ark Royal* had led one of the Far East deployments at the time, all the way out to Australia, it was with that mindset still in place, and an air group of just a handful of Sea Harriers, a clutch of Sea King AEW helicopters, and a squadron of anti-submarine Sea Kings. Massey had taken over from Charles Style as commanding officer of *Illustrious* in the Indian Ocean earlier in the year. Now, again, *Ark Royal*, under his command, was gearing up for another role that would not involve having any fixed-wing aircraft aboard at all. But for Massey this merely underlined the flexibility of these ships.

Unlike in 1991, *Ark Royal* would make it all the way to the Gulf. And Britain's maritime forces there would play a significant part in the early stages of the US-led invasion, both in deploying personnel into southern Iraq and especially keep them supplied. The first conventional coalition forces to arrive on Iraqi soil at the start of the conflict were Royal Marines flying from the deck of *Ark Royal*. And the British Army had to rely on stocks from the Royal Marines to keep its own advance going. But the British naval contingent, despite its scale, would not be a balanced force, with its own organic air power aboard a carrier.

So, in the cases of both Afghanistan and Iraq, Royal Navy forces had played a significant part in the early stages of the campaigns, projecting power ashore in different forms. Much more telling, though, was how both the Afghanistan and Iraq campaigns then unfolded. In each, as the main naval task forces dispersed after the overwhelming and rapid success of the initial assaults, the two conflicts would descend into long, drawn-out, costly, and debilitating campaigns of occupation and counter-insurgency. And this would have a profound impact on the notion and political support for interventionism, and the call on defence resources. And it would renew the debate over the shape and purpose of the armed forces that would be needed in the future.

In early 2002, Jock Slater, now in retirement, would receive some unwelcome news. As the first real hints of a new funding crisis emerged, it was announced that the Royal Navy had decided to retire its remaining Sea Harriers early, in 2006. The Sea Harriers had been a vital part of the carefully-crafted agreement that he and those around him had reached with the RAF, as a bridge to a new generation of aircraft and the new carriers. But that element of it had survived less than three years.

The Sea Harrier had been designed to operate in the NATO area, but the likely environments in which it would be asked to perform now were going to be much hotter than that, literally. It would struggle to cope without an engine upgrade that would cost at least 150 million pounds. The Navy had not made proper provision for it, and it was decided that it would be too expensive. It would take a chance with its air defence until the new generation aircraft and the new Type 45 destroyers arrived. Only the RAF's version of the Harrier, the bomber, would be available. That strike capability was the real priority now. But that would not stop the protests from Sea Harrier champions like Sharkey Ward, who argued that the plane's advanced radar and missiles made it the best fighter in Europe. Jock Slater would see the move as a 'mammoth risk'.

But there was more. The Treasury's continued tight financial control, and the already mounting cost of the operation in Iraq, forced another 'mini-review' in July 2004 that made more inroads into the Royal Navy's forces than the SDR itself. The Navy would lose six more destroyers and frigates and two more nuclear-powered submarines. And the Type 45 programme would be cut by a third. So now there would be just twenty-five destroyers and frigates altogether.

The First Sea Lord, by now, was Admiral Sir Alan West. He would complain publicly about 'piling risk on risk' with this round of cuts, and declare that commitments would have to be re-thought. He would face criticism himself from inside the Navy, and among the retired naval officer community, for not making more of an issue of the reductions. The realization now of just how small the Navy was getting in terms of numbers would start to reignite real concerns about what the future held. Talk of tipping points, of the Navy falling below its 'critical mass' would start to gain wider currency. The carriers may be the key in the Navy Board's thinking, but they also needed to be part of a package to be effective, and would there be enough destroyers and frigates to protect them and carry out all the other tasks that the Navy was supposed to perform?

And what was the news on the carriers themselves? The SDR had spoken of two new ships, much bigger than the Invincibles, of 30,000 to 40,000 tons, able to carry about fifty aircraft. That was certainly going to be a big leap for the Navy. But it seems that the figures did not add up.

At the beginning of 2003, the winning design for the new ships was revealed – produced by a British design team working for the French defence company Thales. It was, in many respects, a rather conventional design. It was like a scaled-down version of the US Navy's ships, with big, blocky overhangs on each side, and two aircraft lifts on the edge of the flight deck. Indeed, the winning design team had been at pains to consult the chief designer of the US Nimitz-class aircraft carriers, Herbert Meier. The Nimitz class was the backbone of the US fleet, the largest and most powerful warships ever built, capable of carrying about seventy-five of the most modern aircraft. Ten of these nuclear-powered ships were built from 1970 onwards. Apart from the nuclear deterrents of the two superpowers, they were the most significant weapons of war of the modern era. Of course, the team also went in search of the drawings from the last full-scale British carrier design, the CVA-01, to learn what it could from those too. The designers found them, almost forgotten, in a remote annex of the National Maritime Museum in Woolwich.

The one big novelty of the new British design was that it incorporated not one but two island superstructures on the starboard side. What was even more striking than that, though, was that the ships were now being described as weighing 68,000 tons. The overall length was 292 metres (958 feet), the engines were four powerful new gas turbines, and the vessels would be able to carry a maximum of forty-eight aircraft. The design also incorporated huge amounts of automation, and very elaborate communications and electronics, including the hugely advanced Sampson multi-function radar – the great grandson, perhaps, of the Type 984 3-D radar that had equipped the Navy's most modern carriers in the 1960s.

So the design, in true Navy tradition, had ballooned substantially. But, whereas Louis Rydill had struggled to work within what he regarded as an absurd artificial weight limit on CVA-01, the designers of CVF had not felt the same constraints. The real issue was the cost. Unfortunately for the design team, that soon became a problem anyway.

It quickly became clear that the shipyards were not going to be able to build the ships within the planned budget. The chief designer, Simon Knight, was in his office in Bath when he received a worried call from his boss. There would have to be a major re-design. Within a week, Knight and his team produced the outlines of a much-modified vessel.

Compared to the original design, Alpha, the new one, Bravo, was chopped down by twenty-seven metres (eighty-nine feet). Out went one entire deck, and much of the radar, electronic, and automation equipment. Two of the gas turbines were replaced by cheaper diesels. The maximum number of aircraft was cut to forty.

However, now the Navy was not happy. The ship did not meet its requirements. It took until the end of 2003 to produce a compromise design, the Delta. The ship grew again, to 282 metres (925 feet), and 65,000 tons. But the maximum aircraft numbers were kept at forty, and the electronics and other systems remained much simpler than before. The struggle over costs would continue. There would be a further major re-think in 2005. But the basic design would remain largely unaltered. And, crucially, it would be adaptable, with a Ski-jump planned initially, but also spaces and compartments below the flight deck and elsewhere in the hull so that catapults and arrester wires could be incorporated relatively easily and cheaply if the plans and requirements changed over what could be a fifty-year life for the ships themselves.

And the new ships would certainly still be vast in scale, the longest, largest, and most expensive vessels ever built for the Royal Navy. It had been Jock Slater, while he was still First Sea Lord, who had pressed early on to give the ships names. He felt it would help their chances of survival in the internal battles in Whitehall, although they were announced publicly only in late 2003.

The first was to be called *Queen Elizabeth*, the second *Prince Of Wales*. Both were great names in the Royal Navy's history. But both, in different ways, had rather unfortunate associations with the story of carrier aviation.

There had previously been only one HMS *Queen Elizabeth*, the first of a class of super-dreadnoughts laid down at Portsmouth Dockyard on Trafalgar Day, 1912. She would serve as a flagship for most of her thirty-year career.

Although it was never announced publicly, *Queen Elizabeth* had also been the name allocated for CVA-01. And maybe its choice for CVF-01 was meant to signify that, as far as the Navy was concerned, this was the righting of a historic wrong. Whether it would prove to be a wise choice was another matter.

There had been seven ships named *Prince Of Wales*. And, of course, the latest had been so wastefully sacrificed when she was sunk along with HMS *Repulse* by Japanese aircraft on 10 December 1941, at least in part for want of carrier air cover.

When the SDR was published, it was not known for sure what new type of aircraft the new carriers would operate. But people had a pretty good idea. Britain had already signed up as a research partner for the new US project for a multi-role aircraft for the US Navy, the Marines Corps, and the US Air Force. The project was known as the Joint Strike Fighter (JSF). There would be three versions – for conventional land operations, conventional carrier operations, and a short take-off and vertical landing (STOVL) version, principally for the US Marines.

For the British, the project would offer the tempting prospect of access into the world of stealth aircraft, and a host of other associated new technology that would amount to the leap of a generation over even the new RAF Eurofighter. But the price would be high – up to ten billion pounds for a share of the development costs and the purchase of up to 150 aircraft for both the Royal Navy and the RAF. In Britain, after various incarnations, the programme became known as the Joint Combat Aircraft (JCA).

At the beginning of 2001, the JSF was duly chosen by the British, but not which variant. However, just over eighteen months later, in September 2003, the government also announced that it had chosen the STOVL variant of the plane.

It was and would remain a controversial choice. Many in the Navy argued that it was not necessary to make a decision on which version of the JSF to go for at that stage anyway. The STOVL plane had advantages for the Navy. It was a generation since it had operated conventional aircraft at sea, with catapults and arrester wires. STOVL would be less of a challenge, closer to the recent experience of flying the Sea Harrier. It would mean more flexibility. And it would make the proposed new carriers cheaper, precisely because there would be none of the complicated equipment associated with conventional carrier operations.

But even among Sea Harrier pilots in the Fleet Air Arm, heads were shaking. Why, when Britain was building full-size aircraft carriers for the first time in half a century, not take advantage of that? The new ships would be more expensive with catapults and arrester gear. But the STOVL JSF would be more complicated and expensive to maintain throughout its life than the conventional versions. And the STOVL JSF sacrificed fuel and weapons payload to make room for an extra engine for vertical landings. The British JSF, which would be the country's principal strike aircraft of the future, would not fly as far or carry as many weapons as most of the other JSFs that would be flying in numerous air forces around the world. It did not help that, by 2004, the STOVL version of the JSF was beginning to suffer serious weight problems in its development that would call into question its performance.

Meanwhile, HMS *Invincible* was clearly entering the twilight of her career. In February 2003, just as key decisions were being made about her successors, she emerged from a refit for what would be her last commission. It had been expected that she would leave service in 2010. In fact, her remaining active life would be much shorter than that. It had been decided that she would, in effect, go into a reserve – officially a low state of readiness – in late 2005. Essentially, in the current circumstances, the Royal Navy could not afford to continue to run and crew her, or indeed maintain enough aircraft to keep another air group going. She had already served longer than the previous *Ark Royal*, the Navy's last strike carrier, to which the term 'venerable' had been attached for what seemed like the majority of her last years of service.

One difference between the two ships was that the old *Ark Royal* had not been kept fully up-to-date with the changes in technology that had been going on around her. Money had been spent to make sure that she could operate the latest aircraft, but on not much else. She really did feel, look, and perform by the end like an old ship out of her time.

Invincible had been worked hard, and in some ways it showed. She had had a very workmanlike air about her throughout her career. In contrast, the new *Ark Royal*, perhaps in part because of her name, had always seemed a bit grander, more elitist, and frankly tidier.

But all the Invincibles had been treated to numerous extensive refits as the world changed around them and the requirements being asked of them also changed. It was a testament to the vision of the original designers that they could absorb so many of the alterations that were made, which had allowed the Navy to get as much as it had out of them. But it had been an enormously expensive business, costing hundreds of millions of pounds altogether, and certainly more than the original price of building the ships.

Invincible would miss out on the Afghanistan and Iraq campaigns. But in another long naval tradition for retiring major warships, she was given a juicy programme of final deployments and exercises. There was a trip to the east coast of the United States in the summer of 2004, including New York harbour for the Fourth of July and a berth quite literally in the shadow of the giant new Cunarder, *Queen Mary 2*. Then there were exercises in the Mediterranean.

The ship's last real operational hurrah began with a departure from Portsmouth on 17 January 2005. Her destination was the waters off Oman and an exercise codenamed Magic Carpet. It was the last opportunity for the ship herself to prove that, finally, she was as equipped as she would ever be to perform the traditional roles of the strike carrier. Her aircraft – a 'tailored' air group in the emerging jargon, to drive home the message of flexibility – would comprise seven Sea Harriers, eight RAF Harrier GR7s, three Sea King AEW helicopters, and another Sea King for other duties, like search and rescue. So, nineteen aircraft in all, including fifteen jets, which would pound the ranges in Oman with the latest satellite-guided bombs -- not bad for a vessel with much more modest origins.

But *Invincible* had one last appointment in the public eye. On 28 June 2005, she took pride of place at the head of an international fleet review at Spithead to mark the 200th anniversary of the Battle of Trafalgar. Of course, there had long been foreign visitors at previous fleet reviews. But, for some, the very international flavour of this one helped mask the fact that the Royal Navy, by itself, did not any longer have enough ships to fill the Solent. Some would also highlight the fact that the Navy had only the third largest warship on view in the assembly.

It was certainly quite a hullabaloo, and attracted much attention. Whether it did anything more than remind people of a glorious past, rather than reconnect the Navy with society as a whole, and with the present and future, is another matter. It all seemed rather self-congratulatory and a little at odds with the emerging grimness of the news from the deserts of Iraq and Afghanistan.

There were lessons, of course, from Trafalgar, inevitably interpreted now through the lens of expeditionary warfare. So it was not just that it had banished the threat of invasion from the British Isles. It was what came after. By cementing Britain's control of the seas, it had enabled the Duke of Wellington to pursue and harass Napoleon's forces on land. The Navy's ability to influence where and how the Army could operate, and how effectively, and thus to influence events on land, was a message that the Naval Staff was clearly anxious to drive home.

Invincible herself was now in to her last days of active service. A clutch of port visits around the United Kingdom and then, on 1 August, twenty-five years and a couple of weeks after that first arrival, a final entry into Portsmouth and the ceremonial of paying off into reserve.

The ship had begun to take shape on the drawing boards at Bath in an age when the Navy was still issuing the tot, when Singapore was still a major British base, humankind had still to set foot on the moon, Margaret Thatcher had yet to be appointed to her first Cabinet job, and the first pocket calculator had yet to appear. She was ordered and her keel laid in the year that Britain joined the European Economic Community, as it was then known. Richard Nixon was still in the White House. Now she was leaving active service in a time when women and the internet were established at sea in Royal Navy warships.

Short of a cataclysmic event, *Invincible* would not sail again under the White Ensign. She would be stripped of much of her equipment, and become an empty grey metal shell in amongst the jumble of the dockyard, almost unnoticed by the multitudes of passengers sailing past aboard the conveyor belt of car ferries which daily docked and undocked barely a stone's throw from where she silently lay.

CHAPTER 15

After *Invincible*

One era was now drawing to a close. Another, the Navy desperately hoped, was opening up. The strains had been showing for some time now in the SDR formula, although it had seemed for many to have been a perfectly plausible blueprint for the future shape of the British armed forces. They would be exacerbated by the growing tyranny of another 'central front', not NATO's from the Cold War, but what President George W Bush was calling 'the central front in the global war on terror', Iraq and Afghanistan.

The entanglements that were developing in both these countries, their descent into bloody insurgencies requiring large garrisons of ground troops facing determined opponents for an indeterminate length of time, were attracting as much anger and anguish from the critics as ever the anti-nuclear campaigners heaped on NATO strategy even in the darkest days of the Cold War. In this atmosphere, the armed forces were becoming both victims and accomplices, believing that they were being starved of the resources that they felt they needed effectively to accomplish their missions, and yet apparently willing and even eager to endorse the interventionist, expeditionary credo.

In the aftermath of the 11 September attacks, the government looked again at the assumptions of its Strategic Defence Review. The 'New Chapter' that emerged in July 2002 concluded that, with some adjustments, the thrust of the original review's conclusions were correct. Somehow, it did not quite feel that way.

The interventionism of Tony Blair had come up against its sternest test in Iraq and Afghanistan. For some, the quagmire into which the United States and Britain had been sucked exposed the true cost of such a policy, in lives and money, or 'blood and treasure', a phrase that seemed to gain currency and which at once seemed to heighten the morality and yet somehow also negate the reality of what was happening.

The public hostility in Britain to the Iraq adventure appeared to call into question the existence of any real consensus about the kind of internationalist, value-based foreign policy that the Prime Minister had espoused. Was this the latest example of delusional folly that had plagued the British establishment throughout most of the twentieth century, and which was now spilling over into the twenty-first? Was it just that hubris had misled both George W Bush and Tony Blair into picking the wrong fight for the wrong reasons at the wrong time? Or was it neither, but rather just a terrible lapse in concentration and planning, which meant that no-one had paid attention to the necessary details of what was being contemplated, so that the execution – whatever its rationale and ultimate outcome – would prove to be vastly more expensive and protracted than needed to have been the case.

Compounding the controversy was the growing drumbeat of public outrage not only at the consequences of these interventions for Iraq and Afghanistan, but also over the predicament of service personnel apparently being asked to fight and die in foreign lands with woefully inadequate equipment and support. And, with the Army inevitably the centre of attention, the admittedly expensive plans and hopes of the Naval and Air Staffs started to be portrayed as part of the problem, when – from their perspectives – they were really part of the long-term solution.

The potency and immediacy of the Army's situation and complaints would be hard to deny – from the lack of body armour and helicopters to the inadequacies of the medical care and soldiers' housing at home. If there was a spending crisis in the Ministry of Defence, surely the right way to deal with it would be to fund the Army properly by cutting the profligate spending on expensive and out-of-control warship and aircraft programmes.

The government talked of sustained increases in defence spending, of emergency provisions for urgent battlefield needs. The services would mutter behind the scenes about spending commitments implied that were never realized. A leader in the *Financial Times* would complain that 'the government's ambitions are out of line with its defence budget'.[1]

It had, of course, been thus for decades. And extra spending was not the answer, some would say, when defence inflation would gobble it up in a few years. But was not the logic of that, then, perpetual under-funding? Not, perhaps, if the real culprits were bureaucratic inefficiencies and massively wasteful mismanagement of the biggest weapons programmes.

And thus the debate, such as it was, circulated. It may not have been either unreasonable or unrealistic to suggest that a country of Britain's wealth, at a time of conflict, might be willing and able to consider spending more on defence. But it was equally true that the other potential calls on government money remained just as unremitting, since Britain was hardly the envy of the world in terms of its creaking infrastructure, health system, and education. British defence spending as a proportion of national income had descended to a level not seen since the 1930s. But was it not also higher still than all its European neighbours? And, if Britain was at war, were these not conflicts of choice rather than direct threats?

Defence, like everything else, had to fight for its place in the arena of government priorities. And a few complaining admirals, generals, and air chief marshals could still make easy targets, a blimpish clique that was merely fighting for its expensive toys and which ultimately sticks together to make sure that none of its number really loses out. If there was to be more money devoted to security, then would it not be better to give it to the police or the intelligence services, to deal with the most tangible threats to the lives of ordinary people, like that of bombs on the public transport system? And the fact was that, even at what seemed like a time of particular trauma in different ways for all the services, none of the mainstream political parties in Britain appeared willing to commit to yet more defence spending. Even if there were to be meaningfully more money for defence, it would seem perverse to most people if the lion's share of it were to go to the Navy in the circumstances.

So where did that all leave the Naval Staff? It was facing perhaps its greatest challenge in half a century. There was the mouth-watering prospect of two new aircraft carriers the like of which the Royal Navy had never seen before, that would lift it back into a different league of capability and clout. And yet these ships remained frustratingly elusive. On top of that, there was the mounting discontent and unease within the service and without, among retired sailors and interested parties, at what was happening to the Fleet in the meantime, and whether the price being paid for the promise of the carriers was getting too high, even assuming they ever appeared. It was not that there had not been lean times before, and periods when the condition of the ships putting to sea was not what it should have been. But now the numbers were getting so low, and the gaps so wide, that there was a question about whether there was any way back. It was the fact that the 'silent service' seemed almost invisible as well.

The year 2007 was to be both tantalising and difficult for the Navy. It was less than two weeks old when the Prime Minister, Tony Blair, as part of a valedictory tour, alighted confidently on the deck of one of the Navy's newest and most substantial warships, the amphibious assault ship HMS *Albion*, alongside in Devonport, to deliver some parting thoughts on the subject of defence.

There was plenty of symbolism here. The fact that the Navy had been chosen as the host for this parting Blair shot. The name *Albion*, echoing with all sorts of overtones. And a vessel that was at the heart of the expeditionary capability that the Blair government was supposedly bequeathing to the nation.

Unpopular but unrepentant in terms of his basic world view, Blair argued that Britain had a choice to make as to whether it would continue to invest in the ability to carry out real war-fighting interventionism, or settle for a lighter shade of peacekeeping, as other similar countries had done. But actually, he argued, there was no real choice between 'hard' and 'soft' power. The two went hand in hand. Indeed, anything less was really 'passive disengagement'. But, if the country was to remain engaged, there would have to be new commitments, including resources.

To the assembled audience in the cavernous 'garage' for military vehicles and landing craft that makes up so much of HMS *Albion*'s interior, it might all have sounded a little ironic. Here was a man, nearly ten years in office, but with only a few months left in the job, who had committed British service personnel to more combat than any prime minister since Churchill, now apparently suggesting that more money needed to be spent on defence, when it would be up to somebody else to settle the bill.

Maybe the outgoing Prime Minister's difficulty was that it had always been up to somebody else to settle the bill. The services were certainly anticipating with some trepidation the presumptive new occupant of 10 Downing Street, the current 'Iron Chancellor', Gordon Brown, supposedly no great friend or supporter of the armed forces.

The strains on defence had already seen cracks begin to appear in the normal reticence of the serving chiefs to complain publicly. The new Chief of the General Staff, Sir Richard Dannatt, had talked of the Army 'running hot', and appeared to question the benefits of the continuing British presence in Iraq. Just a few weeks after Blair had stood upon HMS *Albion*, the new First Sea Lord, Admiral Sir Jonathon Band, weighed in. If the government was not careful, he seemed to be saying, the Navy faced relegation to a lower division in maritime affairs, perhaps alongside Belgium, by implication an appalling thought. The two new carriers were essential for the future, and extra funding to ensure that the Navy could continue to do its assigned job.

But then, just a few weeks after that, the Royal Navy, so long preoccupied with its lack of public visibility, got the kind of attention it could have done without. It had just taken over the command of the multinational maritime security effort in the northern Gulf, what it saw as an overlooked part of the effort to help rebuild Iraq and the stability of the region. As flagship, it had deployed the frigate HMS *Cornwall*, one of the war replacements ordered following the ship losses in the Falklands, and one of the Navy's most heavily-armed and impressive-looking ships, well able to look after herself in any conventional maritime confrontation. But not, it seemed, on this occasion.

It was a little after nine o'clock on the morning of Friday, 23 March, when it became obvious on the bridge of HMS *Cornwall* that something was wrong. The ship had lost contact with its boarding party of fifteen sailors and Royal Marines, which had gone to inspect a vessel a few miles away. They had been surrounded and captured by members of Iran's Revolutionary Guards. The mood aboard *Cornwall* was immediately tense, anxious, and reflective. Those in command knew straightaway that this was a major problem.

And so it was. There followed a fortnight of diplomatic stand-off, paraded captives, claims and counter-claims and exchanges of political outrage. Britain's allies in the Gulf and beyond would shake their heads, and ask how it had handed Iran a propaganda coup that would surely only embolden its leaders in the unstable and potentially combustible regional power-play under way in the Gulf. For the Navy, it only got worse when the captives were returned to the United Kingdom, and a furore erupted over the sale of stories to the media.

Rightly or wrongly, the impression was left of a navy apparently out of touch with the tense and treacherous nature of modern confrontation. The Navy had become soft and slow-witted while the Army had become battle-hardened through bitter and deadly experience. The contrast could not have been sharper. Retired naval officers would loyally stand by the service in public, but privately bemoan a boarding party that looked more like a beach party. In the media, the Army's lobbyists would be quick to make political capital. It was certainly an embarrassment for a service whose mantra for so long had been 'expect the unexpected', that saw itself as ideally placed through experience, tradition, and training to deal with the complexities and unpredictability of the modern world.

The First Sea Lord would acknowledge that it was 'a very, very embarrassing incident', and that it was badly handled in terms of the media, but would insist that it would not have a long-term effect. 'The fact is Royal Naval boarding parties should not be taken by enemies or non-enemies, and of course this was a non-enemy',[2] he insisted, since Britain was not at war with Iran, although relations were strained. It was 'a professional wake-up call,' the admiral said. The Navy had used it 'rigorously' to refocus its preparations for operations.

It would certainly need to do so, since the operation that HMS *Cornwall* was engaged in at the time was one of the primary functions that the Navy saw for itself in this new post-post-Cold-War world, and a large part of what the real story of the Navy down the ages had been. Big battle fleets and decisive actions at sea were one thing. They were all well and good, and crucial in their way, and neither the Navy nor the country could have done without everything that flowed from the supremacy of their ships of the line. But the part played by lonely and distant frigates or cruisers, policing the sinews of empire and keeping the sea lanes safe and secure, was what mattered day-in, day-out. Now these were the sinews of a globalized world in which Britain had proportionally as big a stake as any country.

If the *Cornwall* incident hardly helped the Navy's cause in the short term, it may at least also have been a reminder that there were dangerous and unpredictable waters out there, and that there were risks to be run in not paying attention to the sea and the Navy. As for the Navy itself, human nature is such that everyone and every institution occasionally needs a dose of shock treatment to sharpen the senses and reflexes, and maybe jog the memory, individual and collective, as well. The affair should really be a one-off.

But perhaps what sharpened some of the Navy's sensitivities at this time was that the *Cornwall* incident occurred just as the country was preparing to mark the twenty-fifth anniversary of its great triumph in the Falklands. The anniversary was also prompting the Navy's ministerial nemesis from that period, John Nott, now Sir John, to think about defence and the Royal Navy in a way that he had not for years. He had left active politics at the 1983 general election. But his views about the Royal Navy's ambitions had, if anything, become even more pointed.

At least back in the early 1980s, Sir John had conceded that there was a limited role for ships like HMS *Invincible* for operations beyond the NATO area. But these new carriers that the Navy wanted were just too much, especially as he was a sceptic about the whole policy on which the case for them was founded. Expeditionary warfare he saw as an invention to justify the retention of capabilities and equipment inherited from the Cold War, and it was a trap. If you have such capabilities, he would suggest, 'you are inevitably drawn into interventions, particularly by a persuasive United States'.[3]

The Navy, in his view, was having a catastrophe heaped upon it in terms of ship numbers because of an 'obsession' with maritime air power and a desire 'to hold its head up high in the world'. What as yet unforeseen threat would emerge in the next ten or more years, he would ask plaintively, for which buying two new aircraft carriers would seem like a wise use of resources? 'Our ambitions have to be curtailed', he would plead.[4] For the Navy that meant sticking to the roles of showing the flag, being prepared to evacuate civilians from hot-spots when necessary, and limited amphibious operations with cheap helicopter carriers, frigates, and submarines. Somebody else, either the RAF or the Americans, could provide the air cover.

With rather different motivations, an article published by the Royal United Services Institute for Defence and Security Studies, in April 2007, would also raise the alarm and attract much attention. Entitled 'The Royal Navy at the Brink',[5] it would argue that the Navy 'risks losing irretrievably the capacity which it has had since before Nelson but especially from the time of Trafalgar to the present, to be a decisive force across the globe'. The particular focus of the authors' concerns was the whittling away of the escort force, and especially the industrial capacity to enable that trend to be halted, let alone reversed. In 2007, not a single destroyer or frigate had been commissioned for four years, and only three in the five years before that. This was a plea for a renewed focus on the maritime sphere, rather than for different choices to be made within it.

Grappling with these arguments was a now rather shrunken Naval Staff compared to its heyday. Whatever image the term 'Naval Staff' might conjure up in people's minds, the modern reality would probably come as something of a shock to most. It now mainly inhabited a rather modest open-plan space on the fifth floor of the Ministry of Defence. There were the odd few models of some of the Navy's modern vessels in glass cases. But, otherwise, it could have been the anonymous corporate centre of any medium-sized business. It certainly did not reek of history, let alone extravagance. As for the First Sea Lord's executive-style office, there were certainly pictures of naval heroes like Nelson, Rodney, and Cunningham adorning the walls, and of course a map of the world for that expeditionary look. But the room itself was devoid of historical connections, however much the occupant might still feel the weight of the past.

In truth, the Navy was no longer a service preoccupied by its traditions and history in the way that its detractors were apt to suggest. The scene in

Whitehall mirrored how the service, right down through its ranks, was also profoundly different even from that which HMS *Invincible* had been born into; as with the rest of society, it was a much less deferential, more egalitarian, more informal service. Rightly so, perhaps, as the armed forces should be a reflection of the nation, but not quite as many outside the Navy would have imagined it.

The First Sea Lord himself, Admiral Band, cut an imposing but affable and quite informal dash as well, in public at least. Tall and avuncular, with a deep and gravely voice, a quick and pithy turn of phrase, and a penchant for footballing metaphors, he was a strong and confident presence at the top of the Navy. As his right-hand-man in the job of Assistant Chief of the Naval Staff, to help marshal the strategic case for the Navy, the First Sea Lord had the quiet, thoughtful Rear Admiral Alan Massey, who had commanded HMS *Ark Royal* at the start of the Iraq invasion.

Jonathon Band had thought about joining the Navy ever since, as a youth, he had seen HMS *Victorious* riding at anchor in Mombasa harbour, in the days when that east African port of call was a familiar, welcoming, and busy lynchpin in Britain's lingering presence in the Indian Ocean and beyond to the Far East. He planned to go into the Navy to fly jets. But he actually joined in 1967, the year after the CVA-01 cancellation, when the die had been cast and the Navy's demand for fixed-wing pilots had suddenly collapsed. So he became an ordinary seaman officer, albeit one with an enthusiasm for maritime air power.

The opening words of the First Sea Lord's 'Future Navy Vision' were: 'Britain is pre-eminently a maritime nation'.[6] But that was not really the case as far as public consciousness was concerned, and that was part of the problem. It was not really true either any more in terms of traditional maritime activities, like a thriving merchant marine and shipbuilding industry.

The public may have puzzled what the Navy's role was, with the spotlight focused so sharply on the Army. That was not how the Navy saw it. 'Anyone who looks at having effect in the world and doesn't see the need to police, control, [and] use the sea is barking,' the First Sea Lord would growl.[7]

The country was more dependent than ever for its prosperity on a far-flung and fragile maritime trade. That trade itself had ballooned. The world's population had doubled in forty years. That was astonishing enough. But maritime trade had quadrupled in that time. And the vast majority of the world's population is now clustered near the sea. Here was a highly-strung, intense, but unevenly globalized world in which the stresses and strains were bound to grow. Terrorist groups like Al-Qaeda may not have navies. But they did not have to in order to have an impact, when the 'just enough, just in time' business practice of feeding markets with the minimum of stocks meant that it would not take much to create a ripple effect that would quickly reach ordinary citizens in their daily lives. And then there were dodgy countries like Syria and Iran. Climate change, issues about food and energy security, the growing resource demands of others, piracy, the movements of terrorists and weapons, all added to the volatile mix, and the need to be vigilant on the main physical highway of globalization – the sea.

Equally, the Navy argued, it was wrong to become fixated on the dirty wars in Iraq and Afghanistan. Of course, there was an urgent need to gain success. Planners could also hardly be accused of planning to fight the last war – Afghanistan in particular was ongoing and looking increasingly open-ended. But there was an issue about preparing for the same war again and again. 'There's been a tendency to take the where we are now and to extrapolate today's issues into tomorrow,' Admiral Massey would observe.[8]

Of course, it had not just been Iraq and Afghanistan. The combination of scale and duration of those missions in Afghanistan and Iraq may have come as an unwelcome shock. But the Army had been busy for nearly two decades with various commitments of different size and shape. The Royal Navy's last real taste of sea combat had been a quarter of a century ago, and no other major modern navy had had such experience since the Second World War. However, Iraq and Afghanistan had shown the real and political costs of long occupation. As for a lesson for the future, Massey argued, if the requirement is still there to influence, to be present, and to coerce, preferably at arm's length as much as possible, then maritime forces will offer very flexible options for intervention without entanglement.

The new carriers would certainly be dubbed and derided as 'the Navy's carriers'. But the argument could surely be made more convincingly than before that these would be national assets, in the context of a national policy that still embraced active engagement and the projection of power, and an overall defence doctrine that emphasised flexibility and manoeuvre, and the need to maintain credible forces for deterrence and coercion around the world.

But none of that really solved the numbers riddle. Admiral Band would talk of the balance of the Fleet being at risk both in terms of 'capabilities' and 'scale' – the ability to carry out serious task force operations if need be, and having sufficient ships to maintain a sufficient presence around the world, if possible to deter aggression. But he was reluctant to talk about tipping points in terms of numbers of ships. He had seen the 'red lines' of the past on destroyer and frigate numbers come and go. Numbers mattered. But more than ever, and more even than his predecessors, Admiral Band's focus seemed to be on capabilities.

That meant he faced some difficult questions from officers when he visited wardrooms around the Fleet. 'I say very openly to my people, any navy can run destroyers and frigates. Not any navy can do submarine operations, serious littoral manoeuvre, and carrier strike,' Admiral Band reflected. 'Top league navies take aviation to sea in big blocks, they do brigade-level amphibious type operations, and they coerce and strike from the sea from submarines … That's why I'm in the premiership. That's why I'm not down the bottom of the first division.'[9]

The Band approach seemed to be to accept that his immediate room for manoeuvre was limited, to defend what he saw as the core of the Navy, but to prepare for a time when the pressure might be eased. It was a risky strategy. It got more so the longer the current campaigns went on, and the greater the delays in other key programmes. But it also offered the prospect, for the first time in generations, of perhaps reversing, or at least halting, the decline in escort numbers.

The Naval Staff's sterner critics, both inside and out, long complained that it always came up with the same shape of fleet regardless of the international circumstances – whether colonial, Cold War, or post-Cold-War. The Navy had had one re-design forced on it in the 1960s. What was needed now, some argued, was a further long overdue re-design.

And yet that was what was happening. Superficially, things appeared the same. But within the concept of the balanced fleet, the balance had shifted significantly.

There was still the aspiration for carriers. But, just as the Invincibles were different from their predecessors, the new ships would be different again, more capable but also more adaptable. They would, if they ever appeared, be something of a hybrid, large but relatively simple, at least compared to their American counterparts.

Then there were the hulking, somewhat unglamorous-looking amphibious ships. They had moved from being the half-neglected, struggling add-ons of the Cold War fleet to centre stage, and perhaps the most consistently valuable and cost-effective vessels in the Navy's inventory. The arrival of seven new ships of this type in the space of less than a decade meant that the Navy would have a greater ability to land troops and carry out other amphibious tasks certainly than it had had in the Falklands, and probably since at least the 1960s. They formed a far larger proportion of the Fleet than before.

The key, though, would be the next generation of frigate, the Future Surface Combatant (FSC). The new Type 45 destroyers would be magnificent ships, but they were costing a billion pounds each, and the Navy would probably be getting only half the number that it had originally planned. 'The frigate of the future has got to be cheaper,'[10] Admiral Band reflected. And there would be different versions. One set of studies suggested three types. The Naval Staff seemed to be thinking in terms of two. One would be able to carry out full task force duties, including protecting the carriers. The other would be a smaller and simpler patrol vessel. Crucially, it would take over from some of the current minehunters and survey ships, restoring the frigate numbers that way. Maybe, at long last, the Navy would be getting a cheap frigate. Sceptics might argue that it would not deserve the name 'frigate' in the modern sense. But perhaps it would in the sense that Nelson understood it. The only thing was, the Navy still had to deliver on its promise of a cheap frigate, something that it had manifestly failed to do in the past.

A few miles to the northwest of the Ministry of Defence, Admiral Sir James Burnell-Nugent, relaxed on a comfortable sofa in the elegant surroundings of his official residence, just a short distance from his Northwood headquarters. He reflected on what would be his last few weeks in the Navy as the C-in-C Fleet.

One innovation that he had helped to oversee, and another sign of the times was that the Navy was now using its amphibious ships, support tankers, and even survey ships in roles previously undertaken by frigates. In large part it was out of necessity, as the strains on the frigate force continued to grow. But Admiral Burnell-Nugent was also making a virtue of it. The move seemed an obvious solution when the old, conventional threats at sea seemed to be less pressing, but the new unconventional ones were perhaps even more diverse or dispersed. At the same time, they did not necessarily need as much of the paraphernalia of military capability as had been the case in the past, but perhaps only a helicopter and the space to accommodate a boarding party. Just as the 'wars among the people' on land, and the 'asymmetric threat', meant that there were no frontlines any more, and even the support forces had to be prepared for combat, so the same may also be happening at sea.

But what about the carriers? Perhaps, given all the other pressing calls on the government's resources, it was remarkable not that the promise of the new carriers had still to be turned into steel, but that it had survived at all. And it would continue to do so, perhaps against the odds. For nearly a decade, a succession of chiefs of staff had quietly blamed Gordon Brown for what they saw as the short-changing of defence, and the under-funding of the SDR. He, for his part, seemed to regard them with disdain. And yet, within weeks of his moving in to Ten Downing Street, at the end of July 2007, there was the strongest commitment yet to the two carriers, and a new promise to move ahead with ordering the ships, if not the actual order itself.

CHAPTER SIXTEEN

Carrier Conundrum

The First Sea Lord could not disguise his satisfaction over the latest carrier commitment. It was, he suggested, 'one of those generational decisions'. As significant, in its way, as the CVA-01 decision the year before he had joined the Navy.

The admiral was standing on the quarterdeck of HMS *Ark Royal* in Portsmouth harbour, just after the announcement, as he thought these thoughts and uttered these words. Not far away across the naval base was the sadly empty shell of *Invincible*.

In his mind, he also believed that this was important for the sailors in the Navy now. This announcement implied, as far as he was concerned, that for as long as those currently serving need worry, the Navy would be a global player. This was the Navy's totem. And that was important.

There may still have been uncomfortable echoes of CVA-01 – the long political battle, the unease that the Navy was being too ambitious, the fact that the carrier proposal was tied to a joint RAF/Royal Navy aircraft. But there were plenty of differences as well. One was that this time, compared to the 1960s, the senior leaders in the Navy seemed more committed to and united around the necessity of carrier air power than had been the case before, even though none of them were aviators, and some were from that traditionally sceptical branch, the submariners, like James Burnell-Nugent, and his successor as C-in-C Fleet, Mark Stanhope. And then there was the First Sea Lord himself.

While the dormant *Invincible* and HMS *Ark Royal* were in Portsmouth as the latest carrier commitment was made, the middle sister, *Illustrious*, was three thousand miles away. She was cruising off the east coast of the United States. On her bridge, Captain Tim Fraser looked out as, just a few hundred metres away, two of the US Navy's 100,000-ton giants manoeuvred to keep station on his ship, one on each beam. It made him feel rather humble. But as he gazed across the water at these two American behemoths, he had another thought. Britain's two new ships, he reflected, would in future represent something close to that level of capability. He knew why these vessels would add so much to Britain's defence capabilities even as, back in Britain, many others were still parading their doubts.

Tim Fraser had been just three years old when CVA-01 was cancelled. He joined the Navy in January 1982, straight from school, just weeks before the Falklands War. Julian Oswald, who was then just a few years away from becoming First Sea Lord, had joined Dartmouth to escape Latin. Young Fraser had similarly felt that he did not want to pursue the academic life any longer. He wanted to join the services. It might have been the Royal Marines. In fact, it was the Navy. But he and his fellow new entrants would watch as the ship that they were supposed to go aboard for their sea training, HMS *Fearless*, sailed off to war.

Now, twenty-five years later, he had also felt the lift in spirits aboard his command, the Fleet flagship, following the latest news about the long-promised new carriers. Many of his ship's company had been involved with the planning for the new vessels. For many of them, it had already seemed like a very long road.

But they also had plenty else on their minds just at that time as well. For the past ten days, the ship had been a hive of activity. They had some unusual visitors – fourteen US Marine Corps Harriers and their pilots and support personnel, some 200 people in all.

It was a bitter-sweet experience for the Commander (Air), Henry Mitchell, a former Sea Harrier pilot and erstwhile commander of the now-defunct Sea Harrier force. This was a chance really to put *Illustrious* through her paces with a full complement of aircraft. And there had not been too much opportunity for that lately. But it was thanks only to the Americans.

Of course, there was a war going on, and the British Harrier force was much in demand in Afghanistan. But there was also a sense among the Navy's aviators that the RAF now had more than its fair share of say over what the Harriers did in the new joint set-up, and that it was not being at all co-operative about getting the planes to sea.

For now, though, Henry Mitchell had an enthusiastic group of pilots aboard *Illustrious*, and a contingent of Harriers that were better equipped in many respects than anything now in the British inventory. But this was not just making the best of a bad job. It was unreservedly good in the sense of making a reality of multinational co-operation that would increasingly be the order of the day. For as long as people could remember, British and American naval aircraft had 'cross-decked' on each other's carriers, but never on this scale – an entire air group of foreign jets. *Illustrious* would carry out similar trials in the months ahead with Spanish and Italian naval Harriers as well. Perhaps the Royal Navy did not have to be beholden to the RAF after all, even without its Sea Harriers any more.

Illustrious' cruise off the eastern seaboard of the United States in the summer of 2007 offered another alluring window onto another possible future. In the calm waters, there hove into view what was for the entire crew a totally unfamiliar shape. As it came in to a hover over *Illustrious'* rear flight deck, it looked awkward and ungainly. This was the MV-22 Osprey tilt-rotor, making its first landing on a British ship – a machine that can take-off and land like a helicopter, but fly as fast and as high as a conventional propeller-driven aircraft. It had suffered a prolonged and troubled birth, and had seemingly faced more attempts to kill it off than the Royal Navy's carrier force. It remained controversial.

The Royal Navy certainly coveted the Osprey, particularly as a replacement for its ageing Sea Kings in the airborne surveillance role. It had plenty of advantages over helicopters, but it was also painfully expensive. And money was so tight that the Navy still could not count absolutely on its new carriers.

Such was the scale of the defence funding problem that late 2007 had seen an unprecedented revolt of five former Chiefs of the Defence Staff, stridently calling for increased spending. But, even given the growing anxieties among the general public about the conditions in which service personnel were both fighting and living, the appetite for more defence spending was limited, especially as the general economic climate was turning decidedly unsettled after a long period of sustained growth.

With the budget increasingly overloaded, the tribal survival instincts of the individual services were inevitably re-asserting themselves over the imposed ethos of jointness. In Whitehall, as out at sea on *Illustrious*, the Navy at the highest level would observe that the RAF was being less than fully helpful or enthusiastic about the joint Harrier force. The agreement that Jock Slater had set such store by ten years earlier was certainly fraying at the edges, although both he and his chief assistant then and successor now, Jonathon Band, would insist that they did not regret the move.

Hostility and resistance to the new carriers was also still evident in other parts of the Ministry of Defence. The strange irony was that what seemed to keep the project alive was the backing from the new occupant of Ten Downing Street. Gordon Brown's style on the world stage may have been a sharp contrast to that of his predecessor, and he may have had more of an inclination towards the developmental, softer side of power projection. But, as an old-style, power-broking sort of politician, he also seemed to see the value of what the carrier could bring to the diplomatic negotiating table.

But, with the lingering Iraq and Afghanistan commitments, the urgent demands to equip troops on the front line clearly took priority. Equally clearly, it still left the Naval Staff with a dilemma about how far and how hard to press its own agenda.

In fact, Admiral Band and his colleagues were presented with multiple frustrations: irritation at the continuing attacks from inside and outside the Ministry of Defence on the new carriers; disappointment at what they saw as the apparent public failure to recognize that the Navy really was doing its bit in operations; and dismay that the sacrifices that the Navy had already made in its ship numbers, and even more the support of those that were left, seemed to have been forgotten already. 'I think it's very, very poorly understood,'[1] observed Mark Stanhope. He had just taken over at the Northwood headquarters. He had been based in the United States as the deputy NATO commander for transformation. Now that he was back, he really noticed the shrinkage that had taken place in the Navy while he had been away.

The cuts in maintenance, to help support the Army, were also having an impact. 'Over the last three or four years the Fleet has become more fragile.'[2] Those words from the admiral had found substance in the tribulations of HMS *Illustrious*, which had just had to delay her latest deployment to the Middle East and Indian Ocean, codenamed Orion 08, because of various equipment failures.

There was certainly, from the Navy's point of view, still plenty to do, that was stretching it thin. There were the patrols in the Gulf, and also to help with maritime security in the Indian Ocean. There were commitments to NATO, in the north and south Atlantic, and in the Caribbean. The Navy had at one stage been supplying more than half the forces in Afghanistan, with Royal Marines, helicopters, and its share of the Harrier force. It would be preparing to do so again: Admiral Stanhope was having to find 400 Royal Navy personnel – two frigates' worth – to retrain for operations ashore, to help fill the gaps. But that was certainly not attracting public attention.

The Royal Navy, and indeed all navies around the world, suffer in the age of instantaneous media communication and short attention spans. Being engaged over the horizon, and with long-term presence as a key function, have become structural weaknesses, especially when daily firefights in Afghanistan's Helmand province are beamed into living rooms.

Even the mighty US Navy was feeling it, and grappling with similar issues to the Royal Navy, albeit on a much larger scale. For Britain, the basic choice is whether to be in the carrier business or out of it. For the United States, it is how many carrier strike groups to have. By 2008, the core Pentagon budget, plus the extra money for Iraq and Afghanistan, had reached over 700 billion US dollars. And yet the US Army was at breaking-point. The US Navy, and the US Air Force, faced withering fire in the US Congress over the extravagance of their programmes and ambitions. And all the services were bracing themselves for that time in the indeterminate future when the Iraq and Afghanistan campaigns would start to decline, but so too would the budgets, and the feeding frenzy for funds would really begin.

To prepare the ground, in October 2007, the US Navy and its sister services – the US Marines Corps and the US Coastguard – unveiled a vision for the future: 'A Co-Operative Strategy for 21st Century Seapower'.[3] It would have as many messages for those beyond the United States as it would for its domestic audience.

It began with the familiar – the potency of maritime forces as levers of deterrence: 'preventing wars is preferable to fighting wars', and 'peace does not preserve itself'. It clearly inhabited the same world of globalization as the Royal Navy, in which 'the maritime domain … carries the lifeblood of a global system that links every country on earth'.

The forces it envisaged were clearly familiar too, if not necessarily the way that they might be employed. Even major wars might not be conventional. Climate change, weak governments, population movements, expanding economic frontiers and appetites, and terrorists and pirates, all represented threats to the stability of the system. A powerful fleet gave the United States the edge in terms of being able to respond, and the ability of maritime forces to project soft power for humanitarian relief gained added significance in the wake of the 2004 Indian Ocean tsunami.

This document was clearly meant to underpin the argument for rebuilding the US Navy from fewer than 280 ships to its goal of 313. But it concluded that not even the United States alone could police the sea lanes. So this was also a call for partnership. The original slogan had been co-operation in a 'one-thousand-ship navy'. Perhaps the overtones of that sounded too menacing, but some re-branding had produced 'the Global Maritime Partnership initiative'.

The real spectre for the US Navy, even if it was not mentioned in its new document, was China. That emerging competition was also part of a broader picture of a dynamic maritime region that seemed to be leaving the traditional European naval powers like Britain somewhat floundering. Japan, India, and South Korea all seemed to 'get it' as far as the utility of maritime power, and maritime influence, were concerned, and were all building up navies bigger than the Royal Navy.

That obvious focus for the US Navy on a particular region, and the explicit acknowledgement of the limits of US power, were significant for the Royal Navy in the post-Iraq world. What the broader fallout would be for maritime forces from the Iraq and Afghanistan nightmares was still unclear.

These interventions seemed to highlight the passing of the 'uni-polar moment', when the United States was dominant as the world's only superpower. Instead, the world was becoming non-polar, with a chastened United States in relative decline, but no other power or power bloc in a position to assert its own authority or influence.[4] For Britain, the alternative power centres of the European Union and NATO looked fragile.

The new United Kingdom national security strategy reaffirmed that Britain would in most cases act in future as part of NATO or in coalitions. But it also recognized the need to maintain an independent capability. And the premium on that could increase with the new uncertainties over who may or may not be willing to take the lead in the next crisis. In that context, new aircraft carriers – rather than being a trap that would suck the country into somebody else's intervention – could provide a significant instrument of leverage. They would help maintain a critical link with the United States, a form of power projection that the United States clearly understood and respected, and one which could even make a real difference to the increasingly overstretched US maritime forces. They could impress and influence the new regional powers who were seeking aircraft carriers of their own. But mostly the new British carriers, perhaps in conjunction with the French, could provide the kernel for an independent European military intervention capability, so that Europe would not be beholden to Washington in an intervention of its choosing.

Of course, there are other military instruments or statements of intent that potential partners set just as much store by, not least that of 'boots on the ground'. But the true cost of that has also been brought home. 'Navies are very expensive to build and invest in initially, but actually they're quite cheap to run in comparison to armies when you deploy them,' observed Admiral Stanhope. 'If you build a credible deterrent in a naval sense, and operate it , that's a lot better, a lot cheaper on the balance sheet in the end than not having a deterrent posture in the first place and having to deploy armies to sort your problems out. We know how expensive armies are to deploy, we've been seeing it for the past five years.'[5]

At one level, the Iraq experience did seem to validate a lot of what navies said that they were about. And deterrence was one of those elements. The early intervention with minimum political risks, the ability to remain on hand with low exposure on the ground, in a global political environment where friendly host nations were becoming even harder to find. The pendulum may have swung too far towards the land-based contingency. An adjustment in the other direction, not least to secure the carrier programme and restore a reasonable balance to the rest of the Fleet, might seem justifiable. But to respond to the quagmire by saying 'never again', and trying to push the pendulum in the direction of a purely maritime strategy, would probably be neither wise nor politically possible.

Both in Iraq and Afghanistan experience seemed to teach everyone the lesson that to have real impact, military force is not enough. The US Navy seemed to lead the way in reminding people that maritime forces were excellent vehicles for the delivery of soft power as well as hard power. Its deployment of the giant hospital ship USNS *Comfort* on a humanitarian mission to Latin America in 2007 became an emblem of what could be done.

Again, how far to take the new hearts and minds ethos in the construction of a navy, at the expense of what fighting capabilities, would be a difficult balance. In terms of latent capability, of course, the bigger the ship, the better. A key part of the Royal Navy's approach to its new prize, the CVF, was always to emphasize its flexibility. 'I can't tell you whether the driver is going to be another fifteen years of doing aviation in the Middle East,' Admiral Band would reflect. 'Or whether it's a case of taking all the jets off and putting on lots of helicopters and doing a huge humanitarian "tsunami mark five", which is what this carrier can do.'[6]

That did not stop the critics rolling their eyes with the thought that the Navy's answer to every question was two aircraft carriers. But the admirals were also getting tired of pressing home the argument of just how useful these ships could be, and just how many policy doors and options that they would be able to open. After all, while the British prevaricated, others were going ahead with their plans. The Italians, the Spanish, and the Indians have all been building or buying bigger ships than they already have, albeit not on the scale of the British ones. The Chinese were pursuing their carrier ambitions, while the Russians said that they wanted to start building up their carrier fleet again. Even the Japanese, so long precluded from the carrier business, found the logic of the move for their burgeoning fleet irresistible, and were gingerly stepping on to the ladder of aircraft-carrying warships.

As the debate and delay in Britain continued, one of the protagonists from the battles over CVA-01 re-entered the fray. Michael Quinlan, who went on from the job of private secretary to the Chief of the Air Staff to become the top civil servant at the Ministry of Defence. He had not changed his view that aircraft carriers 'are an expensive way of providing a modest amount of air power'.[7]

But surely the details of the case were rather different now. In Michael Quinlan's day, the Air Staff zeroed in on HMS *Hermes*, which could carry only between five and seven Buccaneer bombers, against a much larger potential array of RAF aircraft. Now, the thirty or so JSFs that the new ships could carry would amount to just about as much as Britain would ever contemplate deploying in the future. That was perhaps one of the reasons why the RAF seemed to be getting edgier again about the prospect of the new ships.

The bill is certainly high, including for the aircraft. But a significant number of them would be needed anyway, with or without the carriers. And the cost of the two ships, although not small, would be less than one new US carrier. The vulnerability question would not go away. The continuing proliferation of new precision weaponry tipped the scales one way, but the likely absence of a general war at sea and the increased protection issues of exposed land bases, assuming they would be available at all, tipped them back the other way. Indeed, the biggest threat to these ships would probably always be in the corridors of Whitehall.

Still, on 3 July 2008, a historic event took place on board HMS *Ark Royal* in Portsmouth harbour. A government minister finally signed a production contract for the two new CVFs, HM Ships *Queen Elizabeth* and *Prince Of Wales*, to be delivered in 2014 and 2016. It was ten years since the intention to build the ships had been announced. It was fully sixty-six years since the orders were placed in the depths of the Second World War for Britain's last two big sister aircraft carriers, HMS *Eagle* and the previous *Ark Royal*.

But it was not quite history turning full circle. For that to happen, the two new carriers would have to be fully at sea under the White Ensign. And the questions persisted. The total bill for the ships alone was 3.9 billion pounds. The country and the global economy were heading for a severe slump. The Ministry of Defence's budget still looked massively over-extended, and the cries about the opportunity cost of the carriers in terms of urgent equipment needs for the Army in Iraq and Afghanistan would not go away. At the same time, there was even less appetite, across any major part of the political spectrum, for a significant boost in overall defence spending.

Even the Navy's own day-to-day presence on the world's oceans seemed even more under threat. Just days before the carrier order, confirmation came that the almost equally cherished new destroyer class, the Type 45, would be limited to just six ships – half the number originally envisaged in the SDR. The Type 45's own mushrooming costs hardly helped matters. But the news also looked like a sacrifice on the twin altars of the carriers and the immediate operational requirements in Iraq and Afghanistan. The number of Navy frigates looked destined to sag to even more strikingly low levels, even if there was still a faint hope of some revival if the FSC programme could eventually deliver on the promise of a more affordable escort ship.

There were also still question-marks over the aircraft that the carriers are designed to operate, the JSF. Was that programme affordable? When would the JSF actually arrive? And was the country even ordering the right version?

But, for all the questions, the carrier advocates maintained that, if Britain still wants to be a major international player able to project real power, there is no better or more flexible military instrument, especially if the stomach for interventions on the Iraq and Afghanistan models is now in doubt, and with a new debate to be entered on just how Western democracies can and should employ their armed forces and apply military power in the future. Within weeks of the CVF order, a small but bitter war in the Caucasus between Russia and Georgia was also a not-so-gentle reminder that this is not just the world of Al-Qaeda and Osama Bin Laden. Just when and how the presence of a British aircraft carrier might be decisive is difficult to predict, but then experience has suggested that scenario planning has always been an imperfect guide to actual need, and that was one of the striking lessons of HMS *Invincible*'s career.

There were at least three ages of Invincible. She was born as a hybrid, established a distinct role for herself in her early years, and then began a slow and tortuous transformation into something that she was never designed to be. She started life operating with five jets, and ended up carrying sixteen. She was tested at the outset, when she was on the disposal list, and she emerged with flying colours as the most recognizable ship in the Royal Navy. Her Falklands fame kept her name in the news, and she also kept busy in the Balkans and the Gulf. In so doing, she helped make a case for the new carriers.

The Navy squeezed more out of *Invincible* and her sisters than it ever expected, and so kept the carrier concept alive. In that sense, the ships were a great success for the Navy. But it then became trapped by their limitations. Others would argue that it has become trapped by its aspiration for something more.

This particular carrier battle has been going on for over fifty years. The baggage of history and inter-service animosity weighs heavily. Whatever her origins, *Invincible* was a proud ship. One way or another, hers will likely be a pivotal period in the saga.

Notes

Reviewing the Fleet
1. Philip Ziegler, *Mountbatten: The Official Biography* (Guild Publishing, London, 1985), p. 522.
2. *Ibid*, p. 550.
3. National Maritime Museum Ships Archive, Woolwich: CVA-01 Ships Cover.
4. National Archives, Kew: ADM 205/192.
5. Lord Carrington, *Reflect On Things Past* (William Collins, London, 1988), p. 160.
6. Ibid, p. 161.
7. National Maritime Museum Ships Archive, Woolwich: CVA-01 Ship Cover.
8. National Archives, Kew: DEFE25/40.
9. National Archives, Kew: AIR20/11242.
10. National Archives, Kew: CAB129/114.
11. *Ibid*.

1966 and All That
1. National Maritime Museum Ships Archive, Woolwich: CVA-01 Ships Cover.
2. Royal Naval Historical Branch, Portsmouth: NHB Study 62–20.
3. National Archives, Kew: DEFE13/589.
4. *Ibid*.
5. *Ibid*.
6. *Ibid*.
7. National Archives, Kew: DEFE13/114.
8. National Archives, Kew: DEFE13/115.
9. National Archives, Kew: DEFE13/589.
10. National Archives, Kew: DEFE13/114.
11. National Archives, Kew: DEFE69/481.
12. National Archives, Kew: DEFE13/589.
13. National Archives, Kew: DEFE13/2937.
14. National Archives, Kew: T225/2963.

'The Cruiser'
1. 'The Defence White Paper 1966', Vice Admiral Sir Peter Gretton, in *RUSI Journal*, May 1966.
2. National Archives, Kew: DEFE24/234.
3. 'Admirals in Dispute with First Sea Lord', Desmond Wettern, in *Sunday Telegraph*, 12 December 1966.
4. 'The Royal Navy in the Next Decade', Rear Admiral Terence Lewin, in *RUSI Journal*, August 1968.
5. National Archives, Kew: DEFE24/385.
6. National Archives, Kew: DEFE24/386.
7. *Ibid.*
8. National Archives, Kew: T225/3471.
9. National Archives, Kew: DEFE24/386.
10. National Archives, Kew: T225/3322.
11. Interview with the author, 2 July 2007.
12. National Archives, Kew: T225/3323.

Invincible and the Sea Harrier
1. National Archives, Kew: T225/3471.
2. Hansard, 10 March 1969.
3. National Archives, Kew: AIR8/2629.
4. National Archives, Kew: T225/3471.

A New Genus
1. Edward Ashmore, *The Battle And The Breeze* (ed Eric Grove) (Sutton Publishing, Stroud, Gloucestershire, 1997), p. 267.
2. A F Honnor and D J Andrews, *HMS Invincible The First of a New Genus of Aircraft Carrying Ships* (paper presented to the Royal Institution of Naval Architects, London, 28 April 1981).
3. National Archives, Kew: T225/3606.
4. National Archives, Kew: DEFE24/1386.
5. National Archives, Kew: DEFE24/1384.

Invincible Emerges
1. Admiral Sir Terence Lewin, 'A Very Good Run For Your Money', in *NAVY International*, August 1978.
2. National Archives, Kew: DEFE19/227.
3. National Archives, Kew: DEFE69/619.
4. Admiral James Holloway, *Aircraft Carriers At War* (Naval Institute Press, Annapolis, 2007), pp. 383–5.
5. National Archives, Kew: DEFE69/619.

Under the White Ensign
1. Margaret Thatcher, *The Downing Street Years* (HarperCollins, London, 1993), p. 249.
2. Interview with the author, 5 December 2007.

No Way Forward
1. Winston Churchill, *The Second World War*, Vol 3 (Reprint Society, London, 1950), p. 343.
2. Admiral of the Fleet Sir Henry Leach, *Endure No Makeshifts* (Leo Cooper, London, 1993), p. 6.
3. Interview with the author, 23 November 2007.

For Sale
1. National Archives, Kew: DEFE13/1198.
2. Interview with the author, 30 October 2007.
3. Op cit.
4. *Ibid.*
5. *Ibid.*
6. Interview with the author, 2 July 2007.
7. Journal of Captain J J Black, RN.
8. Op cit, p. 218.

Invincible at War
1. Journal of Captain J J Black, RN.
2. *Ibid.*
3. John Lehman, *Command Of The Seas* (Macmillan Inc., New York, 1988).
4. *Op cit.*
5. *Ibid.*

What Lessons?
1. The Falklands Campaign: The Lessons, Cmnd 8758.
2. *Ibid.*

Carrier Comeback
1. Interview with the author, 7 March 2008.
2. Admiral Jock Slater, 'A Fleet for the Nineties', in *RUSI Journal*, February 1993.
3. Rear Admiral Peter Abbott, 'A Rationale for Maritime Forces in the New Strategic Environment', in *RUSI Journal*, April 1993.
4. The Fundamentals of British Maritime Doctrine, BR1806 (HMSO, 1995).

The Blair Effect
1. Speech to the Economic Club, Chicago, 24 April 1999.
2. Interview with the author, 3 August 2007.
3. Strategic Defence Review, Cmnd 3999, July 1998.
4. *Ibid.*

After Invincible
1. 'Paying for defence', in *Financial Times*, 12 December 2007.
2. Interview with the author, 9 April 2007.
3. Interview with the author, 30 October 2007.
4. *Ibid.*
5. Jeremy J Blackham and Gwyn Prins, 'The Royal Navy at the Brink', in *RUSI Journal*, April 2007.
6. Future Navy Vision 2006, RN.
7. Interview with the author, 9 April 2008.
8. Interview with the author, 17 September 2007.
9. Interview with the author, 9 April 2008.
10. *Ibid.*

Carrier Conundrum
1. Interview with the author, 10 April 2008.
2. *Ibid.*
3. A Co-Operative Strategy for 21st Century Sea Power, US Navy, October 2007.
4. Richard N Haas, 'The Age of Non Polarity', in *Foreign Affairs*, May/June 2008.
5. *Op cit.*
6. Interview with the author, 9 April 2008.
7. Michael Quinlan, 'We must question the case for carriers', in *Financial Times*, 20 February 2008.

Bibliography

Cable, James: *Gunboat Diplomacy 1919–1991* (Macmillan/IISS, London, 1994).

Eberle, James: *Wider Horizons: Naval Policy and International Affairs* (Roundtuit Publishing, Broompark, Durham, 2007).

Freedman, Sir Lawrence: *The Official History of the Falklands Campaign* (Routledge, Abdingdon, Oxon, 2005).

Friedman, Norman: *British Destroyers and Frigates. The Second World War And After* (Chatham Publishing, London, 2006).

Grove, Eric: *Vanguard To Trident* (Bodley Head, London, 1987).

Grove, Eric with Thompson, Graham: *Battle For The Fiords* (Ian Allan, London, 1991).

Hill, Richard: *Lewin Of Greenwich* (Cassell and Co, London, 2000).

Jackson, Bill and Bramall, Dwin: *The Chiefs* (Brasseys, London, 1992).

Kennedy, Paul M: *The Rise And Fall Of British Naval Mastery* (Macmillan, London, 1983).

Lehman, John F: *Command Of The Seas* (Macmillan Inc, New York, 1988).

McCart, Neil: *Harrier Carriers Vol 1, HMS Invincible* (FAN Publications, Cheltenham, 2004).

Marr, Andrew: *A History Of Modern Britain* (Macmillan, London, 2007).

Massie, Robert K: *Dreadnought* (Jonathan Cape, London, 1992).

Nott, John: *Here Today, Gone Tomorrow* (Politico's Publishing, London, 2002).

Ward, Commander 'Sharkey': *Sea Harrier over the Falklands* (Cassell, London, 2003).

Wettern, Desmond: *The Decline of British Sea Power* (Jane's Publishing, London, 1982).

Index